PRESERVING MEMORIES

PRESERVING MEMORIES

Growing Up in My Mother's Kitchen

Judy Glattstein

FULCRUM PUBLISHING

GOLDEN, COLORADO

Library of Congress Cataloging-in-Publication Data
Glattstein, Judy, 1942-
  Preserving memories : growing up in my mother's kitchen / by Judy Glattstein.
    p. cm.
  Includes bibliographical references.
  ISBN-13: 978-1-55591-473-8 (pbk. : alk. paper)
  ISBN-10: 1-55591-473-X
 1. Jam. 2. Jelly. I. Title.
  TX612.J3G58 2006
  641.8'52—dc22

                                        2006021219

Printed in the United States of America by Thomson-Shore, Inc.
0 9 8 7 6 5 4 3 2 1

Editorial: Faith Marcovecchio, Katie Raymond
Design: Ann Douden
Interior formatting: Patty Maher
Cover image © Index Open

"Canning" from *My Mother's Body* by Marge Piercy, copyright © 1985 by Marge Piercy. Used by permission of Alfred A. Knopf, a division of Random House, Inc.

Fulcrum Publishing
4690 Table Mountain Drive, Suite 100
Golden, Colorado 80403
800-992-2908 • 303-277-1623
www.fulcrumbooks.com

KATZY, HAYA, MIRA.

MOTHER, SISTER, DAUGHTER.

BRAIDED LIVES THAT SWEETLY HOLD

A TIE BETWEEN THE GENERATIONS.

TO THEM THIS BOOK IS DEDICATED,

WITH LOVE.

CANNING

by Marge Piercy

We pour a mild drink each,
turn on the record player,
Beethoven perhaps or Vivaldi,
opera sometimes, and then together
in the steamy kitchen we put up
tomatoes, peaches, grapes, pears.

Each fruit has a different
ritual: popping the grapes
out of the skins like little
eyeballs, slipping the fuzz
from the peaches and seeing
the blush painted on the flesh beneath.

It is part game: What shall
we magic wand this into?
Peach conserve, chutney, jam,
Brandied peaches. Tomatoes
turn juice, sauce hot or mild
or spicy, canned, ketchup.

Vinegars, brandies, treats
for the winter: pleasure
deferred. Canning is thrift
itself in sensual form,
surplus made beautiful, light
and heat caught in a jar.

I find my mother sometimes
issuing from the steam, aproned,
red faced, her hair up in a net.
Since her death we meet usually
in garden or kitchen. Ghosts
come reliably to savors, I learn.

In the garden your ashes,
in the kitchen your knowledge.
Little enough we can save
from the furnace of the sun
while the bones grow brittle as paper
and the hair itself turns ashen.

But what we can put by, we do
with gaiety and invention
while the music laps round us
like dancing light, but Mother,
this pleasure is only deferred.
We eat it all before it spoils.

CONTENTS

FAMILY AND FRIENDS

When I began thinking about this book, before I even began writing, it appeared to be a simple thing centered on my memories of my mother and making preserves. It still is, but in its gestation *Preserving Memories* gathered more and more people around it, just as at a party where family and friends seem to cluster in the kitchen. What's more, they had recipes, memories, and anecdotes of their own to share that were too good not to include in the book. While I do introduce them in the text, it seems like a good idea to provide a small introduction to the people whose memories of their mothers' kitchens also had a role to play in the book. There are other people mentioned briefly and in passing who are not included here. After all, this is a memoir and cookbook, not a Russian novel.

Family

Frances, my mother, who is usually referred to by her nickname, Katzy.

Haya, my sister who now lives in Israel. Older than I, she shared her memories of our childhood summers on Carmen Hill and described making marmalade with ingredients from the Jerusalem *shuk* for me.

Ben, my brother and the youngest of us three siblings, had his own memories to relate and jam-making stories of his own.

Mira, my daughter, remembers as a child picking berries that I would make into preserves. Now mother of three daughters of her own, she continues the tradition with her children as they go apple or berry picking and then make preserves.

Grandma Gussie, my mother's mother.

Aunt Gert, my mother's sister whose summer cottage on Carmen Hill Road #2 in Brookfield, Connecticut, purchased shortly after World War II, is the center of many memories for my sister, my brother, and me, connected with gathering and preserving and much else besides.

Joyce Carleston, my son's wife's mother (isn't *machetayneste*, pronounced mokh-e-TANE-es-teh, a very simple way of saying "the mother of my child's spouse"?), who graciously shared her reminiscences and recipes of making jam in Texas, where her family has lived for generations.

Friends

Sue Brotherton, a computer friend of my husband, who recounted the tale of the great freezer melt down and subsequent marathon jam-making session with her mother.

Nell Jean Campbell of Colquitt, Georgia, who shared her memories and experiences of making preserves with a southern flair.

Jack Lenzo, designer at Fulcrum Publishing, who shares similar good memories of making jam with his mom.

Faith Marcovecchio, my editor at Fulcrum Publishing, who shares my love of homemade jam and jelly.

Joan Means, a gardening friend who once told me of making jam while camping in Nova Scotia, a vignette so compelling that I asked her to relate it again for this book.

DeeDee Stevens, a friend of my daughter, Mira, who passed on to my daughter methods and recipes that DeeDee had learned from her mother.

INTRODUCTION
MEMORIES and HISTORY

This could have been merely a simple book of recipes. I want it to be something even better. Think about when friends share a recipe with you: it comes enhanced with more than a list of ingredients and cooking directions. You get little stories about the first time they made this recipe, how they have tweaked the ingredients and techniques, why it is a favorite, and other tidbits that make it personal. So it is for me with making sweet preserves. Rather than merely following a set of directions, my memories of berry picking in the country with my family and making preserves from them are part of the process.

Kitchens are the heart of our homes, where friends gather for a cup of coffee, a snack, some conversation. I hope you find that my book offers something more than a collection of recipes. Its amalgam of anecdotes and loving memories, along with recipes, tips, and techniques, is intended to offer something more: a shared visit that will inspire you to preserve memories of your own, one sweet jar at a time.

Why make preserves? For my family, it has some weight of tradition. My mother made them, I do, my sister does, my brother has, my daughter does. So while this might be something your mother did and now you wish to follow in this heritage, it could also be a family tradition in the making, something you will share with your children. Making preserves can be creative, thrifty, even a necessity in times of adversity if there's to be something sweet on the table. Interestingly, everyone who shared information with me on making preserves was sharing memories as well: berry picking, preparing the fruit, the satisfaction of glowing jars of ruby-red, deep-purple, and golden amber preserves, memories of time spent companionably together. The cascade of memories is more than just the mechanics of the process. Memories of summer are sealed in a jar of peach butter opened on a winter morning, a visit to Cape Cod preserved in beach-plum jam. Different from the daily routine of preparing breakfast, making lunch, or cooking dinner, making preserves is a bright star in the constellation of our days.

In addition to sweet treats for your own table, homemade preserves make welcome gifts. Joyce Carleston, my daughter-in-law's mother, lives in Texas and told me that as well as giving them as hostess gifts, "I give jams to relatives who don't have access to the dewberries and wild plums that we have in Texas. I also donate baskets of jams to churches and at family reunions, for their silent auctions. My relatives who live southwest of San Antonio in Three Rivers were so happy that I brought the basket of jam at our reunion this last spring. They said they would bid on any I bring in the future. Dewberry jam is their favorite!" Jack Lenzo, designer at Fulcrum Publishing, recalls that "As children, we always gave strawberry jam to our grade-school teachers as Christmas presents. My older siblings often still get holiday care packages containing jams and jellies from my mother. And tomorrow I am sending off a package to a coworker in Seattle. She found out I make my own jam and requested a jar."

"Food," my mother used to say, "is the pleasure that stays with you throughout your life." Hearing and vision might weaken, but tasty fare will always be enjoyed. She would take pleasure from a succulent, ripe peach or a cup of tea, perhaps accompanied by a piece of cake. She wasn't what some today would call a "foodie," nor did she find cooking to be a consuming passion. She was a good plain cook, of the pot roast, meatloaf, and roast chicken bill of fare. Though putting dinner on the table every night might seem rather basic, it was more of an accomplishment for her than it could seem at first glance. Throughout most of my childhood, she worked as a secretary in the New York City public schools, managed a large house in Brooklyn, and cared for her husband and three children of widely separate ages.

Born in 1907 in New York City, the eldest of six girls, my mother, Frances Cohen, grew up in a very different time. Dishwashers were my mother and her sisters. Though convenience food did exist by the 1920s, with more products coming along in the next couple of decades, it was limited compared to today's instant everything. By the time I was born, grocery stores such as the Atlantic and Pacific Tea Company (later known as the A & P) sold cereal, canned soup and canned vegetables, peanut butter, cake mixes, and packaged bread. But there were no microwave-ready dinners—there were no microwaves. The Great Depression had an effect on my mother's character that persisted to the end of her life. When I was a teenager, my siblings and I used to joke that she would walk three blocks out of her way to use a five-cent coupon on something she didn't ordinarily buy. World War II introduced food shortages and rationing. The messages of World War I, the Great Depression, and World War II were that austerity could happen not just once, but again and again. Who could know but that it would happen once more? Thriftiness was prudent.

When I was little, I would ask for stories about "when you were a little girl." "Yes," my mother would start off, with a teasing note in her voice, "when we crossed the plains in a covered wagon." I knew she was joking, but found it fascinating that my mother did remember the last of the horse-drawn streetcars in New York City. It was a very different time. Her grandparents lived in a walk-up apartment with a cast-iron, coal-burning cookstove. A rabbi, the old man's clothes smelled of mothballs, and as a little girl my mother thought that was the odor of sanctity. It was her habit of crawling under the cookstove to play with her grandmother's cat that gave her the affectionate nickname of *katz im kopf*, "cats on the brain," later shortened to "Katzy." Groceries were bought from specialized stores in the neighborhood: meat from the butcher shop, bread at the bakery, produce from the greengrocer. Milk, eggs, and other related items were generally delivered to the house. Produce was also sold from delivery wagons driving up and down the streets, with the driver calling out to the housewives. I remember some of that from when I was a little girl and we would visit Grandma Gussie at the apartment she and Aunt Gert shared on St. Mark's Place in Brooklyn. Mr. Thaler, the greengrocer, would give me a little cluster of grapes to nibble on while the women did their shopping.

Some of the same traditions remained in the 1950s, when we spent our summers in Brookfield, Connecticut. Shortly after World War II, my Aunt Gert bought a small bungalow and a couple of acres of land. In the beginning, the place barely had electricity. There was a bank of glass-tank acid batteries in the dirt-floored, musty smelling basement. We had an icebox. The iceman came three times a week, and if I were polite, he would chip off a splinter of ice from one of the enormous blocks for me to lick and suck on. The milkman also drove up Carmen Hill #2 to deliver milk, cottage cheese, and sour cream (yogurt was unknown to us), and the Duggan's Bakery van also made regular deliveries. I had a sense of déjà vu in the summer of 1973, when I again enjoyed such deliveries. My husband was working on a job in Holland, and our two children and I (plus the dachshund and two cats) joined him for the summer. We lived in Leiderdorp, near Leiden. The milkman came daily and delivered milk, wonderful cheeses, and a delicious yogurt that could be poured over blackberries for an easy, tasty, enjoyable dessert. (He also delivered Heineken and Amstel beer, by the case.) The bakery van came around every day, and the butcher's small truck came two or three times a week. Of course, there were also neighborhood stores to which we could walk and a twice-a-week street market in Leiden. Today it seems we have lost this kind of convenience. Rather than one delivery van making multiple stops, we have multiple cars driving to the store. People lead busy lives, no one's home to take delivery, and many live in isolated suburbs where the houses are too far from a store to walk there.

When my mother was sixteen years old and her youngest sister was only six, their father died. Since her mother, my grandmother, did not go to work, and in later years several of her sisters went to college, things could not have been too dire. Even so, at the time my mother felt it was important to quit school and earn money. She went to secretarial school, then got a job. Those events—the death of her father, the feelings of insecurity that must have come with it, and living through the Great

Depression—had indelible, character-forming effects on her. Thrift was taken for granted. If a meatloaf was in the oven, of course you would make baked potatoes. And since the oven was going, it only made sense to bake a cake at the same time. When fruit was abundant and inexpensive in the summer, it was prudent to put some up. I have memories of watching her in the hot kitchen in summertime with steam wreathing up from large kettles of water as she'd scald and peel a bushel of peaches, make a sugar syrup, and bottle them for winter—and the same with a bushel of pears. And the making of jams and jellies, well, that was sine qua non. My sister, Haya, and brother, Ben, also remember our mother putting up jars of jams and jelly. Many of my friends have memories of their mothers, grandmothers, even great-grandmothers all making preserves. Such memories are shared with family and friends and at times find their way into print, as mine are shared within the pages of this book.

I'm not the first to find that sweet preserves become sweet memories. In *Delights and Prejudices*, James Beard writes about food, from childhood memories in Oregon to his experiences in his adult life as one of America's culinary authorities. His mother, a superb cook in her own right, was a primary, formative influence on his tastes. When I read about the preserves his mother used to make, I know that I am in good company. He writes that each year she would make a hundred jars or more of apricot and pineapple jam, a tiny bit of gooseberry jam, a few jars of elegantly flavored wild strawberry jam, and wild blackberry jam from berries the two of them picked together.

As children, we take for granted how things are done in the family. Were your birthday cakes bought at the bakery, or did your mother bake them for you? Did your mother make jams and jellies, were they gifts from another relative or family friend, or were they purchased at the store? As we grow older and more aware, making friends and seeing how other families do things, then we begin to make comparisons and contrast how we do things with how they do things. As I wrote this book, I found that making preserves was not unique to my family. Cousins shared their memories, friends offered recipes and reminiscences, and some even introduced me to their friends and relatives, creating an ever-widening ring.

My mother had a household of three hungry children, our father, and herself. As well, Grandma Gussie, my mother's mother, and my Aunt Gert, one of my mother's sisters, also lived with us for a number of years. We needed jams and jellies to spread on toast and for peanut butter sandwiches, a staple of our school lunches. Preserves were used as a simple filling for jelly-roll cakes. Good taste was fundamentally important. With so many other demands on her time, simplicity was a significant criterion, and for my mother, cost-effectiveness was also a sensible principle. Involved, intricate recipes with low yield did not inspire my mother. Fruit in season is less expensive, so peach preserves would be made in the summer when the fruit was cheaper and also more flavorful. Citrus makes wonderful marmalade and is available in winter when locally grown fruit is not. She also chose recipes that were quite easy to follow, usually a 1-2-3, start today and finish in a couple of hours process, rather than with involved steps over several days. I don't know who taught my mother to make preserves. I know that I learned the basics by watching her, acquired more background from reading books, and then gained confidence enough to experiment. In the same way my mother taught me, I too had fun teaching my daughter, some friends, and even an occasional class how to make preserves. But it really is something simple enough that you can learn the techniques on your own from a book.

There are many memories of my mother that I carry with me. So why did I choose preserving to be the focus of this book? Preserves are popular and readily available. They are a standard item found next to jars of peanut butter on the supermarket shelves. As well, exclusive gourmet preserves (shelved separately) are sold at exclusive prices. But they are not the same as homemade. There is something comforting about putting up summer's bounty to be enjoyed in winter, welcoming autumn with jars of ruby-red raspberry jelly, wine-dark elderberry jelly, and tart/sweet citrus marmalade. Unlike cooking dinner, which happens day after day—a constant round of preparing, consuming, and cleaning up—homemade preserves offer extended enjoyment. One jar is finished, another jar opened. The fruits are grown or gathered or purchased, providing memories of a special harvest, a day in the country, a visit to a farmers' market. Making preserves offers a grounded sense of keeping: keeping flavors, keeping memories, keeping a sense of the cycle of the seasons. It offers connections. My daughter's friend Kay always depended on her mother to provide the preserves. "Some day" Kay would take time from her busy life and have her mother teach her how to do it herself. Sadly, her mother died, and the opportunity was gone. Now there's a discontinuity in the family heritage. Kay will have to learn from a friend or from a book. But then she and her daughters can share the knowledge and store up memories. You can do this too. You can make distinctive, extraordinary preserves, capturing flavor and memories for yourself, your family, and your friends.

So why do I and my sister and my daughter and some of our friends spend time with vats of boiling water, cooking, mashing, and puréeing fruit and boiling it up with sugar—why do all this? Obviously, we enjoy the process of taking fruit and making something delectable from it. Also, preserves, like memories, are meant for sharing. Don't expect much in the way of thanks if you give someone a jar of Smuckers jam that you bought at the grocery store. But gift friends and relations with a jar of homemade jam, and their thanks will be heartfelt. My friend Nell Jean Campbell said it very well: "I looked in the cupboard to see what kind of homemade jelly we might have. Nurse Sally's grape jelly—not sure if it's wild grapes, I think it may be. Muscadines grow wild here. Marvin and Martha's blueberry jelly from their own blueberries. People in the South are very generous to share jars of jelly, thoughtful little treats that express great love."

CHAPTER ONE

GETTING STARTED WITH PRESERVES

How easy is it to make preserves? So easy that you don't even need a kitchen! My friends Bob and Joan Means used to take summer vacations in Nova Scotia, driving up from their home in New York City. This was back in the 1960s, and they had a little two-seater sports car with a convertible top, an Alfa Giulia. Along with more-typical gear for an end-of-August camping trip, Joan would pack canning jars. They'd pick blueberries, raspberries, and saskatoons (also called serviceberries, a shrubby species of *Amelanchier canadensis*), which Joan remembers as growing especially well along railroad tracks. The same day as they gathered the fruit, she'd boil up a batch of jam on their little two-burner propane camp stove. Joan still chuckles when describing their return to the United States, convertible top down and Bob wearing his "Scottish bonnet," recounting the look on the immigration and customs officer's face as she'd answer "Anything to declare?" with "Homemade jam." Clearly, if jam can be made while on a camping trip, it will be even easier in your own kitchen.

When and where the making of fruit preserved with sugar originated is open to discussion. We do know that sweet preserves, such as marmalades, jams, and jellies, have been around for hundreds of years. Certainly the Romans were preserving fruit with honey centuries ago. Since sugarcane naturally grew in Middle Eastern countries, it was incorporated into the local cuisine. It was probably crusaders returning from the wars who brought these sweet fruit preserves to Europe where, by the late Middle Ages, they had become very popular. Cookbooks, both in Europe and in the United States, included recipes for them. In the United States, fruit preserves sweetened with honey, molasses, and maple sugar were popular by the late 1600s, and housewives would make their own pectin, extracting it from apple peels and cores. With the industrialization of the nation, commercially prepared foods began to be available. It was less than a century ago, in 1940, that the Food and Drug Administration established standards that defined what constituted jam, jelly, fruit butter, and other preserves.

Definitions

There are a number of different cooked, sweetened fruit products that are grouped together as "preserves." At the most basic level, we're talking about fruit and/or fruit juice and sugar boiled to 10° Fahrenheit above the sea-level boiling point of water that combine in a chemical reaction to form a gel. (The word *jelly* comes from the French *gelée*, meaning "to congeal.") Of course, it is a bit more involved than that, but not by much. There needs to be a proper balance of acidity and pectin. Some fruits, such as citrus and apples, have a good balance and jell easily. Others, such as cherries, are so low in pectin that you could endlessly boil them and never get a gel. I am a purist when it comes to making preserves. If tender, sweet blackberries, low in pectin and acid, will not jell on their own, I'd rather prepare my own pectin from green apples than cook up a supersweet product using commercial pectin. I do explore some special flavorings—a little cardamom or cinnamon in apple butter, some dark rum in peach jam, a leaf of lemon-scented geranium in a jar of apple jelly.

Everyone has heard of jam and jelly, but few of us are cognizant of what their actual definitions are. Here, from the simplest, easiest preserves to the more complicated, are some definitions.

Fruit butter is made from fruit pulp that has first been lightly cooked just sufficiently to be made into a purée and then cooked with sugar until it is thick enough to spread. Fruit butters have a lower proportion of sugar to fruit than many other types of preserves, anywhere from one-half to two-thirds as much sugar as fruit. Fruit butters are sometimes flavored with spices such as cinnamon, cloves, ginger, cardamom, or allspice. At room temperature, fruit butter should be thick enough to stand on a plate without running and thin enough to spread easily on bread. The jell point does not apply to fruit butter.

Jam is a fruit conserve made from fruit and sugar cooked rapidly to a thick consistency without any effort to retain the shape of the fruit. Jam is not as homogeneously smooth as fruit butter.

Conserve is a type of jam that includes thin slices of citrus and one, two, or more kinds of fruit. Conserves often contain raisins and nutmeats. The prepared fruit is measured and then two-thirds to three-quarters of that volume of sugar is added. The conserve is cooked until thick but still a little runny, at which time nutmeats may be added. Citrus continues to set up after it is bottled, and if conserves or marmalades are cooked until a firm set is achieved, they are likely to be too stiff when fully matured.

Marmalade is the original sweetened fruit preserve. Its very name, *marmelo*, is derived from the Portuguese for "quince." Today marmalade is used for citrus preserves in which pieces of citrus rind are suspended in a clear jelly. Traditionally, the most time-honored marmalade is made from sour Seville oranges, used on their own. Other citrus, such as sweet oranges, grapefruit, or lemon, may be used, either separately or as a blend of various citrus. The definition of *marmalade* has undergone a sea change as contemporary upmarket chefs in trendy restaurants create a thick, rich caramelized onion with pistachio condiment, or plum spiced with ancho chili. I have no doubt that they are tasty, I'm just dubious about naming them marmalades.

Jelly is made from fruit juice and sugar. A perfect jelly is transparent, clear, and bright. It quivers when turned out of the jar and has a clean, smooth edge when cut with a spoon. Syrupy or sticky jelly is poor quality. As well as sweet jellies, I'm very fond of making savory herb jellies to use as an accompaniment to poultry, pork, and game dishes.

Tools and Equipment

My sister, Haya, wrote to me, "Yes, I too remember Katzy cooking up large pots (they seemed like vats to me, at the time) of wild grape, blueberry, and plum preserves in Aunt Gert's house on Carmen Hill Road." My mother would have thought it wasteful to purchase special pots or pans and utensils for making preserves. There wasn't any need, in her opinion, since any decently equipped kitchen already had a couple of suitable large pots, some ladles, a colander or large strainer, and a measuring cup or two. What else could you need? Maybe some cheesecloth, but a piece of a well-washed, worn-out old sheet would also serve to strain the juice from some cooked fruit. Keep in mind that in those days sheets were all-cotton, and usually plain white. (I remember wash days from our summers in Connecticut, with sheets spread out on the lawn to bleach on the grass. Don't know what, if anything, the grass had to do with it, but my mother said it helped to whiten linens.)

My batterie de cuisine for jelly making is somewhat more elaborate, but that's mostly for indulgence, not necessity. I have two large Dutch ovens, ten inches in diameter and four inches deep. It really is handy to have both of them. Jelly jars can be sterilized in one while I'm making preserves in the other. Wide and shallow is the key, since it allows rapid concentration of the fruit juice and sugar to the jelling point or cooking down of fruit butters and marmalades. My pots are stainless steel and have copper bottoms. What's wanted is a nonreactive pot—that means stainless steel rather than aluminum, which might react with acids in some fruit, affecting the flavor and discoloring the pot. When I'm not making preserves, the pots are great for making soup, cooking pasta, and lots of other things.

Having several measuring cups is also useful. I have one four-cup/quart, two two-cup/pint, and one one-cup. These are Pyrex, with pouring spouts. Such measuring cups

are intended for liquids. The simple round measuring cups that come in nested sets of quarter, third, half, and one cup are intended for dry measurement of sugar and flour. Along with measuring cups, I have measuring spoons—tablespoon and half tablespoon, full, half, quarter, and an eighth teaspoon. A couple of colanders and strainers, some knives, cooking spoons and ladles, maybe a grater, a citrus zester—a handheld tool with four tiny holes at the working end—and that would be sufficient for making preserves.

There are a couple of additions to this array of equipment that are also nice to have. I have a wide-mouthed funnel that makes it easier to pour boiling hot preserves into jars. A jelly- or candy-making thermometer that clips to the inside of the pan with the bulb resting just above the bottom is reassuring, especially the first few times you're making preserves. It provides a helpful assessment of how close the seething mass of jelly is to the jell point of 10° Fahrenheit above the boiling point of water. Jar-lifter tongs have a curved shape that makes it easy to fish jars out of the water. Another neat little gadget is a wand with a magnet at the bottom for lifting the flat metal lids out of the hot water in which they've been sterilized. Pot holders are also handy. A kitchen scale is useful if you want to get compulsively precise about quantities of fruit. Sometimes proportions are given by weight, but that's easy enough to do when you purchase the fruit at the store. Since apples, for example, come in different sizes, this method makes sense to me. Besides, it is the proportion of prepared fruit to sugar that is critical.

A food mill is very useful and makes things easier when making fruit butters in modest quantities or for sieving seeds out of raspberries and blackberries. I prefer a food mill with three removable plates that give a coarse, medium, or fine purée, and I find it superior to a food processor for making preserves. (Additionally, the coarse plate helps make the very best mashed potatoes and applesauce.) Carole Nagy, whose husband, Dick, owns the nearby orchard where I buy peaches, plums, and other fruit, uses a Squeezo for her berry jams. I have a Victorio strainer that's very similar. Both of these devices are easier to use than they are to describe. My Victorio clamps to the edge of a table or countertop. There's a hopper at the top, a horizontal truncated cone-shaped sieve (I have three, with small, medium, and large holes) with a feed screw, and a chute on the side. Basically, you toss the produce into the top hopper and turn a handle to move the fruit into the feed screw. Seeds and any skin come out the side chute while the pulp comes through the sieve. Carole uses her all-metal Squeezo for applesauce, which she makes from three bushels of apples at a time, or for mashed potatoes. I like to use my modestly priced metal and plastic Victorio when preparing a bushel of plum tomatoes for the freezer. Archaic as these devices sound, they are available from several mail-order kitchen gadget sites, fortunate for people like me who sometimes like to do some things the old-fashioned way. (I have a hand-crank ice-cream maker, too.) A food processor gives different results, texturewise, than a food mill or my Victorio.

A jelly bag is necessary when straining fruit juice extracts for jelly. You can simply line a colander with several layers of damp cotton cheesecloth and place it over a pot to collect the free-run juice. Make sure that the bottom of the colander is above the free-run juice or it cannot drain. This is the easiest method, and when the cheese-cloth becomes badly stained, you merely discard it. A more elaborate jelly bag may be made of unbleached, undyed all-cotton muslin. Wash a yard-long length of thirty-six-inch-wide cotton muslin and let dry. Fold in half diagonally. Securely sew the two sides together to make a cornucopia. Use a plastic embroidery hoop of the appropriate size to hold the top open. Pour prepared fruit and juices into the bag, which has been suspended over a bowl, and allow the juices to drain freely, without squeezing or putting any pressure on the bag.

My one true indulgence is a chinois, a conical metal strainer with tiny holes all over its surface, useful for straining liquid. It was a birthday gift from my son, Seth, and daughter-in-law, Kim, one year—the perfect sort of present that you'd really, really like to have but feel it would be too self-indulgent to purchase for yourself. The shape allows for rapid draining of grape or berry pulp, and a chinois even yields superior results with apple or pear purée, since some of the excess moisture is removed mechanically rather than by boiling the purée. Remember to collect the juices—they're too good to just discard.

Of course, these are the tools you'll need to make the preserves. You also need jars to put the finished product in, as well as sealing lids and rings. The prevalent size is eight ounce, but four-ounce jars are also available. The one-cup size is fairly standard, and many recipes give the yield in those terms. Since I like to experiment and try a diversity of recipes, and because there are only two people in our household, I find the half-cup size very useful. So-called jelly glasses have a decorative exterior, either an embossed quilted pattern or a fruit cluster. The same size jars are also available as "can or freeze jars," with a plain surface and a lower price.

As you make preserves and store the beautifully filled jars in your pantry, don't discard the box in which each dozen jars are purchased. You'll need to store both the filled and emptied jars, and the flimsy cardboard dividers keep them nicely compartmentalized, protected from clicking into each other and chipping. As an aside: When I give preserves to family and friends, I make mention of the fact that it is the contents that are the actual gift—I expect that the jars with their metal rings will be returned for refilling.

You may occasionally come across oddly sized or shaped jars. The only thing I'll point out is that it can be impossible to find replacement lids for jars with narrower or wider lids than the standard version. Also, recipes don't always produce a batch of preserves nicely divisible by cup and half-cup sizes. I use baby food jars for the overage. They don't always reseal tightly, in which case they must be promptly refrigerated. These make great little samplers for breakfast. And while Joyce Carleston generally uses the two-piece metal lid and ring method, she mentioned to me that "I also use peanut butter or relish jars if they have the lids that will reseal and I can hear them pop when they seal. Meta Schade, my mother, always used glass jars with paraffin wax to seal them."

General Techniques

Safety First

You are working with boiling water and boiling solutions with sugar in them. This is not the time for small children or pets to be underfoot in the kitchen.

To sterilize jars:

1. Begin by assembling the jars. Check the rims for any chips or nicks, as any jar with even small damage will not seal properly. Guesstimate how many jars you will need for the batch of preserves you are making and add another one or two. Better to sterilize too many than find you are short on jars with preserves still to bottle.

2. Wash canning jars with hot, soapy water and rinse thoroughly with hot water. This step is important, even if the jars are brand new.

3. Set jars in a pot deep enough to cover them with water.

4. Bring water to a boil and keep at a slow boil (bubbling but not seething furiously) for 15 minutes.

5. Turn down the heat and keep the water at a mere simmer until your preserves are made and you are ready to fill the jars.

To fill jars:

1. Lift the jars out of the hot water with a pair of tongs and allow them to drain for a moment.

2. Set the jars upright on a wooden cutting board.

3. Immediately fill all the jars quickly to within $1/8$ inch of the top.

4. Wipe the jar rims and threads with a damp cloth.

5. Working quickly, cover the jars with flat lids and tightly screw on the bands.

6. Stand the jars in a pot of hot water.
    Note: Remove some water from the pot that the jars were sterilized in, or returning the filled jars to it will cause the water to overflow.

7. Bring water back to a boil for 5 minutes.

8. Remove the jars using tongs and stand them on a cutting board until cool.

9. After the jars are cool, check the seals by pressing the middle of the lid with your finger. If the lid springs up when your finger is released, the jar is not sealed. *Refrigerate and use promptly.*

This technique practically guarantees a good seal. When you put the lid on the jar, the $1/8$-inch space between the preserves and the lid is filled with very hot air. As it cools, the air condenses. The circular film of rubber seals the lid against air entering from outside, and the metal of the lid is pulled down, creating a very tight seal, actually a vacuum seal. There is, however, a caveat. The lid may not seal properly if the rim of the jar has a small nick or crack or if there is a drop of jelly on the rim. This is easy to determine. Remove the metal screw band that held the lid in place during processing in the boiling water bath. If the lid is flat, it is not sealed; there should be a depression in the center. Push down on the center of the lid. It should be rigid, already dimpled in the center. If you can push it down and it springs back up when you take your finger away, then the jar is not sealed. When the jar itself is defective—chipped or cracked—it will never make a proper seal. Refrigerate the preserves and enjoy them right away. Or, repack them into an intact jar and reprocess. Since the flat metal lids should not ever be used a second time, use a brand-new lid. If the lid did not seal because there was a drop of jelly on the rim, clean the jar rim and reprocess, using a new lid.

Troubleshooting

Some preserves are easier to make than others and rarely, if ever, have a problem. The sequence of chapters in this book progresses from simple preserves to more difficult. Yes, if you become distracted, you can burn fruit butter or jam, but that is about it. Marmalade, on the other hand, if cooked too long will set up solidly into something even the chickens won't touch. Jelly is the one preserve that offers you the most options for failure, as follows:

1. Jelly may turn out syrupy or sticky, not setting properly, if there is too little pectin or acid in the fruit. Combine fruits, add a little fresh lemon juice, or add home-made pectin for the next batch.

2. Jelly can also turn out syrupy or sticky, not setting properly, if there is too much sugar in proportion to the juice. Use the suggested proportions of sugar to juice to avoid this problem.

3. Jelly may be soft because there is too little sugar in proportion to the quantity of juice. Also, when a large batch is made all at one time, it is more difficult to cook it quickly to the jell point. Working with four to six cups of juice at a time takes care of this.

4. Jelly will be thick and sticky, not setting properly, if rather than boiling it quickly to the set point, the cooking is slow and lengthy, since this damages the pectin. The quicker jelly is brought to the setting point, the better the flavor and texture. Again, working with four to six cups of juice at a time is helpful.

5. Jelly will be thin and syrupy and have a poor set if the jelly is not adequately (and quickly) cooked.

6. Jelly should be transparent. Poorly strained juice or squeezing and pressing on the pulp through the cheesecloth are the most common causes for cloudy jelly.

7. Conserves, marmalades, and jam should have evenly distributed pieces of fruit. If the fruit floats to the top, it may not have been sufficiently cooked or was not well packed into the jars. Turning the jars upside down after taking them out of the hot water bath for the first stage of cooling down can help. Remember to turn the jars right side up before the conserve or marmalade sets.

8. Jelly may have sugar crystals settling out after it has been stored for a while if there was not enough acid in the juice or if there is too much sugar in the jelly. Grape jelly is a special case. The jelly may develop crystals of tartaric acid if the grape juice was not allowed to stand overnight in a cool place before the jelly was made.

9. Jelly may weep after it has been stored for a while if there is too much acid in the juice. Use the correct proportion of ripe to underripe fruit or the appropriate blend of different fruits. It may also weep if it is stored in too warm a place.

10. If jellies and jams such as raspberry and strawberry turn brown, it means they have been stored at too warm a temperature or in a sunny place. Flavor fades along with the color. Cool, dark, and dry conditions are best for storing preserves.

11. If the jelly ferments, it means the jars were not properly sealed, the jelly was not hot enough when it was put into the jars, or too little sugar was used in making that batch of preserves. Make sure you sterilize the jars, keep them hot until they are filled with hot preserves, and process in a water bath. Once they have cooled to room temperature, check that the jars are sealed before you store them.

12. Moldy jellies and jams are more of a problem when paraffin is used to seal the jars instead of two-piece metal lids and sealing rings. It can be a problem even with this type of jars if they are not properly sealed. Mold can be more of a problem when preserves are stored in damp places. Sterilized, properly sealed jars that were filled with hot jelly then processed in a hot water bath should not develop mold. Low-sugar preserves develop mold more easily than traditional preserves.

About Fruit

Read the label on a jar of store-bought preserves: corn syrup, high-fructose corn syrup, and an alphabet soup of additives that homemade preserves avoid. Fruit and sugar, perhaps some fresh lemon juice, sometimes some homemade apple or citrus pectin are the only required ingredients in homemade preserves. Be mindful that memorable preserves can only be made from excellent ingredients. Sure, canned peaches can be turned into peach jam, but do you really believe it will taste as delicious as the real stuff made from ripe fruit? Do you want grape jelly made from grapes loaded with flavor or from grape juice? At their most basic, preserves are made from fruit and sugar. However, since each fruit is unlike the others, different fruits need different handling in their preparation. Apples must be cooked first, while soft, juicy berries, grapes, and peaches can simply be crushed. Choose the best fruit you can find. Use a mix of three parts ripe fruit to one part underripe fruit for the best gel. Rinse clean before starting preparation.

In the beginning is the coaxing of juice out of the fruit. Berries are easy; so are peaches. Apples are firmer, and quinces are denser yet. So sometimes you need to add water. Soft fruit, such as berries, and juicy fruit, such as grapes, require no or very little water, perhaps a quarter cup to a quart of fruit—just enough to get the juices flowing.

Once brought to a boil, five or ten minutes at a simmer in a covered pot should be adequate. Apples need sufficient water to barely cover the fruit, or even a little less. Once they are brought to a boil, apples will require twenty to twenty-five minutes at a simmer in a covered pot before they are sufficiently cooked to proceed to the next step in making preserves. As a general rule, one pound of fruit will yield one to one and a third cups of juice.

About Pectin

Pectin is a substance that, combined with fruit acid and cooked with sugar, causes fruit juice to form a gel. Some fruits are naturally higher in pectin than others, and under-ripe fruit is higher in pectin than very ripe fruit. Pectin-rich fruits include sweet apples and quinces, both of which are low in acid that can be supplied by adding a small amount of fresh lemon juice. Fruits that are naturally high in both pectin and acid include crab apples, cranberries, red currants, grapes, lemons, and most plums. Fruits low in pectin but high in acid include apricots, cherries, pineapples, and strawberries. Fruits low in both pectin and acid include raspberries, peaches, and almost any very ripe fruit. Low-pectin fruits, such as raspberries, may be combined with high-pectin fruits, such as apples, to produce delicious jelly.

Commercially prepared pectin is available in grocery stores as either a liquid or in powdered form. Both types come with a recipe sheet. It is important to follow the specific recipes provided for a particular product—you cannot use a recipe given for the powder if you are using the liquid, and vice versa. The powder is available in both a standard and a lower sugar form.

If you are concerned that your preserves will not set up or jell properly and you would rather not take the time to make your own pectin from apples or citrus rind, there's always the fallback of commercial pectins. If you do decide to use commercial pectin, I would recommend that you choose the lower sugar versions, which I feel offer a brighter, more fruit-flavored preserve. Keep in mind that it is not possible to simply take one of my recipes and add commercial pectin in an attempt to ensure a gel.

For personal reasons, I prefer not use the standard formulation of commercially produced pectin, though I do use the lower sugar formulation when making savory herb jellies. What I don't like is the fact that in making jelly, these commercial pectins require the use of more sugar than fruit juice, and the resulting jelly is anywhere from 55 to 85 percent sugar. Instead, I prefer to blend high-pectin and low-pectin fruit juices, obtaining good gels with flavorful results. I also prepare my own homemade pectin extract from green apples or from the white pith of citrus rinds. It is easy enough to do, and I bottle it in eight-ounce-capacity glass canning jars to have on hand when raspberry, blackberry, or cherry season comes around.

Successful jellies have the right balance of sugar, pectin, and acid. In the beginning, it may seem confusing—which fruit has what level of pectin to easily reach the jell point? This is really important for making jelly, less so for fruit butter and jam,

which have lots of fruit pulp or purée, or marmalades and conserve, which contain citrus that is high in pectin. Keep in mind that fully ripe fruit is lower in pectin than underripe fruit, which is why it is always a good idea to include some underripe fruit in each batch of jelly.

If you want to make jelly from fruit low in pectin, there are several options. My preference is to use a combination of fruits. For example, a blend of cranberry and raspberry makes a delicious jelly. I use homemade apple or citrus pectin with low-pectin fruit. Of course, that's another step in the process of jelly making, something that's done in advance. I usually make enough homemade pectin at the start of the preserving season to supply my needs. Or, you can use commercial pectin. Many people use these products and find the results delicious. So there are several options, and it's your choice. For those of you wishing to try the recipes in this book that use homemade pectin, here is the recipe.

Homemade Apple Pectin

INGREDIENTS:

4 lbs. or 7 to 8 large green (immature) apples or Granny Smiths

1. Wash apples. If immature apples are not available, Granny Smith apples can be used. Do not peel or core, just cut into quarters or eighths, depending on the size of the apples. Place in a suitable-sized pot and add water to just cover the cut-up fruit.
2. Bring to a boil, then turn heat down to a gentle simmer. Cook until the fruit is soft.
3. Line a colander with several layers of damp cotton cheesecloth, place over a clean saucepan, then add apples and liquid. Allow liquid to drain freely. Do not squeeze or twist the cheesecloth, as this can force small particles through the cheesecloth and the liquid will become cloudy.
4. Return the pulp to the kettle and add an equal amount of water (for example, 2 quarts of pulp, 2 quarts of water). Bring to a boil, then keep at a high simmer for 20 minutes. Strain as before. Combine the two extractions and measure.
5. Boil rapidly to reduce the liquid by two-thirds. If you started with 3 quarts of liquid, boil down to 1 quart.
6. Sterilize eight 4-ounce canning jars. Bring filtered liquid to a high simmer, fill jars, and cap with two-piece metal lids.
7. Place filled, capped jars in a hot water bath, bring to a boil, and boil for 10 minutes.
8. Let cool, label, and date. The pectin should be used within a year.
9. This will provide enough homemade pectin for 8 batches of jelly.

Homemade Lemon Pectin

INGREDIENTS:

Seeds and pith from 8 large lemons

1. Collect any seeds that may be in the lemons (or oranges or other citrus) you are using. Some citrus have many seeds, others have a few, and some are seedless.
2. Place in a glass jar, cover with twice as much water as seeds, and refrigerate overnight. A jellylike substance will form.
3. Peel the colored rind off the citrus and coarsely chop the white pith.
4. Cover with twice as much water as pith. Put in a glass jar and refrigerate overnight.
5. Place seeds, jelly stuff, chopped pith, and water in a pot.
6. Bring to a boil, then turn heat down to a gentle simmer. Cook until white pith is very soft, about 15 to 20 minutes.
7. Line a colander with several layers of damp cotton cheesecloth, place over a clean pot, and pour in seeds, pith, water, and all. Allow to drain without putting any pressure on the pulp.
8. Return pulp to the pot and add an equal amount of water (for example, 1 cup of water for each cup of pulp).
9. Bring to a boil and keep at a strong simmer for 20 minutes.
10. Strain as in step 7, then combine the two extractions. Measure.
11. Boil down by half. (For example, if you started with 4 cups, cook down to 2 cups.)
12. Sterilize eight 4-ounce canning jars. Bring filtered liquid to a high simmer, fill jars, and cap with two-piece metal lids.
13. Place filled, capped jars in a hot water bath, bring to a boil, and boil for 10 minutes.
14. Let cool, label, and date. The pectin should be used within a year.
15. This will provide enough homemade pectin for 8 batches of jelly.

Necessary Acidity

In addition to pectin, preserves need acid. You can easily raise the level for low-acid fruits by adding a tablespoon of fresh lemon juice to each cup of prepared juice. This adds tartness without significantly affecting the flavor.

Here are lists of fruits with their pectin and acid balance:

- Fruit high in both pectin and acid includes crab apples and sour apples, citrus, cranberries, currants and gooseberries, underripe grapes, and tart plums. Those fruits that are moderate in both pectin and acid include elderberries, ripe grapes, and sweet plums.
- Fruit high in pectin but low in acid includes sweet apples and quinces.
- Fruit low in pectin but high in acid includes apricots, pineapple, and rhubarb.
- Fruit low in both pectin and acid includes berries such as blackberries, raspberries, and strawberries, cherries, figs, pears, and peaches.

Sugar

Sugar is necessary to produce a gel. In addition, it functions as a preservative for all kinds of sweetened preserves. Low-sugar preserves need to be frozen to keep them from spoiling. When you use anything other than white sugar made from sugarcane or sugar beets, it will affect the flavor of your finished product. This includes brown sugar, light corn syrup, honey, or molasses, all of which are often used in making chutneys and other strongly flavored preserves.

Of late, there are recipes available for preserves made without any sugar at all. Honey or concentrated fruit juices are used for sweetening, and these products are thickened with glycerin or low-methoxy pectin that requires a calcium solution to create a gel. One cookbook for no-sugar preserving gives recipes using boiled-down bottled grape juice, frozen juice concentrate, and canned fruit. I find this entire concept somewhat offensive and cannot fathom why someone would want to put the effort into making such absurd, imitation preserves as "Jam-Pot Jam" using "odds and ends of fruit such as canned peaches, apricots, pears, etc." After all, preserves are eaten in small amounts. Other than diabetics and people following currently fashionable low-carb diets, there are few of us who could not/should not/would not enjoy a spoonful of apple butter on Sunday morning toast.

Sugar

Today we take sugar and its easy availability for granted. Do you want granulated white sugar, light brown or dark brown sugar, confectioners' sugar, or superfine sugar? We think nothing of buying clean white sugar in a two-pound box or a five- or ten-pound bag. In my suburban/rural area, at certain times of year sugar is obtainable at the supermarket in twenty-five-pound bags, a size that is available year-round at a shopping club warehouse store nearby. At the other end of the spectrum are little paper packets of sugar set out for the taking with restaurant coffee. Sugar sneaks onto our tongues in many disguises, not just in sweet things, such as candy and baked goods, but also in soda and soft drinks, salad dressings, canned vegetarian-style beans, and much, much more. Once upon a time, sugar was a luxury for the rich, who used it as a seasoning rather than a sweetener. Where did it come from, and how did it so thoroughly establish itself in our food?

Sugar has two primary sources. It can be extracted from sugar beets, which are grown in temperate parts of the world, or from sugarcane, *Saccharum officinarum*, originally from tropical southeastern Asia. Cultivation of sugarcane may have begun in southern India, spreading into Asia and the Middle East before reaching northern Africa and Spain. When the crusaders first tasted this new "spice" in the Middle East and brought it back to Europe in the thirteenth century, it was used, along with cinnamon, cloves, saffron, and other spices, as a culinary additive. "Sugar and spice and everything nice" is a fragment from a children's nursery rhyme that happens to describe sugar's original usage. We don't think of sugar as a spice today, and it has certainly always been anomalous compared to other seasonings. It does not have the fragrance we associate with spices such as pepper and nutmeg, cloves and cinnamon. But like these spices, in the thirteenth century and up until the close of the fourteenth century, sugar was an exotic condiment only procurable from faraway places and at great cost.

Sugar's primary use was medicinal. Conserves and preserves, names that were used well before *jam* and *jelly*, were thought to be an admirable remedy for winter coughs and colds and an excellent digestif after a banquet. These conserves and preserves were much stiffer than the softer, more spreadable versions of today. Recipes from the late seventeenth century for *quidony*, made of quinces, pears, or apples, have the fruit cooked until soft then wrung through a cloth so there would be tiny particles of fruit in the juice, rather than the clear liquid used for jelly making. This would then be boiled with sugar until thick and poured into wooden or tin molds. These might have a decorative form on the bottom, to print the *quidony* with a pattern that would be revealed when it was turned out of the mold. Today's equivalents would be a quince, damson plum, or even cranberry cheese or fruit leather. Fruit cheese is a cooked-down version of fruit butter, firm enough when set to turn out of an oiled mold and slice.

Sugar was used in the kitchen only sparingly, as a condiment in cooking. It is still used in this manner in Chinese cooking, where a small amount of sugar, perhaps a teaspoonful or less, is added to the other marinade or sauce ingredients for a dish intended to serve four people. The effect is not so much a sweetening of the dish as one that creates a rich brown glaze, affects the texture of the sauce, and influences the meat's ability to take up the seasonings.

Sugarcane grows relatively easily in the Mediterranean region. It was produced in the Kingdom of Jerusalem in the twelfth century, and the Venetian Cornaro family had a vast sugar operation in fourteenth-century Cyprus. It is not surprising that Venice was involved in the sugar trade, as it was the center for the flourishing spice trade. By the fifteenth century, production shifted from Sicily to the Algarve and then to the newly settled islands of the eastern Atlantic: Madeira, the western Canaries, the Cape Verde Islands, and those of the Gulf of Guinea. By the end of the century, it became the basis of the islands' economies, a high-value product that could compete with the spices of the East. However, though it was more readily available and beginning to replace honey, cane sugar was still a luxury even in the last quarter of the fifteenth century. Sugar confections were still an indulgence, written down in the household accounts of Isabella the Catholic as Christmas gifts for royal children.

By the next century, it was introduced to the New World, to the Caribbean Islands, and to Brazil. The triangle of molasses, rum, and sugar was made possible to a large extent by the African slave trade. Sugar became the sweetener of choice in the Western world, even for the masses. It changed from a luxury and a curiosity to something commonplace that was considered to be a necessity. Think about this: in the England of 1700, the estimated annual consumption of sugar was four pounds per person. That's everybody, rich and poor, so obviously a few consumed more and others much less, if any at all. This tripled to twelve pounds per person by 1780, and was

up to eighteen pounds of sugar per person per year by 1800, a better than 400 percent increase in less than 100 years. By then, most sugar was used to sweeten coffee, tea, and hot chocolate to European tastes. I find this use to be rather interesting, since the Chinese, who began drinking tea thousands of years ago, did not sweeten it, nor did the Aztecs sweeten chocolate. (Coffee, discovered in Ethiopia, taken to Arabia—hence to Turkey and thence to Europe—was drunk as a sweetened beverage by the Turks.) But it was in the seventeenth and eighteenth centuries, when sugar began to be used to preserve fruits and marmalade, jams, and jellies hit the market, that demand really took off. By the 1890s, the consumption of sugar was just slightly less than ninety pounds per person per year.

Until well into the nineteenth century, sugar was an expensive luxury eaten in relatively small amounts. The major change came about when sugar was transformed from a rare and costly substance into a cheap and commonplace one, from a frippery for royalty to the teatime jam pot on working-class tables. Sugar's ability to function as a preservative escalated its consumption in the form of sweetened preserves. Marmalades, jams, and jellies need no refrigeration to keep them from quickly spoiling. As the cost of sugar dropped, it was the fruit that became the expensive ingredient. Any sort of cheap vegetable, carrots primarily, but also beets and others, was made into a sweetened pulp with a small amount of flavoring added and sold off as jam. It was cheaper than butter. And it was eaten every day.

In the sixteenth and seventeenth centuries, sugar was sold more or less refined, pressed into lumpy blocks or cones. It was clarified at home. A quantity of sugar would first be heated with water until it dissolved. Next an egg white would be well beaten in a small amount of water and added to the sugar water. Once the sugar had melted, it would be brought to a boil. As the egg white coagulated, it would trap the scummy bits. Next the sugar syrup would be strained through a thick wet napkin to catch the bits of egg white. Only then you could begin cooking fruit with the syrup to make jam or marmalade. For other uses, sugar might be scraped off the block and then sifted. My brother, Ben, brought me some block sugar from Mexico, small, coarse, crumbly dark-brown cakes that tasted faintly of cinnamon. It gave me an entirely new appreciation for the clean, refined, granular white sugar that is so cheaply and easily available today as a staple rather than a luxury.

Testing for the Jell Point

Preserves are best made in small quantities. It keeps the flavor fresh, not overcooked or caramelized. Telling when a fruit butter or jam is ready is an easy determination: a spoon leaves a track when dragged through the mass. For jelly, use no more than four to six cups of juice at a time; the modest volume quickly reaches the correct temperature to produce a gel. When you've been making jelly for a while, it becomes easier to tell when the blend of fruit juice, sugar, and pectin acidity amalgamates into jelly, but jelly making is trickier than making other kinds of preserves.

Katzy did it by eye: a boiling liquid has relatively large bubbles, while boiling jelly is a seething mass of small bubbles that cannot be stirred down. Carole Nagy mentioned that the fine bubbles also have a shiny, glassy look. Testing by appearance works for me when I'm making jelly that I know sets easily. In fact, some jellies—grape, for example—will continue to firm up a bit after they've been bottled, so something that's on the soft side when it first cools off will be just right a month later.

A low-tech method that works only with jelly is to dip a metal soupspoon into the boiling liquid. Lift the spoon out and turn it sideways so jelly runs off the side. Blow gently on the liquid to cool it more quickly. When the jell point has been reached, the mass flows off the spoon in a sheet. If it falls as a couple of drops, the jell point is close but has not yet been reached.

Here's another simple method. Before starting to make jelly, put several china saucers in the freezer to chill them down. When you think the jell point has been reached, remove the pan from the heat. (You don't want cooking to continue while you make the test.) Put about a tablespoon of jelly on the plate and put it back in the refrigerator for two or three minutes. Then push the jelly with your forefinger. If it wrinkles ahead of your finger, the jelly is done and may be bottled. Carole turns the plate upside down to see how well it clings.

Lastly, and perhaps easiest, is to use a jelly or candy thermometer. At or near sea level, when the boiling liquid reaches 220° Fahrenheit, the juice and sugar mixture (with good pectin and acid levels) has reached the jell point. Remember to drop the temperature approximately 2° for every 1,000 feet above sea level.

ALTITUDE	JELL TEST TEMPERATURE
sea level	220° Fahrenheit
1,000 feet	218° Fahrenheit
2,000 feet	216° Fahrenheit
3,000 feet	214° Fahrenheit
4,000 feet	212° Fahrenheit
5,000 feet	210° Fahrenheit
6,000 feet	208° Fahrenheit

And if your jelly doesn't jell? You could remake it using commercial pectin. If using Certo liquid pectin:

1. Mix ¾ cup of sugar with 2 tablespoons of fresh lemon juice and 2 tablespoons of liquid pectin in a measuring cup and set aside.

2. Bring 4 cups of jelly to a full rolling boil in a large saucepan, stirring constantly.

3. Remove from the heat and quickly add the pectin mixture. Bring back to a full boil over high heat and cook for one minute, stirring constantly.

4. Remove from heat, skim off any foam with a teaspoon, and ladle into hot, sterilized jars. (Another option to skimming off the foam is to add a spoonful of butter to the hot liquid before adding sugar, and the foam will not form.)

5. Cap and process in a boiling water bath for 5 minutes.

If using Sure-Jell powdered pectin:

1. Combine $^3/_4$ cup of sugar with $^1/_2$ cup of water, 2 tablespoons of fresh lemon juice, and 4 teaspoons of dry pectin.
2. Bring ingredients to a full boil, add 4 cups of jelly, and bring back to a boil, stirring all the while.
3. Boil for 30 seconds, remove from heat, and skim off any foam.
4. Remove from heat, skim off any foam with a teaspoon, and ladle into hot, sterilized jars. (Another option to skimming off the foam is to add a spoonful of butter to the hot liquid before adding sugar, and the foam will not form.)
5. Cap and process in a boiling water bath for 5 minutes.

Another option is to do as I do when my jelly doesn't jell and call it syrup, great over ice cream or pound cake. It also makes a refreshing drink by pouring a tablespoon or two over a glass of ice, then filling with water or club soda.

Canning Jars and Sealing Options

When I was a child, jams and jellies were usually put up in recycled jars that once held some other item. This was common practice: My friend Sandra Green from Orrington, Maine, recalls that her mother did all of her preserving in glasses or small jars, using paraffin wax to seal them. Jack Lenzo learned about making preserves from his mother. He recalls that "I was too little to be near the stove while she made preserves, but I loved being in the kitchen, so I was her number-one fruit masher. We used glass jars sealed with paraffin wax." Faith Marcovecchio remembers that "We always bottled our preserves in glass jars that we had saved over the years (not jars purchased specifically for preserving) and sealed them with paraffin wax." From the 1950s on, even jars sold specifically for jelly making were designed for use with paraffin wax. They had straight sides without any threads that would take a screw-on cap. These purchased jars had a metal cap that fitted over the top. While it did protect the paraffin seal, its primary purpose was to cover the jar once it was opened.

And at that, paraffin wax is an improvement over earlier techniques. *The Cottage Kitchen, A Collection of Practical and Inexpensive Recipes* was a title in the Common Sense in the Household Series, written by Marion Harland and published in 1883 by Charles Scribner's Sons. Here is how she suggests bottling your preserves: "Have your jelly-glasses all ready, roll each in hot water, and fill while wet inside and out. When the jelly is firm, press tissue-paper closely on top, working out all the air from beneath, and paste stout papers over the glasses." Now comes the good part: "Should mould form on the tissue-papers it will not injure the taste of the jelly. Indeed, it will help to exclude the air, and when the papers are removed, the surface of the jelly will appear bright and clear." She does add that "A teaspoonful of brandy on the tissue-paper is said to assist in preserving the jelly." Trust me, we do it differently today. In all fairness, I must say that occasionally, if the inside rim of the jar has not been sufficiently cleaned, there would be some mold beneath the little cake of paraffin wax on the surface of the jelly or jam. As I recall, that would be scooped off with a spoon, making sure to take some of the adjacent preserve, and we'd go ahead and eat the rest.

The occasionally purchased, purpose-made jelly glasses my mother infrequently bought when I was growing up were simple, straight-sided jars that also were sealed with paraffin wax. I have an old box of the stuff, manufactured by Gulf Oil Corporation. An end flap bears text that says Gulfwax is "A highly refined paraffin wax especially made for sealing jams, jellies and preserves in open top containers and for home candle making" and also that it "Conforms to F.D.A. Regulations." The box also has the following instructions:

1. Fill glasses or jars to within $1/2$ inch of top.
2. Clean inside top rim of container to remove any preserves from surface.
3. While contents are hot, cover with $1/8$ inch of melted Gulfwax.
4. When cold, add another $1/8$-inch layer of melted Gulfwax, tilting and rotating to seal completely.

Paraffin wax does seal the contents against the air and against contamination by dust and mold spores. It could be recycled, melted down, and reused season after season. Faith recalls that her mother "kept the wax in a small saucepan in the cupboard. She just put the saucepan on the stove over very low heat and, voilà, melted paraffin!" That is a somewhat hazardous way to melt the wax, as the temperature differential between melting point and igniting the wax is narrow. A much safer method is to put the wax in a clean, dry tin can set into a saucepan filled with water, and then heat. This quasi–double boiler method may be somewhat slower, but it is also more prudent.

My sister, Haya, still uses paraffin wax to seal her jars of homemade preserves, but that is out of necessity. She mentioned to me that "I wish that mason jars like the ones in your photo from the state fair [it was actually the fabulous Madison, Wisconsin, Saturday farmers' market] were available here in Israel. I'll use what smaller jelly jars I have from preserves that you've sent to us (now empty) because I have a box of unused lids I brought home from my last visit to the States. I do have some paraffin and can use it to seal larger jars that I'll fill with most of the marmalade."

The layer of wax is somewhat brittle and can crack, which may be a problem. For about five years in the late 1960s, I had a pet skunk, which we bought from a pet store as a baby. Skunks are clever, have a keen sense of smell and a sweet tooth. Stinky (I know, I know, but that's what my toddlers named him) sniffed out a box with a dozen jars of preserves stored in the kitchen. He dug through the wax to sample each and every one. Partly my fault, since the box was on the floor. But I imagine that mice could also gnaw through the sealing layer of wax and contaminate the contents. This is not a concern today, because the paraffin wax method is pretty much abandoned by now. The USDA recommends only the use of two-piece metal lids, which are not only easier to use, they also seal the contents much more safely. Accordingly, this is also the

standard required for grange fairs, country fairs, and anywhere else that preserves might be entered into competition. Jars can be used again and again and again, for as long as they are sound and the rim is free of any nicks or chips. The flat lids can only be used once and are then discarded. Replacements are available in boxes of a dozen, as are the metal rings that seal them down to the mouth of the jar. While the screw-down rings may be reused, they eventually become discolored and pitted, usually replaced for aesthetic reasons rather than through necessity.

The Development of Canning

What is today a pleasant, optional, leisure-time occupation was once dire necessity. Food was grown or gathered, raised or hunted. Putting food by, saving the summer and fall bounty for winter's scarcity, was fundamental to survival. Food had to be kept for months on end, and not all food can be stored "as is." Some produce, potatoes, for example, could be heaped up, covered with a layer of straw and a covering of earth, and they would last out in the field. Root cellars, earth-floored basement rooms with shelves and bins for apples, carrots, turnips, potatoes, and so on, were once part of every farmhouse, and even common in town. Even though bacteria and fungi were unknown as microorganisms at that time, their effects—the results of bacterial contamination—were obvious. Food became moldy, it rotted, it was no longer edible. People discovered that salted, dried, and pickled food lasted better and remained edible for a longer time. Different methods of preserving—pickling, salting, drying, freezing—were developed as methods of keeping food that would otherwise spoil. Sugar also makes food less subject to decay, and sweet preserves, combinations of sugar and fruit, became another method of food preservation.

Today cans and bottles are the norm. It seems that almost everything comes in a can or a bottle: soft drinks and motor oil, tuna fish and Spam, tomatoes whole, diced, crushed, or puréed, pickles and preserves, pet food … the list is endless. While recycling is the ideal, we take containers so much for granted that their empty shells litter highway verges. Yet where did the idea of putting food in a bottle or a can come from? The impetus began late in the eighteenth century, when the emperor Napoleon Bonaparte, concerned with supplying his troops with safe, convenient rations, offered the handsome sum of 12,000 francs to anyone who developed a reliable method of preserving food. An army, it is said, travels on its stomach. And Napoleon had not only his large army, but also a navy to victual. It was Nicholas Appert, a French chef who had also worked as a brewer and distiller, who developed a process whereby food was sealed in a bottle, like wine. If the food was first heated, bottled, sealed with a cork that was covered with pitch and wired down, and then heated gently in a water bath, voilà, the food did not spoil. Appert concluded that it was the exclusion of air and the application of heat that preserved the food. In a way, he was correct. The heating process killed bacteria present in and on the food and in the air. Sealing the containers kept additional bacteria from contaminating the bottles' contents. Keep in mind that Appert, who perfected his technique around 1810, was fifty years ahead of Louis Pasteur and his theory of germs.

Canning Jars

As with anything else, canning jars have evolved over time. The major change and useful innovation was the development of a threaded neck that mated to the threads in a screw-on cap. Invented by John Landis Mason, it received a patent in 1858. So popular were his jars that *mason jar* became a colloquial term for the glass jars used for home canning. Then there was Mason's Improved, which also used a sealing rubber ring, with a flat glass lid and a separate metal (often zinc) screw-on band. Another technique, patented in 1882 by Henry W. Putnam, also used a glass lid and a rubber sealing ring. However his design used two sturdy wires: one, the bail, went over the top of the lid and was held in place by a pair of raised dots. A second wire was snapped down to tighten the bail and secure the lid. A further variation was the Lightning Dimple Neck Seal, patented by Anthony McDonnell in 1908. Rather than having a tie wire circling the neck of the jar, his design used two small indentations on opposite sides of the jar's neck to hold the snap-down locking wire. Ball Ideal jars made use of this technology.

Collectors pay extraordinary prices for rare examples. An American Improved Preserve Can from the mid-1800s in aqua glass might sell for $2,500 or more. A popular collectors' guide to old fruit jars by Douglas M. Leybourne Jr. has more than forty-two pages of Ball canning jars and more than sixty-eight pages for Mason's. Examples of Kerr jars fill six pages. And endless examples of jars from America, Canada, England, Belgium, Australia, and elsewhere reveal just how enthusiastically the manufacture of supplies for home canning took off.

CHAPTER TWO

FRUIT BUTTERS

If you can make applesauce, you can make fruit butter. Fruit butter is, beyond a doubt, the easiest type of preserves you can make. Simply put, apples or other fruit are lightly cooked just sufficiently to make into a purée, which is then cooked with one-half to two-thirds as much sugar (by volume) until it is thick enough to spread. The texture should be uniform and fine. At room temperature, fruit butter should be thick enough to stand on a plate without oozing or running and thin enough to spread easily on bread. Sometimes fruit butters are flavored with spices such as cinnamon, cloves, ginger, cardamom, or allspice. My mother, ever the thrifty cook, would sometimes use the pulp left after cooking and puréeing fruit then straining it to extract the liquid for making jelly. Thus grape pulp leftover from the early stages of making grape jelly would become grape butter. Because fruit butters are made from a thick purée, they bubble and pop when cooked on a burner. I prefer to cook some fruit butters in an oven. It takes longer, but there's no hazardous spattering. Also, there's less likelihood of scorching the purée and spoiling the flavor.

My sister, Haya, remembers a story of our mother, Katzy, at about age seven. She had an annoyingly loose tooth. Grandma Gussie gave her a slice of rye bread spread with applesauce (which maybe we can think of as a kind of fruit butter). In chewing the hard crust, the tooth came out, and at first Katzy thought it was an apple pit that had somehow been left in the applesauce. Haya also remembers watching our

Grandma Gussie making applesauce, sometimes seasoned with cinnamon. Her first-born daughter, our mother, told Haya that when she was a girl and Gussie was preparing a batch of potato pancakes, she'd grate the potatoes into a *schissel* (Yiddish for "dishpan") in order to have sufficient quantity for her six daughters' hearty appetites. And, as is traditional, the potato pancakes would be served with applesauce.

Perhaps it never rains in California, but winter still brings cool, damp days when a quiet weekend with some comfort food is more than welcome. An e-mail from my brother one Sunday morning late in December shares his pleasure in a dish of apple butter that I'd sent him in November: "I hadn't opened the apple butter, knowing that there would be a right time for it. And it came this morning … Somehow the slowness of the morning, the pleasure of staying inside with the Sunday papers, seemed just right. And … we even had some leftover challah. The apple butter was just fabulous on toasted, slightly stale challah—smooth, moist, fragrant, and, above all, delicious!"

Apples

Apple Butter

Rating: Easy

Special Instructions: Partway through the recipe, the liquid must be boiled down and reduced to half its volume. This quantity makes two batches of apple butter.

Yield: Six 8-ounce jars plus one 4-ounce jar for each batch

INGREDIENTS:

2 small lemons

8 C. apple cider

15 Granny Smith or other tart, firm apples

4 C. dark brown sugar

Spices: Your choice of $^1/_4$ tsp. nutmeg and $^1/_4$ tsp. cardamom or $^1/_2$ tsp. cinnamon and $^1/_4$ tsp. cloves for each of the two batches

1. Wash lemons. Cut into quarters and then into thin slices. Place in a small saucepan, cover with 1 cup of cider. Put a lid on the pot and simmer, covered, for about 15 minutes, or until the lemon slices are soft. Set aside.

2. Wash apples and cut into quarters. Do not peel or core. Place in a large saucepan or Dutch oven. Add prepared lemon slices and liquid. Add remaining 7 cups of apple cider.

3. Simmer until the apples are very soft. Strain, saving the liquid.

4. Purée fruit pulp through a food mill with the coarse screen to remove the seeds. Yield should be about 10 cups. Set aside.

5. Measure liquid. Yield should be about $9^3/_4$ cups. Boil down liquid until reduced by half.

6. To 5 cups of purée, add 2 cups of dark brown sugar and 1¹/₂ cups of the cider reduction. Repeat for second batch.

   Note: I like to divide the purée into two batches since the smaller volume can be cooked in a shorter time. It also means that I can season one batch with cinnamon and cloves, the other with nutmeg and cardamom.

7. Cook, uncovered, in a large pot or Dutch oven in a 225° Fahrenheit oven for about 6 hours, stirring occasionally. The apple butter is ready when a spoon dragged through the purée leaves a track. You may prepare and cook both batches at once if separate posts are used.

8. If you would like a delicately spiced apple butter, now season the purée with nutmeg and cardamom. Alternatively, season with cinnamon and cloves.

   Note: Some recipes call for adding the spices at the start of cooking down the sugared purée. I feel that the finished product has a brighter flavor when the spices are added at the end of the cooking process.

9. Fill and process prepared jars as described on page 6.

Rhineland Apple Butter

I once read a definition for apple butter, its source now forgotten, that said, "Apple butter, which is applesauce concentrated by boiling it down with cider, was a traditional European product associated especially with the Dutch. It was they who introduced it to America, now its principal stronghold." So, of course, I had to ask Carla Teune, my Dutch friend who lives in Leiden, about this. And she replied, "*Appelmoes* is apples, not peeled, cut in four parts and cooked in a pan with sugar (like you cook cranberries) and eaten warm or cold or with cinnamon powder on it, a great favorite of children. When I was younger, my answer to the question 'What do you want to have for your birthday dinner?' was always 'Roast chicken, French fries, and *appelmoes*.' I think you call that 'applesauce.' You can keep bits of apple in it or put it through a sieve. Even cold on bread it is very nice.

"What I think you call 'apple butter' is what we call '*appelstroop*,' but it is much thicker than syrup (not like maple syrup, which is quite thin). It is quite dark, like shoeshine, and really looks a bit like molasses, but smells and taste appley. It is 'apple molasses,' and it was my great favorite when I was young to put on my bread. It is usually not served with a dish, but sometimes it is used in other recipes."

Well, that doesn't sound like the apple butter I'm familiar with, but I did manage to turn up a recipe that sounds like what Carla is talking about for *Rheinisches Apfelkraut*, Rhineland Apple Butter, in *The Good Cook, Techniques & Recipes: Preserving* published by Time-Life Books in 1981. While certainly doable at home, it is one of those things generally bought. Apparently *apfelkraut* can still be found without problems in any supermarket in Germany or Holland.

Rating: Moderate, can easily scorch

Special Instructions: This recipe takes two days. The second day, when you boil the liquid down, will require close attention.

Yield: Two 8-ounce jars

INGREDIENTS:

10 quarts apples

2 C. water

1. Wash and quarter apples and steam with water until they dissolve into a purée. If a steamer is not available, simmer the apples and water in a large covered pot until they are quite soft, about 40 minutes.

2. Pour the apple mush into a jelly bag and allow it to drip, undisturbed, for 24 hours, saving the liquid. You should have about 3 quarts of liquid.

3. Put the liquid into a large, heavy pan, bring to a boil, and cook, uncovered, until the liquid has been reduced to about 2 cups. This will take between 90 minutes and 2 hours. Toward the end of that time, it will require constant stirring to keep it from scorching. The *apfelstroop* will turn dark brown and become quite thick, having the consistency of honey.

4. Fill and process prepared jars as described on page 6.

Quinces

Quince is a wonderfully delicious fruit—if you cook it first. Even when ripe, they are astringent and inedible, too hard to bite into, even more so than the most underripe of pears. However, their fragrance and the flavor of the cooked fruit are unique and special. This is the fruit from which marmalade was originally developed. (There is more information on marmalades in Chapter Five.) Once relatively common, quinces are now more difficult to find. They are sometimes available in supermarkets in late fall or winter, and the occasional farm stand may sell them. If you are buying quinces at the supermarket and find them rather costly (they are priced per fruit, rather than by the pound), keep in mind that quince combines beautifully with apples or pears.

Quinces: The Golden Apple

Now, *quince* is a name used as the common name for the fruit of a couple of different shrubs or small trees. The true quince is *Cydonia oblonga*. Like apples and pears, it is a fruit that originated in the Caucasus. Its cultivation spread to the Levant, the lands bordering the eastern shores of the Mediterranean and the Aegean Seas. It was cultivated in Palestine as early as 1000 B.C. "Stay me with flagons, comfort me with apples: for I am sick of love" from the Song of Solomon is more likely a reference to quinces, also called golden apples. It is quite possibly the fruit that Paris awarded to the goddess Aphrodite, leading to the Trojan War.

Shaped somewhat like an apple or a rounded pear, the large, fragrant fruit is covered with a soft fuzz, like a peach plucked directly from the tree, and turns golden yellow when mature. Quince is also the name commonly used for flowering quince, *Chanomeles speciosa,* a deservedly popular garden shrub with beautiful flowers that bloom in mid- to late spring. The roundish green fruits that develop in autumn can be used for preserves. In addition, I discovered that a nearby arboretum has a couple of ornamental Chinese quince trees, *Pseudocydonia sinensis,* which bear huge oval fruits, much larger than the true quince, in fall. No one was interested in them until I came along and politely asked if I might glean the fallen ones. As long as I was inconspicuous about this, I was told, go ahead. Over time, I have learned to be prudent about this sort of largesse. The first time out I collected all the fruit that had fallen beneath both trees, and most of it went to waste; there was simply too much. Now, I take only three or four of the best quality, and I find that this quantity is more than ample. Not inevitably, but frequently, the pale flesh of all of these quinces turns a lovely Venetian red when cooked into fruit butter and jelly.

Quince Butter

Rating: Easy

Special Instructions: The peels and cores are cooked separately from the fruit. You will also need a cheesecloth bag made by taking a large square of cotton cheesecloth, doubling it over, then doubling it over again. Once you put the peels and cores in the center, gather up the corners into a pouch and tie them with kitchen twine.

Yield: Variable, depending on the size of the quinces

INGREDIENTS:

6 or 8 large quinces

> *(Note: If you have only a couple of quinces, make up the difference with apples or pears.)*

Juice of 1/2 lemon

Water

Sugar

1. Wash the quinces. Scrub them with a coarse kitchen towel to remove any fuzz. Peel, cut open, and core, using a melon baller to scoop out the seeds and membranes and setting aside the peels and cores. Drop the prepared fruit into enough water to cover them and mix with the lemon juice to keep the quinces from turning brown.

2. Put the peels and cores, which are high in pectin, into a cheesecloth bag as described in the Special Instructions above.

3. Lift the fruit from the acidulated water and put it in a Dutch oven with enough water to cover. Add the pouch of cores and peels. Bring to a boil, then simmer

for about 45 minutes, or until the fruit is easily pierced with a skewer.

4. Strain, saving the liquid but discarding the pouch of peels and cores after pressing on it to remove as much liquid as possible.

    Note: You may use the liquid to make Quince Jelly as described on pages 76–77.

5. Purée the fruit using the coarse plate of a food mill. Measure the purée and add between two-thirds and an equal amount of sugar, depending on your preference for a sweet or less-sweet product.

6. Cook over moderate heat, stirring constantly to prevent scorching, until the spoon leaves a track when dragged through the purée.

7. Fill and process prepared jars as described on page 6.

Paradise Butter

This tasty fruit butter makes use of the puréed pulp leftover from making Paradise Jelly (pages 77–78).

Rating: Easy
Yield: Variable

INGREDIENTS:
Puréed pulp leftover from making Paradise Jelly
Sugar

1. Purée the set-aside quince, apple, and cranberry pulp through the coarse plate of a food mill.

2. Measure. Add $2/3$ cup of sugar for each cup of pulp.

3. Cook over a low flame, stirring frequently, until fruit butter is thickened and a spoon dragged through it leaves a track. Or, process in a 225° Fahrenheit oven, stirring occasionally, until thick.

4. Fill and process prepared jars as described on page 6.

Pear Butter (also known as Pear Honey)

This is sometimes called pear honey, perhaps for its smooth texture and sweet taste.

Different pears have very different flavors. They used to be grown for specific uses: for eating out of hand, for cooking, or for making perry, pear cider. Today we generally find only a few all-purpose kinds of pears in the market: Anjou, Bartlett, Bosc, Comice, perhaps Packham, and the little Seckel pears. Unlike other fruits, pears must be picked while still immature. Allowed to ripen on the tree, they develop gritty stone cells at the center that make the fruit unpleasant to eat. Putting fruit into a brown paper bag with the top rolled over and clipped shut will speed the ripening process. For preserving, pears should be firm-ripe. Beyond that point, they fall apart when cooked.

My two favorites for making preserves are Bosc and Comice. Recognizable by its long neck and russet skin, Bosc is a great winter pear with a juicy, aromatic flesh when ripe. Comice is a plump, green-skinned pear with a red blush, sweet, aromatic, and juicy flesh.

Rating: Easy

Yield: Four to six 8-ounce jars

INGREDIENTS:

2 to 2^1/$_2$ lbs. pears, Bosc or Comice preferred

1 to 2 Tbs. fresh lemon juice

^{1}/$_4$ C. water

Sugar

1. Peel pears. Cut each one in half and use a melon baller to scoop out the core. As each pear is prepared, drop it into a bowl of water with the lemon juice added. This keeps the fruit from discoloring.
2. When all of the pears are prepared, chop them into coarse chunks and measure. You should have about 6 cups. Put in a large saucepan, add about ^{1}/$_4$ cup of water, and simmer, covered, over low heat, for 15 minutes, or until the pears are soft.
3. Purée through the coarse plate of a food mill. Measure.
4. For every cup of purée, add ^{1}/$_3$ cup of sugar. Return to the large saucepan.
5. Cook over low heat, stirring frequently, until the mixture thickens and a spoon dragged through the mass leaves a slowly filling track. Or, process in a 225° Fahrenheit oven, stirring occasionally, until thick.
6. Fill and process prepared jars as described on page 6.

Variations: Use a combination of pears and quinces. Or, flavor with one or two tablespoons of candied ginger, chopped very fine and added to the pear purée together with the sugar. Or, flavor with three or four strips of fresh orange zest (the colored peel only, no white pith), cut into fine slivers, and one teaspoon of vanilla extract. Add the orange zest together with the sugar; add the vanilla extract just before bottling.

Plum Butter

I can tell autumn has arrived when the little Italian prune plums once again show up in the supermarket. A smallish plum with a whitish bloom on its deep blue-black skin, rich amber flesh, and freestone rather than one clinging to the pit, this was my mother's favorite for simple cakes. Inexpensive, it's one I also enjoy using for baking— and even more for preserves. Pick out your plums carefully, one by one, rather than scooping them up by the handful. Firm-ripe with a good bloom are better quality and more flavorful than soft and overripe plums whose skin has generally lost its whitish bloom and gone purple-black.

Rating: Easy

Yield: Six to seven 8-ounce jars

INGREDIENTS:

3 to 3^1/$_2$ lbs. Italian prune plums

^{1}/$_2$ C. water

Sugar

1. Rinse plums, split them in half, and discard the pits. You should have about 6 or 7 cups of prepared plums.
2. Put the plums in a preserving kettle or a large saucepan together with the water.
3. Simmer, covered, over low heat for 20 minutes, or until the plums are soft.
4. Purée through the medium plate of a food mill. Measure. Add ^{1}/$_2$ to ^{3}/$_4$ cup of sugar for every 1 cup of purée, depending on the sweetness of the plums.
5. Cook over low heat, stirring constantly, until the purée has thickened and a spoon dragged through the mass leaves a slowly filling track. Or, process in a 225° Fahrenheit oven, stirring occasionally, until thick.
6. Fill and process prepared jars as described on page 6.

There are recipes for fruit butters in other chapters. The recipe for Blackberry and Raspberry Butters are in Chapter Eight: Delectable Berries (pages 98 and 100), for Grape Butter in Chapter Nine: Native Harvest (page 117), and for Rose Hip Butter in Chapter Ten: Backyard Harvest (pages 142–143).

CHAPTER THREE

JAMS

Katzy had firm opinions about a number of things. And when it came to making preserves, she felt that certain fruits were better for certain types of preserves. Citrus, sine qua non, was for marmalade. Grapes were best used for jelly, with the residual pulp thriftily turned into grape butter. Apples: apple butter. Ever my mother's daughter, I have some opinions of my own. Berries are better for fruit butter than for jam, as the sieving process used for puréeing removes those annoying hard little seeds that otherwise get stuck between your teeth. However, when it comes to peaches, I agree with my mother, who was convinced that they are ideal for peach jam. The succulent tidbits of peach are like an extra flavorful bonus. Really simple and easy to make, jam is only a step away from fruit butters in complexity. The primary difference is that it is made from crushed or cut rather than puréed fruit, and jam lacks the uniform texture of fruit butter. Jams usually have a higher proportion of sugar. They make a thick spread that holds its shape, to a certain extent, but is not as firm as jelly.

Peaches

Only a few miles from where I live in New Jersey, Dick and Carole Nagy have an orchard where they grow fruit for sale: peaches, pears, plums, apples, and blueberries. Their customers are devoted—who wouldn't be, given the superb quality of their tree-ripe harvest? Every year around mid-July, I call and, my mouth watering in anticipation, eagerly ask, "Is Dick picking peaches yet?" The very best peaches are picked "tree-ripe." Of course, they are then so tender that they bruise with ease. For the usual commercial shipment and distribution, peaches are picked, at best, hard-ripe. Putting them in a brown paper bag and rolling over the top will help the ripening (I am tempted to instead say "softening") process. However, such fruit cannot even begin to compare to the peaches I get from Dick and Carole's orchard only minutes from home, so succulent and juicy that I assure them a peach must be eaten naked, in a bathtub.

There are two kinds of peaches: clingstone and freestone. You can tell them apart by the difficulty or ease with which the flesh separates from the pit. Peaches are most commonly available as yellow-fleshed varieties, and I think they are better for preserves or, indeed, anything that is cooked, including cobblers and pies. Yellow-fleshed freestone peaches that Dick Nagy favors include 'Salem,' 'Loring,' 'Redhaven,' and its sports (a gardening term for a mutation), such as 'Cresthaven' and 'Sunhaven.' While excellent for eating out of hand, white-fleshed peaches, such as 'Belle of Georgia,' 'Summer Rose,' 'Mountain Rose,' and 'Snow Giant,' have a delicate flavor that is too modest for preserves. Besides, they easily discolor and do not make as attractive a preserve. Nectarines are fuzzless peaches.

Peach Jam

Rating: Easy

Yield: Seven to eight 8-ounce jars

INGREDIENTS:

3¹/₂ to 4 lbs. ripe peaches

4 C. sugar

1. Prepare the peaches: Bring a large pot of water to a boil. Drop in a few peaches at a time. Let them seethe for a scant minute, dip them out, and drop them into an ice-water bath. Lift them out of the cold water and slip off their skins. Repeat until you've processed them all.

2. Slice the peaches into quarters or sixths (depending on the size of the peaches) and then measure. You should have about 6 cups. Mix with 4 cups of sugar in a large pot.

3. Slowly bring to a boil, stirring constantly, until the sugar has dissolved.

4. Crush with a potato masher, then bring back to a boil. Cook, stirring frequently, until thick.

5. Fill and process prepared jars as described on page 6.

Note: When my mother made peach jam, she would crack the hard pits and add a few of the almondlike seeds while the jam was cooking. They'd be removed before bottling. I do the same thing. While they do add to the flavor of the peach jam, I would be remiss if I did not mention that the seeds do contain minute quantities of cyanide. Modern recipes never include them. I don't think there is really any danger, especially since the seeds are left whole and are removed before bottling. The choice to include them or not is a personal one, and you'll certainly make excellent jam leaving out the pits and using just peaches and sugar. If you want to mimic the flavor of the peach seeds but are concerned about safety, add a little almond extract instead. Or, use a table-spoon of Amaretto, spooning it into each jar just before filling with jam.

Ginger–Peach Jam

You can make a spiced-up version of peach jam by adding candied ginger.

Rating: Easy
Yield: Seven to eight 8-ounce jars

INGREDIENTS:
$3^1/2$ to 4 lbs. ripe peaches
1 Tbs. candied ginger, or to taste
$^1/2$ C. sugar
1 Tbs. fresh lemon juice
$2^1/2$ C. sugar

1. Prepare the peaches: Bring a large pot of water to a boil. Drop in a few peaches at a time. Let them seethe for a scant minute, dip them out, and drop them into an ice-water bath. Lift them out of the cold water and slip off their skins. Repeat until you've processed them all.
2. Slice the peaches into quarters or sixths (depending on the size of the peaches) and then measure. You should have about 6 cups.
3. Combine $^1/2$ cup of sugar with a generous tablespoon of candied ginger in a food processor. Pulse until the ginger is coarsely chopped.
4. Combine peaches with ginger sugar, the additional $2^1/2$ cups of sugar, and lemon juice in a Dutch oven. Stir thoroughly and cover well. Allow to sit for an hour. The sugar will start the juices flowing from the peaches.
5. Bring the mixture to a boil, stirring frequently. Boil gently until the jell point is reached.
6. Fill and process prepared jars as described on page 6.

Sweet yet tangy, this jam is sophisticated in a cream-cheese sandwich. My favorite use, and the real reason I make it, is as an ingredient for marinades and glazes used with meat. See Chapter Twelve: Using Preserves.

Chili-Peach Jam

Sweet and spicy, Chili-Peach Jam is great brushed on barbecued meat, especially pork, just before it comes off the grill. Good for glazing ham and pork chops, too.

Rating: Easy

Special Instructions: Different types of chili peppers have different Scoville heat index ratings, from the incendiary little Scotch bonnet and chile pequin to the much larger, mildly hot ancho chilis. Choose the type that best suits your preferences, and/or adjust the quantity added to the peaches. Also, beware that chili peppers can burn skin, lips, mouth, and eyes. Handle with care and wash hands with soapy water after handling.

Yield: Seven 8-ounce jars

INGREDIENTS:

3¹/₂ to 4 lbs. peaches

2 fresh red chili peppers

2 limes

3 C. sugar

1. Prepare the peaches: Bring a large pot of water to a boil. Drop in a few peaches at a time. Let them seethe for a scant minute, dip them out, and drop them into an ice-water bath. Lift them out of the cold water and slip off their skins. Repeat until you've processed them all.

2. Slice the peaches into quarters or sixths (depending on the size of the peaches) and then measure. You should have about 6 cups.

3. Wash, stem, and seed the chili peppers. Mince finely.

4. Finely chop limes (peel, pith, and juice) and measure ¹/₄ cup.

5. Combine peaches with the chili peppers, lime, and sugar in a Dutch oven. Stir thoroughly and cover well. Allow to sit for an hour. The sugar will start the juices flowing from the peaches.

6. Slowly bring to a boil, stirring constantly, until the sugar has dissolved.

7. Crush with a potato masher, then bring back to a boil. Cook, stirring frequently, until thick.

8. Fill and process prepared jars as described on page 6.

Jam is so easy to make that it was a disaster-relief method for Sue Brotherton and her mother. The family lives in Fairfield County, Connecticut, and this happened back in 1985, in the fall. As Sue related to me, the great meltdown situation went as follows: "My father grows blueberries, raspberries, apricots, peaches, and apples. (The pears usually get nabbed by the squirrels.) At the time, he also grew strawberries. My mother has long frozen the blueberries, raspberries, peaches, and apricots in four-cup portions for making pies or jam. Berries are just rinsed and put in freezer bags; tree fruits are skinned, sliced, and then measured. (Apples get made into sauce before being frozen in plastic containers, but they are the exception.) Numbers on the order of forty or fifty bags of fruit are not unusual for a season.

"All this produce has always been kept in a standing freezer unit. Well, before the old unit was retired, the gasket was finicky and sometimes did not seal properly. (The new unit has a key to lock the door!) The freezer was also used for ice cream—my father is a big consumer. Anyway, one morning, my mother woke me with, 'We've had a disaster.' My first thought was water in the basement. But no, the freezer door had been left ajar all night. And once fruit has gotten to a certain point in the thawing process, it's ruined if you try to refreeze it. So we had many, many sad bags of fruit staring us in the face.

"Mom has been making various jams for years. I don't believe it is something she learned from her German mother; she has a number of books that she consults for recipes. She likes to cut down on the amount of sugar, so she usually puts in something like two-thirds or even half of the suggested amount, and she does use commercial pectin. Mom's actually quite fond of making jam on cold days, and I recall us joking that it was not quite cold enough that day to meet her criteria but, oh, well.

"I can't even remember what we began with, but I'm sure I remember blue, gold, and red, so we must have done some of everything. We may even have had two pots going at once, with another of boiling water for sterilizing the jars. I do remember a very brief discussion about whether to wash the pots, but Mom said something like, "Nah, who cares, we've got so much to do." I believe we were so industrious that Dad was sent out to buy more jars. I think we must have made at least half a dozen batches, and I think each typically produces five jars or so.

"Actually, I asked today, and Mom said that it is not uncommon for her to make multiple batches without washing the pot between. She usually starts with the lighter colors and works her way darker. Her point is that once you get set up and going, it's kinda easier to keep in the groove of things. As for distributing the booty, Mom never has a problem getting people to take the jam. It is a little on the runny side, since she doesn't add all the sugar, but her favorite use for it is mixing with plain, nonfat yogurt for her own fruit blend. So it's actually better if it's runny. Mom has experimented with peach and apple butter but does not like the results as much as she does her jam sessions … "

Apricots

I adore apricots. The best I ever had was on a visit to Portland, Oregon, for the annual meeting of a plant group I belong to. A girlfriend and I drove out to Lincoln City, on the coast and a lot farther away than we had thought. On the way back, Jayne Roberts and I stopped at a farm stand, buying field-ripened cantaloupes, cherries, and apricots. We each got a Styrofoam fruit box from the back of the stand and packed our produce into it before sealing it up with duct tape. In those days, there was no problem checking such odd packages aboard an airplane. As I walked in the door after arriving home, luggage wheelies loaded with a Styrofoam box as well as suitcase, my husband looked at the box in bemusement. He is used to my hauling home plants, but what could be in here? When the tape was cut and the lid lifted off, the fantastic aroma of perfectly ripe fruit came rushing out. One or two apricots had gotten crushed but were still edible, so I ate them right away to keep them from spoiling.

Here in the Northeast, apricots are usually offered for sale underripe. Sometimes so much so that I've seen them literally green as grass. If you do find beautifully ripe—delectably, meltingly ripe—velvet-skinned apricots and can bring yourself to defer the gratification of eating them fresh to making jam for a winter's day, well, here's a simple recipe for apricot jam.

Apricot Jam

Rating: Easy
Special Instructions: Fruit will need to sit for several hours or overnight before cooking.
Yield: Three 8-ounce jars plus one 4-ounce jar

INGREDIENTS:

2 to 3 lbs. ripe apricots (Apricots are small, with usually 4 or 5 and up to 7 apricots to the pound.)
2 to 3 Tbs. fresh lemon juice
Sugar

1. Rinse apricots and cut in half to remove the stones, but leave the skin on. Slice in eighths lengthwise, then cut each slice in quarters. Place the prepared fruit in a large saucepan. One pound of apricots yields 2 cups of prepared fruit, and it is preferable to work with 4 to 6 cups of fruit at a time.

2. To each 2 cups of prepared fruit, add 1 cup of sugar and 1 tablespoon of fresh lemon juice. Stir gently but thoroughly to coat the apricot slices with sugar. I prefer to use a wooden spoon. Cover and let sit for a few hours or overnight. This draws some of the juices from the fruit.

3. When the sugar is soupy and pretty much dissolved, heat the fruit to just below a boil. Turn the heat down so the apricots simmer gently. Stir frequently, gently mashing the fruit as it softens.

4. The apricot jam is done when it has thickened to the point where a spoon dragged through the mass leaves a track, about 20 or 25 minutes.

5. Fill and process prepared jars as described on page 6.

Note: My mother's recipe calls for cracking the stones, blanching and slicing the nuts, and adding them to the jam just before it is put into the jars. This is no longer recommended, as the nuts contain trace amounts of cyanide and slicing them makes the cyanide more likely to permeate the jam. I use a teaspoon of almond extract for 4 cups of prepared apricots in place of the stones.

Dried Apricot Jam

If you cannot find good-quality fresh apricots, then you can use dried apricots to make jam instead. It is worthwhile to choose organic Turkish dried apricots, which are of the best quality. Supermarket apricots are first bleached with sulfur dioxide, and I find that this does affect the flavor of the jam.

Rating: Easy

Special Instructions: The dried apricots will need to be soaked for 12 to 24 hours.

Yield: Approximately three 8-ounce jars

INGREDIENTS:

2 lbs. dried apricots (organic Turkish preferred)

Fresh lemon juice

Sugar

1 tsp. almond extract (optional)

1. Cut fine the dried apricots. Using a pair of scissors works well to snip them up, but first rinse the scissors with boiling water poured over the blades to be sure they are clean. Add 1 tablespoon of fresh lemon juice to every cup of prepared dried apricots.
2. Cover the apricots with tepid water and let them sit overnight to plump up. Be patient. If they were very dry, this may take 24 hours.
3. Add 1 cup of sugar to every 2 cups of softened apricots and remaining liquid.
4. Bring slowly to a boil, then quickly turn down the heat to a gentle simmer. Cook slowly, stirring frequently, until the preserves are thick.
5. If you would like, add a teaspoon of almond extract to the mixture just before bottling.
6. Fill and process prepared jars as described on page 6.

Figs

I adore fresh figs. Here in New Jersey, they are an indulgent treat, sold individually or as threesomes. Compared to apples and peaches, they are uncommon as backyard fruit trees, though a few people do grow them in the Northeast, cosseting the little trees to get them through the winter. The man who owned a few acres next to my Aunt Gert's summer bungalow in Brookfield, Connecticut, was, like us, also a seasonal resident. He had a small greenhouse of sorts, with a fig tree. Thinking back, I remember the grown-ups making dismissive comments about this: after all, he was Italian. I didn't then, and still don't today, understand why this was somehow risible.

Fig trees are near to hardy in New Jersey and Connecticut. The difficulty is not so much the cold on the aboveground branches as much as it is winter wet killing the roots. So good drainage with a sandy loam soil is helpful. An Italian gardener I knew in

Norwalk, Connecticut, had a large, productive vegetable garden, a grape arbor, and a fig tree. Late in autumn, after the leaves had dropped, he and his brothers would dig along one side of the tree and loosen the roots from the ground. The tree would be tipped over and laid on the ground, then covered with a mound of dirt. In spring it would be resurrected, dusted off, and readily begin growing. Another family wrapped their tree. The branches would be gently forced in toward the trunk, then a rope would be spirally wrapped to hold them in place. The tree would next be swaddled, first with a layer of tar paper that was in turn enfolded with a sheet of plastic. The whole thing would then be crowned with an inverted metal bucket to keep the rain off.

Figs may be yellow-green skinned with amber or violet flesh, such as 'Kadota,' or deep purplish black skinned with red flesh, like 'Mission.' They come in various sizes, from large 'Brown Turkey,' also known as Black Spanish or Texas Ever-Bearing, a midseason variety with brown-violet skin and pink flesh, to dainty early season 'Celeste,' with bronze skin and sweet amber to pink flesh. Celeste is also known as Malta or honey fig. There are exotic varieties of figs with romantic names, such as 'Pied de Boef' and 'Rattlesnake Island.' Two I would dearly love to sample are 'Violette de Bordeaux,' described as purple skinned and red fleshed with a taste like the best raspberry jam you ever ate, and 'Panachée,' whose bright yellow skin is striped with green, with a strawberry-like aroma to its red flesh.

Clearly, when figs are sold one at a time or when the trees require valiant efforts to keep them alive and harvest a crop, well, then the figs will be a delectable treat eaten fresh, perhaps with crème fraîche as an embellishment or poached in red wine. In California, figs are so plentiful that they fall to the sidewalk to be squashed underfoot. And where they are so plentiful, you can do as my brother did in his bachelor days and make fig jam. He recalls that, "In Woodland, the county seat of Yolo County, about twelve miles north of Davis, there was a community cannery. It was run by a government project to encourage home canning by the poor in rural areas, and indeed, there were a number of Mexican families bringing in loads of tomatoes to make salsa to store. I recall the large water baths in which the jars could be immersed for sterilization and processing, and also the convenience of the long stainless-steel counters, making it easy to wash up after preparing the preserves. It did allow people to cook up big batches of preserves at once, larger quantities than one could handle in a single batch at home." Around that time, a Lebanese colleague gave him a recipe for fig jam made with fresh figs, sesame seeds, and walnuts, which Ben recalls as having a lovely texture and color as well as flavor.

Commonplace in the South, fig jam is a popular preserve. Nell Jean told me, "The preserves of choice in this household are fig preserves, along with pear preserves and apricot jam. My husband has learned to make his own fig preserves. The recipe is vague, learned by doing. The ratio of figs to sugar is roughly one to two parts figs to one part sugar, depending on whether you want thick or thin syrup. Wash the figs, add sugar, let sit for a few hours or overnight, and boil until they look and smell like preserves. I prefer my figs fresh and just eat them from the tree in season. We have the little brown figs. We used to go over to Cyrene and pick white figs. The cousins who own the property where the big fig tree was had it bulldozed to make way for irrigation equipment to run. Pity."

Fig Jam

Where figs are a commonplace fruit, as in California, Texas, and Georgia, fresh fig jam is a familiar option for preserving. While dried figs are readily available nationwide, I find their taste too different from the fresh fruit to consider them as a tit-for-tat substitute. Which is not to say that dried fig jam isn't good. It is, but the two are unlike one another.

Rating: Easy

Special Instructions: If the figs are freshly picked, they will need to soak for about an hour, as described below. The jam will need to be cooked twice, standing overnight in between.

Yield: Four to six 8-ounce jars

INGREDIENTS:

2 lbs. fresh figs

1 to 2 Tbs. baking soda

Juice of 1 lemon

3 C. sugar

1. If the figs are freshly picked, they will need a preliminary step to clear them of the sticky sap. Dust the figs with a spoonful or two of baking soda and place them in a sturdy plastic bag. Fill the bag with cold water, tie it shut, and place it in a picnic cooler for about an hour. Drain, discarding the water, and rinse the figs well.

2. Trim away any stiff stems from the top of each fig. Cut them into chunks. You should have about 4 cups. Put the figs into a large, heavy-bottomed saucepan and mix with sugar and lemon juice.

3. Stir gently yet well. Let sit for at least two hours to draw out the juice.

4. Bring the mixture slowly to a boil, then simmer gently for about an hour, stirring occasionally.

5. Remove from heat and let sit overnight.

6. The following day, reheat the mixture back to a boil, then turn down the heat to a slow boil until the jam has thickened sufficiently, stirring frequently.

7. Fill and process prepared jars as described on page 6.

Variation: Lebanese-Style Fig Jam

Yield: Five to six 8-ounce jars

INGREDIENTS:

2 lbs. fresh figs

1 to 2 Tbs. baking soda

Juice of 1 lemon

3 C. sugar

$^1/_4$ C. pine nuts

$^1/_2$ C. walnuts

1 tsp. ground anise seed

1$^1/_2$ tsp. black sesame seeds

1. Follow steps 1 through 5 for Fig Jam (page 37).
2. The following day, coarsely chop the walnuts. Toast the sesame seeds in a dry pan until they begin to pop and become aromatic.
3. Reheat the fig mixture back to a boil, then turn down the heat to a slow boil until the jam has thickened sufficiently, stirring frequently.
4. Approximately 5 minutes before you think the fig jam will be sufficiently thickened, turn the heat down to a simmer. Add pine nuts, walnuts, anise, and toasted sesame seeds.
5. Stir constantly until thickened.
6. Fill and process prepared jars as described on page 6.

Dried Fig Jam

Rating: Easy

Yield: Approximately four 8-ounce jars

INGREDIENTS:

1 pound dried Smyrna figs

1 large lemon

2$^3/_4$ C. water

1$^3/_4$ C. sugar

1. Put figs in a large saucepan. Juice the lemon, measure out $^1/_4$ cup, set aside. Tie the lemon seeds in a piece of cotton cheesecloth and add to the figs, along with water.
2. Cover the pot and bring it just to a boil before promptly removing it from the heat. Let the mixture sit for an hour or more until the figs are plump.
3. Drain the figs, reserving the liquid. Squeeze the bag of lemon seeds to extract as

much juice as possible, then discard the bag and contents. Trim and discard any stems from the figs, then chop them into medium coarse pieces.

4. Add the lemon juice and sugar to the reserved liquid. Bring it to a boil, reduce the heat, and simmer for 10 minutes.

5. Add the chopped figs to the liquid and return to a boil. Reduce heat and simmer for 15 to 20 minutes, or until the jam begins to thicken.

6. Bring the mixture back to a boil, cooking quickly for 5 minutes and stirring constantly.

7. Fill and process prepared jars as described on page 6.

Orange-Fig Jam

Where figs are scarce, they become a companion to other fruits to make a jam.

Rating: Easy
Special Instructions: Wait a month before sampling this jam to allow the liqueur to permeate it.
Yield: Six to seven 8-ounce jars

INGREDIENTS:
4 Valencia oranges
$^1/_2$ lb. fresh figs
1 Tbs. fresh gingerroot, or to taste
Sugar
6–7 Tbs. Cointreau or other orange-flavored liqueur

1. Choose Valencia oranges with good color that are heavy for their size. Remove the colored zest, chop it finely, and set aside. Juice the oranges and set aside the juice.

2. Chop the white pith and measure it, together with any seeds. Put pith and seeds in a saucepan with twice the amount of water. Simmer the mixture for 20 to 30 minutes, then strain.

3. Combine chopped zest, juice, and pith/seed extract in a large saucepan.

4. Rinse, stem, and coarsely chop the fresh figs. They should measure 1 cup.

5. Peel and grate gingerroot. Add to mixture.

6. Bring mixture to a boil, reduce heat, measure, and add $^3/_4$ cup of sugar for every cup of prepared fruit. Stir well and return to a boil.

7. Boil, stirring all the while, until the mixture thickens sufficiently.

8. Prepare the hot, sterilized jelly glasses for filling by adding a tablespoon of Cointreau or other orange-flavored liqueur to each jar.

9. Fill and process prepared jars as described on page 6.

Rhubarb

Rhubarb-Fig Jam

Rhubarb, though treated as a fruit, is actually the stem of the rhubarb plant. Happiest in colder climates, rhubarb has a tart love-it-or-hate-it taste. One difficulty with this fruit, in my opinion, is that rhubarb is frequently overcooked into an unappetizing, disintegrating mess. When handled with respect and given a proper partner—now that's a different story.

Rating: Easy

Special Instructions: Prepared fruit will need to sit for about 4 hours before cooking. This jam can take two weeks or more to set.

Yield: Four 8-ounce jars

INGREDIENTS:

7 skinny stalks or 4 fat stalks rhubarb

$1/2$ lb. fresh figs

1 lemon

3 C. sugar

1. Wash rhubarb, trim the ends, and cut into 1-inch pieces, preparing sufficient stalks to measure 3 cups. If using the fat stalks, cut them in half lengthwise before trimming into small pieces.

2. Rinse figs. Remove any stems and chop them into coarse pieces by cutting each fig into quarters from top to bottom, then cutting each section in half or into thirds, depending on the size of the figs and your preference.

3. Juice and zest the lemon.

4. Combine the prepared fruit with the sugar, lemon juice, and lemon zest. Stir well and allow to sit for about 4 hours so that the juices start to flow.

5. Bring the mixture to a boil, then turn down the heat to a simmer, stirring frequently. When the sugar has completely dissolved, skim out the pieces of rhubarb and fig, setting them aside.

   Note: I like to use the brass wire skimmers from Asian grocery stores, as they allow the liquid to promptly drain back into the pot.

6. Bring the liquid back to a boil and cook it to the jell point.

7. Fill each prepared jar with set-aside fruit sufficient to reach the bottom of the threaded portion of the jar. Fill loosely; do not pack firmly.

8. Pour jelly over fruit in prepared jars and process as described on page 6. This technique results in tender pieces of fruit floating in a syrupy jelly. If you leave the fruit in the liquid while cooking it to the jell point, the fruit will disintegrate some-what and the jam will be firmer.

9. Turn the jars upside down and let them sit until cool enough that the jam just begins to thicken, then turn them right side up.

Note: Sometimes there is a significant amount of jelly left after filling the jars over the pieces of rhubarb and fig. Strain the hot jelly through a mesh sieve to remove the little fig seeds and bottle. Even if you don't have enough for a full 4-ounce jar, you'll still have some tasty, rosy red jelly as a bonus.

Rhubarb-Strawberry Jam

Katzy liked rhubarb. She'd cook it gently in a covered saucepan with some water, a little sugar or honey, and perhaps some raisins. This might be served as a compote or be spooned over a slice of plain cake. In spring, when rhubarb was plentiful and strawberries were in season, sometimes she'd combine the two. This jam is an adaptation based on the flavors I remember.

Rating: Moderate
Special Instructions: Prepared fruit must sit overnight before cooking.
Yield: Approximately four 8-ounce jars

INGREDIENTS:
7 skinny stalks or 4 fat stalks rhubarb
3 C. sugar
Juice of 1/2 large lemon
2 C. strawberries

1. Wash rhubarb, trim the ends, and cut into 1-inch pieces, preparing sufficient stalks to measure 3 cups. If using the fat stalks, cut them in half lengthwise before trimming into small pieces.
2. Sprinkle rhubarb with sugar and lemon juice. Mix thoroughly, then let sit in a large covered saucepan overnight.
3. When ready to proceed, rinse strawberries and remove the green hulls. If they are small, leave the strawberries whole. If they are large, slice them in half.
4. Bring the rhubarb mixture to a boil, then promptly add the prepared strawberries. Reduce the heat so that the mixture simmers, stirring well to incorporate the strawberries.
5. Simmer, stirring periodically, until the mixture thickens and a spoon dragged though the mass leaves a track.
6. Fill and process prepared jars as described on page 6.

Variation: Rhubarb-Strawberry Conserve

Yield: Approximately four 8-ounce jars

INGREDIENTS:
7 skinny stalks or 4 fat stalks rhubarb
3 C. sugar
Juice of 1/2 lemon
1/2 lemon
1/2 C. raisins
2 C. strawberries

1. Follow steps 1 and 2 for Rhubarb-Strawberry Jam (page 41), adding the second half of the lemon, thinly sliced and quartered, and the raisins to the macerating rhubarb and sugar before allowing the mixture to sit overnight.
2. Proceed as directed with the rest of the Rhubarb-Strawberry Jam recipe, only now call it a conserve.

Rhubarb Jam with Ginger

One time Katzy ended up with a lot of rhubarb. I don't remember if someone gave it to her or just how she got it, but it was more than we could eat. After all, rhubarb is not something you can enjoy out of hand, like a peach, and there are limits to rhubarb consumption within a short time frame. So Katzy made some rhubarb jam. It was just rhubarb and sugar, and as I recall, nobody liked it very much. When I was similarly gifted with a huge brown paper shopping bag of rhubarb, I had this in mind and came up with this recipe for Rhubarb Jam with Ginger.

Rating: Easy
Special Instructions: Prepared fruit must sit overnight before cooking and again after cooking, for a total of 48 hours of preparation time.
Yield: Approximately four 8-ounce jars

INGREDIENTS:
9 skinny stalks or 5 fat stalks rhubarb
1 ounce fresh gingerroot
3 to 6 ounces crystallized ginger, to taste
Juice from 1/2 large lemon
4 C. sugar

1. Wash rhubarb, trim the ends, and cut into 1-inch pieces, preparing sufficient stalks to measure 4 cups. If using the fat stalks, cut them in half lengthwise before trimming into small pieces.

2.   Peel and grate fresh gingerroot.

3.   Toss rhubarb and gingerroot with the lemon juice and sugar in a large Dutch oven. Let stand overnight.

4.   The next day, strain off the juice into a saucepan and return the rhubarb to the Dutch oven. Bring the juice to a boil and boil for 10 minutes.

5.   Pour the syrup back over the rhubarb and let sit for 24 hours.

6.   The next day, coarsely chop the crystallized ginger. Use between 3 and 6 ounces, depending on how much you like ginger and how "hot" you want the jam to be.

7.   Add chopped ginger to rhubarb and syrup, bring it to a boil, and simmer briskly until it is thick and a spoon leaves a track when dragged through the mass.

8.   Fill and process prepared jars as described on page 6.

CHAPTER FOUR
CONSERVES

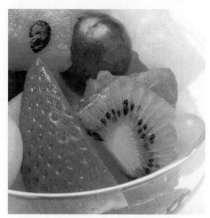

Conserves are not something my mother ever really made. I have a feeling that she considered them somewhere in between a jam and a marmalade, so why not simply make one or the other? There are times, though, when a conserve is a more interesting alternative to one or the other. Conserves are made by blending together two, or perhaps three, kinds of fruit. I've seen recipes for conserves made of four or more fruits, but I think this sort of hodgepodge must make it difficult to decide what you're tasting. Perhaps, it's like finger paints. Blue and yellow make green. Keep adding colors, though, and you get muddy brown. If two flavors are good, more is not necessarily better.

Conserves should be soft and easily spreadable, with a soft jelly or very heavy syrup around the pieces of fruit, but no appreciable liquid. Conserves' texture is uneven because some or all of the fruit is sliced, shredded, or in little pieces. Usually one fruit predominates and the other(s) blend in and underscore that flavor. Citrus is a frequent minor ingredient in conserves, as are raisins. Walnuts or pecans are sometimes included, but I don't like them. For one thing, the nuts are softened by the cooking process and I don't like their texture. Second, unless the nuts are first blanched in boiling water, they frequently blacken the conserve right around them, spoiling its appearance. Conserves are only a step more involved than jam, which is only a little different from fruit butters, which are only cooked-down, sweetened purées.

All of these preserves are really easy to make. In fact, you can pretty much transmogrify a jam into a conserve with the addition of citrus and raisins. It's that easy, and conserves don't take long to prepare. One morning, my daughter, Mira, went blueberrying with her mother-in-law, Huguette. Briefly stopping by our house at midday, Mira dropped off some of the blueberries. When she returned again in late afternoon, I presented her with a couple of jars of blueberry conserve that I'd made. Mira still remembers how astonished she was that the blueberries had become conserve so quickly.

Blueberry-Orange Conserve

A Sunday morning trip to the supermarket in early July revealed a bonus sale in the produce department: a cardboard tray holding six pints of blueberries that, with the sale price and my shopper's discount card, cost only $4.99. At a mere 83 cents a pint, how could I go wrong? Adding two large Valencia oranges to my cart, I went through the checkout while mentally thumbing through recipes. Once home and after checking to see if my recollections were accurate, I decided to make some blueberry conserve.

Rating: Easy

Special Instructions: This is a very mild preserve. One option to consider would be replacing $3/4$ cup of sliced and diced orange with an equivalent quantity of lemon. Another variation uses $1/2$ cup of dark raisins added to the orange zest and pulp while it is simmered.

Yield: Six 8-ounce jars and three 4-ounce jars

INGREDIENTS:

1 Valencia orange

$1/2$ C. water

6 C. blueberries

4 C. sugar

1. Take one large unpeeled Valencia orange and cut it in half from top to bottom, stem scar to blossom end. Cut each half into 10 narrow strips, again from top to bottom. Then cut each strip crosswise into 12 or more segments. There should be approximately $1^1/2$ cups of these small pieces.

2. Place them in a small saucepan and add the water. Bring to a boil, cover, and turn the burner down so it just maintains a slow simmer. Let simmer for 10 minutes. Turn the burner off and let the pot sit, still covered, for an additional 15 to 20 minutes.

3. Prepare the blueberries. One pint at a time, rinse three pints (6 cups) of blueberries in a colander. Pick over and discard any small green berries, but keep any that are reddish and somewhat underripe. Remove any stems. Turn the berries into a large Dutch oven. Add the softened bits of orange and their liquid. *Do not* add any additional water. The orange liquid and any water clinging to the berries is sufficient.

4.   Bring the fruit to a boil, stirring occasionally—especially in the beginning before the juice starts to flow from the blueberries.

5.   As soon as the mass of fruit and liquid in the pot begins to boil, add the sugar. Stir to incorporate it. The mass will boil up to fill the entire pot.

6.   Keep boiling, stirring frequently, until the mass thickens.

7.   This is a messy preserve to bottle because of all the lumpy bits. What is more, the blueberry liquid stains fabric really well. To avoid hot spatters that will hurt and could also dye your clothes, use a ladle and a wide-mouthed funnel rather than pouring the conserve from a measuring cup. Fill the jars to within $^1/8$-inch of the rim.

8.   Fill and process prepared jars as described on page 6.

Peach–Orange Conserve

Making preserves is not a tedious, time-consuming affair. A Saturday morning foray into peach conserves only took about two hours, start to finish.

I had a box of dead-ripe peaches from a local orchard, so ripe that they should really be eaten while naked in the bathtub for easier washing up afterward. At this stage of ripeness, something was necessary to keep the preserves from being insipidly bland. I thought a conserve, incorporating both orange and lemon, would be a good choice. Other options and possibilities would have been a ginger-peach conserve or one heated up with chili peppers.

Rating: Easy
Yield: Three 8-ounce jars and one 4-ounce jar for each of two batches

INGREDIENTS:
1 large Valencia orange
2 medium-sized lemons
$^1/2$ C. water
$3^1/2$ to 4 lbs. ripe peaches
Sugar

1.   Prepare one large Valencia orange and two medium-sized lemons by thinly slicing them from top to bottom, then crosscutting each slice into small pieces, peel, rind, and pulp together.

2.   Citrus needs to be simmered before incorporating it into a conserve, to soften the white rind. That's the part high in pectin, which helps the conserve thicken up. Put the chopped citrus into a small saucepan together with $^1/2$ cup of water and simmer this mixture while preparing the peaches.

3.   Peaches need to be skinned. The easiest way is to scald them, transfer the fruit into a cold water bath, and then the skin just slips right off. Fill a Dutch oven half full of water and bring it to a boil. Scrub out the sink and partially fill it with cold

water and a couple of lumps of ice. (In the summer, I keep a few pint containers of ice in the freezer to use when cooling scalded fruits and vegetables. Pints don't melt as quickly as cubes.) Ripe peaches only need 10 or 20 seconds in the boiling water bath before moving them to the ice-water bath to cool them down.

4. These were clingstone peaches, so once skinned, I cut the flesh off the pits in large lumpy pieces. (The flesh of freestone peaches separates cleanly from the pits.) These peaches were so ripe that I could mash them through the coarse plate of a food mill, getting $5^1/2$ cups of pulp and juice. Decision time.

5. If I combined the softened citrus mush with the peach purée, I'd have more than I'd like to preserve in one batch. Therefore, I divided the peach purée, adding half to the preserving kettle together with half the citrus mush. After adding the remaining citrus mush to the rest of the peach purée, I covered it tightly with plastic wrap to keep air away from the peaches, which would darken the pulp.

6. Conserves are difficult to time. A jelly thermometer really doesn't work well, and the pulp makes the sheet test also inaccurate. My gauge of doneness is dragging a spoon through the mass and watching to see if it leaves a clear track for a moment or two. That's another reason to work with small quantities—they'll thicken up faster than a larger volume, which might caramelize before cooking down. Since the peaches were so sweet and ripe, I decided on a minimal amount of sugar, only 2 cups of sugar to 3 cups of prepared fruit.

7. Measure the fruit, start the fruit heating, then add the sugar. Watch the pot, stirring frequently. After bottling the first batch, I rinsed out the preserving kettle before making the second batch.

8. Keep boiling, stirring frequently, until the mass thickens.

9. Fill and process prepared jars as described on page 6.

Plum Conserve

Italian prune plums make a delectable fruit butter as well as a delicious conserve.

Rating: Easy
Yield: Three to four 8-ounce jars

INGREDIENTS:
1 large Valencia orange
$^1/_2$ C. water
2 lbs. Italian prune plums
1 C. raisins
3 C. sugar
1 C. pecans (optional)

1. Peel the orange and slice it into fine strips. Set aside. Remove the white pith and chop up the orange.
2. Coarsely chop the white pith and, together with any seeds, put it into a saucepan with the water. Simmer for 20 minutes and let sit while you prepare the plums, then strain, setting aside the liquid.
3. Rinse the plums. Cut them in half to remove the pits, then chop them into coarse pieces. You should have a little more than 4 cups.
4. Combine the chopped plums, orange zest, chopped orange pulp, strained liquid from the orange seeds and pith, and the raisins.
5. If you want to include pecans, prepare them now and set them aside to be added later on: Bring a medium saucepan filled half full of water to a boil. Add the nutmeats and boil for 4 minutes. Promptly remove the nuts from the boiling water and drop them into a bowl of ice water. As soon as the pecans have cooled off, remove them from the water and drain them on a kitchen towel. They are now ready to chop into quarters and add to the conserve, stirring to mix well.
6. Start cooking the mixture over moderate heat. As it approaches a boil, add the sugar.
7. Continue cooking the mixture, stirring occasionally, until it begins to thicken. Then stir constantly.
8. When a spoon dragged through the mass leaves a track, the plum conserve is ready to bottle.
9. If you want, now is the time to add the pecans.
10. Fill and process prepared jars as described on page 6.

Grape Conserve

Rating: Easy
Yield: Four to six 8-ounce jars

INGREDIENTS:
2 lbs. Concord grapes
$1/2$ C. water
1 orange
1 lemon
1 C. raisins
3 C. sugar
$1/2$ C. walnuts (optional)

1. Slip the grapes from their peels, sort of like popping eyeballs in horror flicks. Do not discard the skins.
2. Cook the skins with the water for about 15 or 20 minutes, until they are soft.
3. Cook the peeled grapes over low heat until they are soft.
4. Combine the cooked grapes and grape peels, then purée them through a food mill with the coarse or medium plate to remove the seeds.
5. Zest the orange and the lemon and juice them both.
6. Combine the purée with the orange and lemon zest and juice.
7. If you want walnuts in the finished conserve, prepare them now to be added later: Bring a medium saucepan filled half full of water to a boil. Add the nutmeats and boil for 4 minutes. Promptly remove the nuts from the boiling water and drop them into a bowl of ice water. As soon as the walnuts have cooled off, remove them from the water and drain them on a kitchen towel. They are now ready to chop into quarters and add to the conserve, stirring to mix well.
8. Put grape purée, citrus zest and juice, and raisins into a large Dutch oven. Add sugar. Bring slowly to a boil, stirring constantly until the sugar dissolves.
9. Raise the heat and cook rapidly until the conserve thickens, approximately 15 minutes.
10. If desired, at this point you could add the walnuts to the conserve, stirring well to mix.
11. Fill and process prepared jars as described on page 6.

Apple Conserve with Nutmeg

Apple conserve is better as an accompaniment to an entrée of pork, duck, or roast chicken than it is spread on toast. It makes a great addition to acorn squash that's been baked in the oven, too.

Rating: Moderate

Special Instructions: The brandied raisins and concentrated cider should be prepared one day in advance.

Yield: Six to seven 8-ounce jars

INGREDIENTS:

1 C. yellow raisins

Brandy to cover

1 C. cider

3 lbs. tart apples, such as Granny Smith

$^1/_4$ C. fresh lemon juice

4 C. sugar

$^1/_2$ tsp. nutmeg

$^1/_2$ C. walnuts or pecans (optional)

1. The day before you want to make this preserve, prepare the brandied raisins. Place the raisins in a glass jar and cover with brandy. Let sit, occasionally shaking the jar, until you are ready to make the preserves.

2. Also a day in advance, reduce the cider. Pour the cider into a small saucepan and boil until reduced to $^1/_2$ cup. Let cool, pour into a glass jar, and refrigerate until you are ready to make the conserve.

3. If you intend to add walnuts or pecans, prepare them now: Bring a medium saucepan filled half full of water to a boil. Add the nutmeats and boil for 4 minutes. Promptly remove the nuts from the boiling water and drop them into a bowl of ice water. As soon as the nuts have cooled off, remove them from the water and drain them on a kitchen towel. Dry well, chop the nuts into quarters, and put them into a plastic bag, refrigerating them until you are ready to add them to the conserve.

4. On the day you will be making the conserve, rinse the apples. Cut them in half and remove the cores, stems, and blossom ends. Chop medium-fine. You should have about $4^1/_2$ to 5 cups.

5. Place the apples in a large Dutch oven together with the concentrated cider and the lemon juice. Stir well.

6. Start cooking the apple mixture over high heat, stirring constantly. Reduce heat, cover, and simmer for 10 minutes.

7. Bring the mixture back to a full rolling boil, stir in $^3/_4$ cup of the brandied raisins and the sugar.

8. Continue stirring while returning to a full boil.

9.   Boil for 1 minute; stir in nutmeg.

10.   If desired, at this point you could add the walnuts or pecans to the conserve, stirring to mix well.

11.   Fill and process prepared jars as described on page 6.

Gingery Apricot Conserve

I love the warmth that ginger adds. One of these days, I'll find a way to incorporate fresh, candied, and dried ginger all in the same recipe. Meanwhile, I'll enjoy the manner in which candied ginger adds a pleasant warmth to apricots in this preserve. Nice with grilled chicken, this conserve also adds a Moroccan flavor to lamb.

Rating: Easy

Special Instructions: This conserve may take as much as two weeks to set up firmly.

Yield: Five to seven 8-ounce jars

INGREDIENTS:

1 large navel orange

1 lemon

2^1/$_2$ to 3 lbs. fresh, ripe apricots

^{1}/$_2$ C. water

^{1}/$_2$ C. crystallized ginger

3 C. light brown sugar, packed firmly

1.   Wash the orange. Trim and discard the ends, but do not peel. Cut into thin slices, then cut each slice into 6 wedges.

2.   Rinse the lemon. Peel off the yellow zest and sliver it, then juice lemon. Discard the white pith.

3.   Wash, pit, and chop the apricots. They will measure about 6 cups.

4.   Combine orange wedges, slivered lemon zest, lemon juice, and water in a large saucepan. Cover, bring to a boil, then turn down heat and simmer for 15 to 20 minutes, or until the peel of the orange sections can easily be pierced with a toothpick.

5.   Add the apricots, cover the pot, and simmer until the apricots are tender.

6.   Cut the crystallized ginger into slivers.

7.   Add the brown sugar and the crystallized ginger to the citrus and apricots.

8.   Stir until the sugar dissolves, then raise the heat to boiling. Boil, uncovered, for 35 to 45 minutes, or until a track is left when a spoon is dragged through the mass, stirring frequently.

9.   Fill and process prepared jars as described on page 6.

Cactus–Date Conserve

It was late July, and the local Shoprite supermarket had cactus fruits, also known as cactus pear, *tuna* if you are in Mexico, or *sabra* in Israel. My sister, Haya, who happens to live in Jerusalem, said the *shuk*, or street market, had *sabra* for about $1 a kilo. Discussing this with Raymond in the produce department, I decided to get twenty-one. At three for $1.99, mine were considerably more expensive than my sister would pay, but, looking at the nice-sized fruits, I figured there would be ample to play around with. I stopped off at Jerry Barad's, cacti and succulent maven and a good friend, to show him my haul. There went three, as he showed me how the street vendors peel the fruit and give it to you, ready to eat. "Spit out the seeds," he said. Seeds. Think of a pomegranate. A cactus fruit consists of a thin peel, a very seedy core, and a sparse fleshy bit of juicy, deep-red flesh sandwiched between the two. My estimated yield of cactus preserves was quickly revised downward.

Here is the recipe, originally from the Southern Union Gas Company of Albuquerque, New Mexico, as I found it in the 1972 edition of the Cactus and Succulent Society's *Cactus Cook Book*, which was compiled by Joyce L. Tate (and thanks to Jerry for lending me this intriguing publication).

Rating: Moderate

INGREDIENTS:

2 C. cactus pear (aka *tuna*, *sabra*, cactus fruit)

1 C. dates

1 orange

4 Tbs. fresh lemon juice

1$^1/_2$ C. sugar

1. Cook all the ingredients together slowly until you reach the right consistency for conserve.
2. Five minutes before removing from fire, add $^1/_3$ cup walnut meats.
3. Seal in glasses as for any conserve.

After reading the recipe, I went back to the store where I bought a ten-ounce container of pitted dates, most of which I had to chop up to make one cup. I peeled and juiced one large Valencia orange. I also grated the lemon's rind and added it with the juice. Then I added the cactus fruit. I peeled the fruit as thinly as possible and used a teaspoon to scoop away the seeds, which mostly came off as a cohesive lump. (Peels and seeds were collected in a bowl for later experimentation.) It took a dozen cactus fruits to yield two cups of sliced pulp. This was becoming an expensive proposition. Prepared cactus fruit, chopped dates, grated citrus peel, and citrus juice were combined in a stainless-steel pot, together with one and one-half cups of sugar. I brought the mixture just to a boil, and then simmered it over very low heat. Trying to decide when "five minutes before removing from the fire" was not that difficult. I just waited, stirring infrequently, until the spoon began to leave a clear track on the bottom of the pot, then I added a one-quarter cup of pecans, the halves broken into four pieces.

And the results were not really worth my time and the cost. I had one eight-ounce and four four-ounce jars of a pleasantly innocuous, deep-red conserve. There is nothing except the label that identifies it to me as Cactus Date Conserve.

CHAPTER FIVE

MARMALADES

It's one thing to be on a jam- and jelly-making binge in summer. There are all sorts of soft fruits and berries, from peaches, plums, and cherries to blueberries, blackberries, and currants. Autumn rolls around with grapes, apples, pears, and quinces. And then we get to winter. It is true that when winter locks the land in ice and cold, we can find all sorts of locally-out-of-season fruit available for sale at the grocery store. But they are certainly not as flavorful. Fortunately, there is a fabulous fallback. Whether they are lemons, limes, oranges, grapefruits, any other kind of citrus, or a blend of two or more, they all make marvelous marmalade.

A Diversity of Citrus

What a fabulous variety of citrus fruit we find available. There's the familiar grape-fruit, with pale yellow or red flesh. Oranges, all sorts, from sweet to sour, blood, and navel. Sweet oranges have that delicious citrus aroma; the most common are Valencia and Jaffa. Sour oranges, also called bitter oranges, are not so much for eating out of hand as for making marmalade and some sauces. Blood oranges, so called, have deep-red flesh. Mandarins are smaller than oranges, usually flatter, and have stringy white pith under their loose skin. Kumquats are thought of as citrus, but they're not truly citrus, small, oval in shape, with a soft skin and tart flesh. There are lemons and limes, both the larger, more familiar Persian lime and the tart, aromatic little Key lime. Ugli fruit are large, but most of the fruit consists of thick rind, puckered up at the top. And then there's citron.

Citron, *Citrus medica*, is duplicitous, with its large fruits yet minimal yield of juice. A small, thorny evergreen tree native to India, it grows as an irregular, open-headed shrub or small tree with large, light-green leaves. Cultivated for its large, warty fruits, this was the first citrus fruit that was introduced to Europe by the armies of Alexander the Great in about 300 B.C. It found a suitable home in the Mediterranean region, where it has been cultivated from that time to the present. The flowers are stained purple on the outside and are followed by large, oblong or elliptical fruits. The peel is very thick and rough, yellow on the outside and white inside. The pulp is small and greenish and the juice is scanty and very acid in most types. They were originally grown in Europe out of interest for the fragrant fruits. Somehow, the name came to be applied to the lemon, called *citron* in France and *zitron* in Germany. Additionally, *citron* became the common name used for a kind of small watermelon with solid white flesh used in making pickles. The huge fruits of the true citron, up to a foot long, are unfamiliar to most people.

Even less well known is Buddha's hand, a variety of citron in which the fruit grows in five or more fingerlike lobes. Grocery stores offer a goodly selection of oranges and grapefruits, mandarins and kumquats. For the less-common citrus such as Seville oranges, Key limes, and citron, specialty growers in Florida and California's Central Valley that mail-order are a better choice.

My mother considered citrus marmalade a cinch, something that could be made in winter when other fresh fruit was difficult to obtain. In later years, as fruit other than apples and pears became available, she felt it was too expensive. In her opinion, peaches, for example, that had traveled north across the equator were a costly enterprise as ingredients for preserves. Besides, they never had the flavor of summer-ripe fruit. And, pleasing to her thrifty soul, the yield from citrus into marmalade is high, because the white pith under the rind is very high in pectin. It is also bitter, so the cook must balance the bitter and the sweet.

So toward winter's end when the summer harvest of preserves was getting low, it was an easy bet that citrus marmalade would fill in the gap. Sometimes Katzy would make marmalade from a single kind of citrus, and other times she'd blend two or even three types—orange with lemon, maybe with grapefruit.

Just what is marmalade anyhow? Today it is a term attached to all sorts of inappropriate concoctions—onion marmalade on some upmarket trendy restaurant menu, for example. Historically, marmalade was the designation for a sweet preserve made from quinces, and, over time, it became the name given to sweetened citrus preserves.

Marmalade through the Ages

Marmalade, it is frequently said, is where preserving began. In ancient Greece, in the first century A.D., Dioscorides described how to tightly stuff *melomeli*, quince, into a container of honey and let them sit for a year, after which they would soften. The "recipe" is in his *De Materia Medica* because sweetened quince paste was used as a digestive aid. Three centuries later, in *Opus Agriculturae*, Palladius suggested cooking peeled, cored, and shredded quince in honey and sprinkling it with black pepper. Fast-forward to another recipe, this time from late-fourteenth-century France (*Le Ménagier de Paris*), that continues to combine quinces, honey, and spices. *Marmelada* was exported to England toward the end of the fifteenth century, and recipes for making it at home soon followed. It is in England (*A Leechbook*) that a written recipe first mentions sugar. The first of three recipes for *charde-quynce* (good for the stomach, the author says) is a concoction of quinces and pears boiled in ale, mashed in a mortar, then sieved, mixed with honey flavored with black pepper, boiled again, and stirred vigorously while cooked. When stiff, it is flavored with cinnamon and ginger, allowed to cool, and then sliced. This would be more along the lines of fruit leather and much more heavily seasoned than contemporary tastes prefer. It would have been served as an after-dinner digestif and sweetmeat. The next recipe uses two parts honey and three parts sugar, "and shall this be better than the other … " The third recipe "is the best of all" and uses equal parts by weight of sugar and quinces.

Marmalade has a long and honorable history. By the sixteenth century, recipes for "drie Marmalade" [*sic*] of quince or peaches made from fruit, rosewater, and sugar turn up. In a manuscript book of recipes written by Margaret Savile of Methley dated 1683, there is a recipe for "Lemon Marmalet." It sounds quite practicable, and could well be used today:

Pare the lemons very thin, and put the rinds in water for four days, changing it twice a day. Then boil them in several changes of water.

Pick the seeds out from the pulp, and squeeze out the juice, and set aside the pulp and juice.

Take a half-pound of prepared lemon rind and a half-pound of pippin [apple] pulp, and mash them up in a mortar.

Weigh the pulp, and to every pound of pulp add half the weight of sugar and a pint of pippin-liquor.

Bring to a boil, and when almost boiled enough, add the lemon pulp and juice.

There's a casual note in the recipe book that "Thus you may do oranges." And there we have it, a recipe for a preserve made from citrus, one that we would recognize today as marmalade.

In *The Sephardic Kitchen*, Rabbi Robert Sternberg explores the culinary traditions and recipes of Sephardic Jews. They brought this type of jellied confection made from cooked, puréed, sweetened quinces to the Ottoman Empire. Expelled from Spain in 1492 during the Inquisition, the Sephardic Jews settled primarily around the Mediterranean, in Italy, France, Algeria, Greece, and Morocco. Their distinctive cuisine was developed from the foods and flavors of Spain and Portugal. And it is from the Portuguese language, where *melomeli* became *marmelo*, that marmalade got its name. Dulces, sugary sweets made from puréed fruit and sugar cooked to a stiff paste, resemble the original *marmelada*. The form made from quince purée continues to be popular in various Middle Eastern countries, as well as Mexico and Latin America, where it is called *dulce de membrillo*. Today other fruits, such as apples, apricots, peaches, guava, and mangoes, are also used.

Oranges: Options, Theme, and Variations

Even today, the traditional ending to a proper English breakfast of eggs and bacon and perhaps a grilled tomato is tart orange marmalade spread lavishly on toast.

The British fondness for marmalade dates back better than two centuries. James Keiller began making and selling orange marmalade in 1797. Several decades later, in 1864, James Robertson & Sons entered the marmalade business. Both of these companies were originally based in Scotland, while Frank Cooper began selling marmalade from his shop in Oxford in 1874. In modern times, mergers, buyouts, and acquisitions have narrowed the playing field. In 1988, Keiller's marmalade production was taken over by James Robertson & Sons, now of Manchester, which itself is now part of RHM (Rank Hovis McDougall) Foods. Frank Cooper marmalades are distributed by Bestfoods, Ltd. after Cooper's was acquired by CPC. Wilkins of Tiptree continues as an independent family firm whose offerings of Seville orange marmalade are available on American supermarket shelves.

Seville Orange Marmalade

In seventh century Spain, Isidore of Seville, circa A.D. 570–636, wrote of *malomellus*, a sweetened purée of quinces cooked to a stiff paste and served as a digestive aid at the end of a meal. Fruit—damson plums, pears, apples, medlars, service tree (related to rowan), and even strawberries, would be cooked until soft before boiling a second time with sugar. The apples, in order to have the desirable, necessary higher pectin content, must be not too sweet, not too ripe. In the Middle Ages, a recipe for conserve of oranges was printed in 1587. Others for a combination of apples and sour oranges or lemons appear, and some that used candied orange peel. Recipes for bitter orange marmalade began showing up a century later, in 1681.

Sour Seville oranges are a rarity today. They might occasionally appear in fancy grocery stores at a high price. A more reliable way to obtain them is by mail order from the few specialty growers in Florida. The season for Seville oranges is brief, with its peak in February, though some may be offered for sale in late January. These will be less mature than the oranges used in the past, probably in part because their skin thickens as the season advances. Excellent marmalades can be made from sweet oranges, lemons, limes, mandarin or tangerine oranges, grapefruit, satsumas, kumquats, or, as my mother did and my sister still does, with a blend of two or more kinds of citrus fruit.

Late one January, I happened to be in Wegmans, an upmarket grocery store in Somerville, New Jersey. And in the produce section, I found sour oranges. As they say, nothing ventured, nothing gained, so I bought four Seville oranges at a pricey $1.99 apiece. The same store was selling Cooper's Fine Cut Seville orange marmalade at $5.29 for a one-pound jar, Chivers Olde English marmalade at $3.39 for a twelve-ounce jar, and Wilkin & Sons Double One (Seville orange and tangerine) marmalade at $3.99 for a twelve-ounce jar. After making the marmalade, it turned out that the actual cost for my homemade Seville orange marmalade came to less than a dollar per jar.

Most of the sour oranges in the bin had a bright orange, somewhat wrinkled, rather warty skin. The first few that I picked up seemed rather light for their size, an indication that they would be less juicy. I chose four that appeared somewhat heavier by comparison; these also seemed to have a smoother skin. Later, I found out that there are a couple of varieties of sour oranges. 'Poorman' was first used as a rough-skinned kind, then later grafted to the smooth-skinned 'Flat Seville.'

Rating: Moderate

Special Instructions: This recipe takes two days to prepare.

Yield: Eight 8-ounce jars. This is the yield from half of the prepared sour orange peel, juice, and soaking liquid. Repeat with the remaining citrus and an additional 3¹/₂ cups of sugar or use another marmalade recipe.

INGREDIENTS:

4 Seville oranges

5 C. water, plus additional water for pith

3¹/₂ C. sugar

Day One

1. Wash the oranges. Use a vegetable peeler to remove the zest from all 4 oranges, which should equal about 1 cup.

2. Cover the strips of zest with 2 cups of water in a small saucepan and simmer gently until quite soft, about 2 hours. Let cool in pan.

3. Drain, reserving the liquid, and snip the peel into slivers with scissors or a sharp knife. Put the zest in a glass jar, add the cooking liquid, cap it, and refrigerate.

4. Cut all 4 oranges in half and use an electric juicer to juice them. They will yield 1 cup of juice. Pour the juice in a separate glass jar, cap it, and refrigerate.

5. Scrape the seeds out of juicer. (Seville oranges are seedy. There should be about 2 tablespoons worth of seeds.) Cover them with 1 cup of water, pour into a glass jar, cap it, and refrigerate.

6. Put the white pith in a food processor together with 2 cups of water, then pulse until coarsely chopped. Yield should be about 2²/₃ cups. Put the pith mixture into a quart-sized glass jar and add sufficient water to cover the pith. Refrigerate.

7. You now have, collected in various jars in the refrigerator, 1 cup of slivered peel, 1 cup of juice, 2 tablespoons of seeds (pips if you are English), 2²/₃ cups of coarsely chopped rind, and a total of 6 cups of soaking water from soaking the seeds and the pith.

Day Two

8. The next day, use a sieve to collect the seeds, pouring the liquid into a pot. Wrap the collected seeds in cotton cheesecloth, tie it with string, and toss it into the pot.

9. Add the chopped pith and its soaking liquid to the pot.

10. Bring everything to boil, then briskly simmer for 20 to 30 minutes.

11. Strain while everything is still hot, squeezing out as much liquid as possible. The yield will be 2 cups.

12. Juice, slivered peel and liquid, and pith/seed extract in their separate containers should have a total volume of about 6 cups. Three cups is sufficient for one batch of marmalade.

13. Place 3 cups of the mixture in a Dutch oven. Refrigerate the remaining 3 cups.

14. Start heating the mixture in a large Dutch oven.

15. Add 3^1/$_2$ cups of sugar and stir it into the citrus preparation.

16. Turn up the heat and bring to a rolling boil. Watch carefully—even with this small volume of ingredients in this large a pot, it can boil over. Three cups of prepared fruit and 3^1/$_2$ cups of sugar will boil up to fill a 5-quart pot, even boil over.

17. Bring to a hard rolling boil (which reminds me of the head on a pint of freshly pulled Guinness in an Irish pub). It will quickly reach the jell point.

18. Fill and process prepared jars as described on page 6.

The Seville Orange Marmalade was delicious. Now I was on a roll and wanted to experiment some more. However, I felt that purchasing Seville oranges directly from a grower might be a better way to go. (Katzy would have been puzzled by my insistence on using Seville oranges. Sweet oranges are so much less expensive and make a fine marmalade. What can I say, except that there is not too much else that you can buy for less than eight dollars that not only provides hours of entertainment while you make it, but tastes this good, too.) Florida Citrus offered a quarter bushel as their smallest package, so I found a friend to go halves with me. After all, if four Seville oranges produced eight jars of marmalade, even a half of a quarter of a bushel was going to be a lot of marmalade. The oranges arrived in early February, twenty, nicely boxed. I shared them with my friend and neighbor Carol Thompson Clarke and started inventing variations on a theme of marmalade. While waiting for the oranges to arrive, I decided to try my hand at Ginger Marmalade.

Ginger Marmalade

Candied ginger can be quite expensive if you buy it in tiny little jars found among the spices at the grocery store. Interestingly, it is significantly less expensive at health food stores. Or, you can prepare your own from fresh gingerroot. Ginger Marmalade needs pectin from an outside source, and it is therefore not a true marmalade. More accurately, it should be called ginger jam or ginger preserves.

Rating: Easy
Special Instructions: This recipe takes several days to prepare.
Yield: One pound of gingerroot yields two 8-ounce jelly jars of ginger in syrup.

INGREDIENTS:
1 lb. fresh gingerroot
Water
8 oz. candied ginger
2 C. sugar

1. Choose fine plump "hands" of ginger. Break the gingerroot into finger-sized pieces where it branches and scrape off the thin brown skin with a small paring knife or the edge of a teaspoon.
2. Put the pieces in a saucepan, cover with water, and bring to a boil.
3. Boil for 5 minutes. Let cool in the water for an hour or more. Repeat 3 to 5 times with fresh water, depending on how gingery you want the final preserves to be.
4. Make a strong syrup of 2 cups of sugar to 1 cup of water for each pound of gingerroot—bring the sugar and water to boil in a saucepan, boil for 5 minutes, and put the chunks of gingerroot into the syrup.
5. Turn off the heat, cover the pan with a china plate (not plastic) to keep the ginger submerged, and let it sit overnight.
6. The next day, dip the ginger out of the syrup and set it aside. Bring the syrup to a boil, boil for 5 minutes, and turn off the heat. Return the pieces of ginger to the saucepan, cover with a china plate, and let it sit for 2 days.
7. Remove the ginger from the syrup and cut it into smaller pieces, from $1/2$- to 1-inch long, or as desired. Bring the syrup to a boil, return the gingerroot to the saucepan, and simmer both together for 5 minutes.
8. Let stand for 2 days. Strain off the syrup, which will be quite thick by this point.
9. Pack ginger in sterilized, hot jelly jars. Heat syrup to the boiling point and pour it over the ginger.
10. Process the filled jars as described on page 6.

Gingery Orange Marmalade

Rating: Moderate

Special Instructions: This recipe takes two days to prepare.

Yield: Four 8-ounce jars. This is the yield from half of the prepared sour orange peel, juice, and soaking liquid. Repeat with the remaining citrus and an additional 3¹/2 cups of sugar or use another marmalade recipe.

INGREDIENTS:

4 Seville oranges

5 C. water, plus additional water for pith

8 oz. candied ginger

3¹/2 C. sugar

1. Follow steps 1 through 13 for Seville Orange Marmalade (pages 59–61).
2. Use a food processor to pulse/chop the candied ginger together with enough sugar from the 3¹/2 cups to keep the blade from gumming up.
3. Add the chopped ginger and remaining sugar to the Seville orange mixture.
4. Bring to a boil and boil fast, to the jell point.
5. Fill and process prepared jars as described on page 6.

Gingery Orange Marmalade with Barbados Molasses

Seville Orange Marmalade segued into Gingery Orange Marmalade, and next I took things to a third-stage variation with the addition of Barbados molasses.

Rating: Moderate

Special Instructions: This recipe takes two days to prepare.

Yield: Four 8-ounce jars of marmalade, with that lovely warm taste that ginger has to offer, darkened in color and with the flavor enriched by the molasses. Repeat with the remaining citrus and an additional 3¹/2 cups of sugar or use another marmalade recipe.

INGREDIENTS:

4 Seville oranges

5 C. water, plus additional water for pith

8 oz. candied ginger

3¹/2 C. sugar

8 oz. candied ginger

3 Tbs. Barbados molasses

1. Follow steps 1 through 3 for Gingery Orange Marmalade (above).
2. Add Barbados molasses.

3. Bring to a boil and boil fast, to the jell point.
4. Fill and process prepared jars as described on page 6.

Orange Marmalade Flavored with Liquor

My cupboard shelves were filling with marmalade, but there were yet more Seville oranges to experiment with. I suppose I could have simply grated the zest, juiced the oranges, and frozen the combined juice and zest in little ice cubes to make Sauce Bigarade, a delicious sauce for roast duck, at some future time, but we only have duck occasionally. I decided to go for marmalade flavored with liqueurs.

Rating: Moderate
Special Instructions: This recipe takes two days to prepare.
**Yield: Four 8-oz jars. Repeat with the remaining citrus and an additional 3^1/$_2$ cups of sugar
     or use another marmalade recipe.**

INGREDIENTS:
4 Seville oranges
5 C. water, plus additional water for pith
8 oz. candied ginger
3^1/$_2$ C. sugar
8 Tbs. liqueur such as Drambuie or Grand Marnier

1. Follow steps 1 through 17 for Seville Orange Marmalade (pages 59–61).
2. Add 2 tablespoons of liqueur to each prepared jar. I used a variety of liqueurs: orange-flavored Grand Marnier; Drambuie, a Scotch whiskey liqueur; and The Famous Grouse, a superior Scotch whiskey.
3. Fill and process prepared jars as described on page 6.

Clearly, these were a favorite with anyone fortunate enough to sample them. For example, I'd sent a three-pack of preserves to Marlene Blessing and got the following "taste report" in return: "Okay, my favorite, the Scotch whiskey orange marmalade. This would be delicious on anything, but I ate it on homemade English muffins. The best! The tang that the Scotch gives this, along with the richness of concentrated orange, an explosion of flavor."

Seville Orange Marmalade with Brandy-Soaked Raisins

Getting by this time somewhat desperate (remember the sorcerer's apprentice in *Fantasia*?), I made one last batch of marmalade, this time incorporating a generous tablespoon of brandy-soaked raisins per jar. I happened to have on hand brandy-soaked dark raisins, and (after the fact) thought that golden raisins would probably look better. Brandy-soaked any-dried-fruit is absurdly easy to make and convenient to have around.

This reminds me of Katzy's compote of dried fruit. In the days of my childhood, rather than an electronic igniter, gas stoves had a pilot light for every pair of burners, a tiny flame beneath the porcelain drip grates. Katzy would fill a quart-sized glass jar with a mixture of dried fruit—mostly prunes and raisins, but including some dried peaches and pears. She'd add a slice or two of lemon somewhere in the middle, top the fruit with a couple of tablespoons of sugar, and fill the jar with water. She'd do this in the evening, then set the jar on the warm spot over the pilot light. By morning, the ever-so-gentle heat would have caused the fruit to plump up and swell into a delicious compote.

Rating: Moderate

Special Instructions: This recipe takes two days to prepare.

Yield: Four 8-ounce jars

INGREDIENTS:

1 C. golden raisins

Brandy to cover

4 Seville oranges

5 C. water, plus additional water for pith

8 oz. candied ginger

3^1/$_2$ C. sugar

1. Place one cup of golden raisins in a glass jar. Cover with brandy. Cap and set aside for 24 hours.
   Note: Brandied raisins are nice to have on hand to serve with ice cream or pound cake. It is just as easy to make a jar full as a cup's worth.
2. Follow steps 1 through 17 for Seville Orange Marmalade (pages 59–61).
3. Add a tablespoon of brandy-soaked raisins to each jar.
4. Pour hot marmalade into jars, filling to within 1/4 inch of the top.
5. Stir gently with a spoon to distribute raisins.
6. Process prepared jars as described on page 6.

Blood Orange Marmalade

One year, at the very end of February, my local supermarket had superb blood oranges at four for $1.99, only a third more expensive than navel oranges at six for the same price, and one-quarter the price of Seville oranges. I could not pass them by. Blood oranges, also known as pigmented oranges, have nothing to do with blood; they're named for the intense deep-red color of the pulp. The deepest-colored ones, I believe, often have a red blush on the peel. They are a sweet, seedless orange with a hint of berry flavor. They make a lovely juice, an attractive addition to a fresh fruit cup, and, what else?—a luscious marmalade.

Rating: Easy

Special Instructions: This recipe takes two days to prepare.

Yield: Four 8-ounce jars. Repeat with set-aside zest and liquid, plus an additional 3^1/$_2$ cups of sugar, for a second batch.

INGREDIENTS:

4 blood oranges

3^1/$_2$ C. water, plus additional water for pith

2 lemons

3^1/$_2$ C. sugar

Day One

1. Wash the oranges. Use a vegetable peeler to remove the zest from all 4 blood oranges.

2. Cover the strips of zest with 1^1/$_2$ cups of water in a small saucepan. Simmer until tender, about 45 minutes.

3. Drain, reserving the liquid, and snip the peels into slivers. Combine slivered peel and liquid in a jar (there should be about 1^3/$_4$ cups altogether), cap it, and refrigerate.

4. Cut all 4 oranges in half and, using a juicer, extract the juice. These big, heavy oranges yield 2 cups of dark-ruby juice, a larger yield than sour oranges would provide. Since they are sweet and seedless, peel and juice 2 lemons in addition for the necessary acidity to produce a good gel. Pour the combined 2^1/$_2$ cups of juice in a glass jar, cap it, and refrigerate. Set the remaining white pith and the lemon seeds aside.

5. Pulse/chop the white pith of both the blood oranges and lemons in a food processor with 2 cups of water. Put in a glass jar together with any lemon seeds and additional water as needed to cover the chopped pith, cover, and let sit overnight.

Day 2

6. The next day, put the chopped pith, lemon seeds, and their soaking water into a pot. Bring the mixture to a boil, cook at a brisk simmer for 30 minutes, then strain, setting aside the liquid.

7. Combine the slivered zest and its cooking liquid, blood orange and lemon juice, and pith extract, then measure. Altogether there should be somewhere between $6^1/_4$ and $6^1/_2$ cups. Divide it in half. Put one half into a Dutch oven and set the other half aside.

8. Bring citrus mixture to a boil. Add sugar, stirring well. Cook rapidly to the jell point.

9. Fill and process prepared jars as described on page 6.

Key Limes

Key Lime Marmalade

When my daughter, Mira, and her family were living outside Houston, Texas, in The Woodlands, we would visit them for Thanksgiving, a lovely time of year for families to get together. I discovered that the local Texas supermarkets had Key limes as a common item in November and December, which meant I could return to New Jersey with a couple of bags of the small, green citrus fruit. Now limes and Key limes are two different things. The first is about the size of a small lemon, with a pleasing fragrance and flavor. Key limes are very small, with a distinctive, more intense fragrance, flavor, and acidity than the more common Persian limes. When Mira and her family moved to Connecticut, it was much more convenient for visiting, but more awkward for the procurement of Key limes. Then Carol Thompson Clarke, her husband, and brother-in-law went to Florida for a pre-Thanksgiving visit. Good friend and neighbor that she is, Carol returned home with three bags of Key limes and kept only one bag for herself. Each bag contains twenty-eight to thirty Key limes. The price usually ranges from $2.99 to $3.59 a bag. As the label clearly states, the fruit is "coated with vegetable-, petroleum-, beeswax, and/or shellac-based wax or resin to maintain freshness." So the first step in making Key lime marmalade is to wash the fruit in soapy water, rinsing the fruit thoroughly afterward.

Rating: Moderate

Special Instructions: This recipe takes two days to prepare.

Yield: Four 8-ounce jars

INGREDIENTS:

Approximately 25 key limes

2^1/$_2$ C. water

Sugar

Green food coloring (optional)

Day 1

1. Wash the fruit. Use a citrus zester to remove the green zest, continuing until you have about ^{1}/$_4$ cup of finely shredded peel. If you don't have a zester, use a regular vegetable peeler and then sliver the peel with scissors or a sharp knife. Be careful to remove only the colored portion of the peel and none of the bitter white rind. Put in a small jar or plastic bag and refrigerate.

    Note: I do not soak or pre-cook Key lime zest.

2. Next, roll the Key limes between the palm of your hand and a cutting board. This helps release the juice. Cut the fruit in half and juice. Due to the small size of Key limes, there is not much juice in each one. I find an electric juicer very helpful, as my hands get tired after manually squeezing half a dozen Key limes, and there are more yet to go for the necessary amount of juice. The yield should be about 1 cup of juice. Set the remaining white pith and the seeds aside.

3. Combine the juice and shredded peel in a glass jar with a tight lid and refrigerate. Use a piece of plastic wrap to cover the juice and peel if the jar has a metal lid.

4. Pulse/chop the white pith in a food processor together with 1 cup of water. You should have about 2 cups of liquid. Place in a one-quart glass jar.

5. Add the seeds to a different jar. Use an additional 1 to 1^1/$_2$ cups of water to rinse anything, such as the juicer and measuring cup, that held Key lime pulp. Add the water and retrieved bits of pulp to the chopped rind and seeds, cover, and refrigerate for 12 to 24 hours.

Day 2

6. The next day, put the chopped pith, seeds, and their soaking water into a pot. Bring the mixture to a boil, cook at a brisk simmer for 30 minutes, then strain, setting aside the liquid.

7. Measure the extract and add 1 cup of sugar for every cup of combined Key lime material.

8. Bring citrus mixture to a boil. Cook rapidly to the jell point. The color will not be as bright a green as the fresh fruit. You may, if desired, tint the marmalade with food coloring before bottling and processing.

9. Fill and process prepared jars as described on page 6.

Triple Citrus

Triple Citrus Marmalade

My sister, Haya, lives in Israel, a country where a goodly assortment of citrus is grown. She also likes to make marmalade, and late one winter she sent me the following e-mail: "As for my own preserves, I put up a variety of marmalades during citrus season here. I use whatever combination suits my fancy and whatever citrus I have at home when in the mood to cook up a batch, but my favorite marmalade is a blend of grapefruit, orange, and lemon, which I call 'Triple Citrus Marmalade.'"

Rating: Easy

Yield: Six 8-ounce jars

INGREDIENTS:

1 small grapefruit

1 orange

1 lemon

6 cups water

Sugar

1. Peel colored rind off grapefruit, orange, and lemon and cut into thin strips about 3 inches long. Cut the fruit pulp into slightly thicker pieces. Altogether there should be about $2^1/_2$ cups of peel and pulp.

2. Place peel, pulp, any juice, and 5 cups of water into a large pot. Let the mixture sit for 2 hours or more.

3. While the mixture is steeping, put any seeds in a small saucepan. Add 1 cup of water and boil for 10 minutes. Let sit for 10 minutes. Then strain, reserving the liquid.

4. After the fruit has been sitting for a minimum of 2 hours, add the reserved liquid and bring to a boil, then turn down the heat to an active simmer.

5. Let the mixture cook for about an hour, or until the peel is tender.

6. Measure the cooked mixture and add an equal amount of sugar.

7. Stir well until the sugar is dissolved.

8. Divide the mixture into two batches. Working with one at a time, boil over high heat until the marmalade reaches the jell point.

9. Fill and process prepared jars as described on page 6.

Etrog

Etrog Marmalade

A particular kind of citron, grown only on ungrafted trees and with an intact calyx (the outer green leaflike whorl at the base of a flower, sometimes remaining like a little cup or cap at the base of a fruit), is called *etrog*. In Israel, Orthodox Jews use it as a symbol of the Lord's bounty during Sukkot, the Festival of Tabernacles, when *lulav* (palm branch), willow, and myrtle are bound together and the *etrog* is kept separate. And, after the better-than-weeklong holiday was over, my sister used some to make a most exotic marmalade. *Etrog* has a thick, rather dry skin, with a singular, resinous fragrance. There is not much juice to the weakly lemon-flavored pulp.

Haya wrote, "I decided that this would be a good time to slice and soak the *etrogim* for cooking up the marmalade tomorrow afternoon, rather than Friday morning. Now, ninety minutes later, the job is done. There's going to be a lot of jam once I cook it. I'd thought one large pot would be big enough to soak all the thin slices overnight, but they were packed in so tight that I divided them between two pots so that there'd be more water around them. There is a lot of sliced rind and only a small amount of fruit pulp. I plan to drain the scanty fruit and ample quantity of sliced peel tomorrow afternoon, boiling it up twice, changing water between each one." Since the rind is very bitter, Haya was using an older technique wherein the rind is covered with water, brought to a boil, and then taken off heat and allowed to soak overnight. The next day she drained it and repeated the process. She continued, "Then I'll cook up at least some of the marmalade. I may try adding ginger to one batch à la the recipe you sent to me for the melon-type citron preserves—that is, putting the fresh gingerroot into a cloth bag while cooking and removing it before portioning the cooked jam into jars."

Of course, I had to get into the act and had some suggestions of my own to make. Since Haya had not made *etrog* marmalade before, I proposed that she cook up one small batch, perhaps even as little as 2 cups of peel and pulp, to see how she liked the taste. Then, once it had a chance to set and been sampled, other batches can either be the same or be revisions: more or less sugar, blended with other fruit, flavored with ginger or other seasonings. Since *etrog* is much less juicy than other citrus fruit, I asked Haya if she thought she should add fresh lemon or orange juice to the *etrog* peel. Moreover, I added, should she be concerned about the prepared but uncooked "stuff," I could reassure her, because I've kept a marmalade base in the refrigerator for an extended period, like a couple of weeks, and it was fine. Not, mind you, that I recommend this as a standard practice.

And one day, a jar of *etrog* marmalade showed up in my mailbox. It had a most delicate, translucent pale green color. When opened there was a very distinctive aroma of citrus, lemonlike, but different. And it had a subtle flavor not at all unpleasantly underlain with a hint of bitterness, giving my morning toast a loving connection between sisters.

CHAPTER SIX

SWEET JELLIES

It is somewhat of a conundrum that out of all the different kinds of preserves, jelly is the one that comes first to most people's minds. Of all the different kinds of preserves, jelly is the one that, in my opinion, takes the most skill to make well. I'm talking here about a jelly made from fruit juice and sugar, perhaps with a touch of added acidity from lemon juice, perhaps some supplemental pectin made at home from apples or citrus pith. It's true that commercial pectin will create a gel from practically anything—fruit juice, wine, even water, for all I know. But they do so using more sugar than juice. It is the flavor of the fruit I want to savor, and preserves made using less sugar than juice to perhaps equal parts sugar to juice are my preference.

There are times when only jelly will do. Grape jelly is one of those and is my husband's favorite among all the preserves I make. My mother, Katzy, used the liquid strained from puréed apples or other fruit to make jelly—great tasting jelly, and it suited her thrifty habits. Sometimes it is the fruit itself that creates the demand. Elderberries, blackberries, and raspberries, not to mention currants and gooseberries, all have tiny seeds that get stuck between my teeth in an aggravating manner. Sure, I could purée the berries into jam, but there's something about a perfect jelly, transparent, clear, and bright. It quivers when turned out of the jar and has a clean, smooth edge when cut with a spoon. And there is something so fundamental about jelly, made as it is from fruit juice and sugar.

The tricky part of jelly making is determining the jell point. Even though I provided this information in Chapter One: Getting Started with Preserves, I feel it is important and will be helpful to reiterate it here. Easiest and most reliable of all is to use a jelly or candy thermometer. At or near sea level, when the boiling liquid reaches 220° Fahrenheit, the juice and sugar with good pectin/acid levels will have reached the jell point. A low-tech method of testing the jell point is to dip a soupspoon into the boiling liquid. Lift the spoon out and turn it sideways so that a little of the seething mixture runs off the side. Blow gently on the liquid to cool it more quickly. When the jell point has been reached, the mass flows off the spoon in a sheet. If it falls as a couple of drops, the jell point is close but has not yet been reached.

Even easier is Joyce Carleston's method. (Joyce is the mother of my daughter-in-law, Kim. In Yiddish, she would be my *machetayneste* [pronounced mokh-e-TANE-es-teh], a very simple way of saying "the mother of my child's spouse.") She explains, "I determine doneness by putting a fork into the juice and when I lift it, the jelly stays between the tines if it is ready." Another simple method is to put a tablespoon or so of boiling jelly on a refrigerated plate. Put it back in the refrigerator for a few minutes. Use your finger to push at the jelly from the edge of the little puddle. If it wrinkles up, the jelly is done. Carole Nagy turns the plate upside down to see how well it clings. If you try this, do it over the sink, just in case the jelly isn't quite done. And when you gain enough experience, perhaps you'll be able to do it as my mother Katzy did, by eye. Ready-to-set jelly is a seething mass of shiny, glassy-looking small bubbles that cannot be stirred down, very different from the relatively large softer bubbles of a boiling liquid.

In addition to the recipes in this chapter, recipes for many additional jellies are to be found in other chapters: blackberry and raspberry in Chapter Eight: Delectable Berries; grape and elderberry in Chapter Nine: Native Harvest; cornelian cherry in Chapter Ten: Backyard Harvest. As well as sweet jellies, I'm very fond of making savory herb jellies to use as an accompaniment to poultry, pork, and game dishes, and those recipes appear in Chapter Seven: Savory Jellies and Conserves.

Back to the basics. As a general rule, two pounds of prepared fruit will yield approximately a pint of juice. A pint of juice mixed with one pound (that's two cups) of sugar will produce three or more eight-ounce jars of jelly, depending on the fruit. Prepare jelly in small batches, working with no more than four to six cups of juice at a time. Quality, not quantity, should be your guiding principle. Good jelly is transparent and quivery, while cloudy, syrupy, or sticky jelly is poor quality. Clarity is achieved by using only free-run juices, since squeezing the jelly bag or putting pressure on the pulp forces fine particles into the juice.

PREPARING FRUIT FOR JELLY MAKING

Fruit and Preparation	Added Water per Pound of Fruit	Time to Simmer
Apples, cut in quarters	1 cup	20 to 25 minutes
Blackberries, mashed	none or $^{1}/_{4}$ cup	5 to 10 minutes
Crab apples, cut in half	1 cup	20 to 25 minutes
Currants, mashed	$^{1}/_{4}$ to $^{1}/_{2}$ cup	10 to 15 minutes
Grapes, crushed	none or $^{1}/_{4}$ cup	5 to 10 minutes
Plums, cut in half	$^{1}/_{2}$ cup	15 to 20 minutes
Quinces, cut in pieces	2 cups	25 to 30 minutes

Apples

Apple Jelly

This is an easy jelly to make, since apples are high in both pectin and acid. I remember Katzy using crab apples, even more tart than the familiar eating or cooking apples. Crab apples are occasionally available at supermarkets in the fall, but only as a specialty item and not in the generous quantities I recall from my childhood. If you decide to grow your own (and crab apple trees are beautiful when in bloom), be careful to choose a variety with decent-sized, useable fruit. Ornamental crab apples have tiny fruit that birds love to eat, but they are too miniscule to bother with for preserving.

Rating: Moderate
**Special Instructions: Apple jelly is one of the easiest to make, but determining the jell point
is a steeper learning curve.**
Yield: Six to eight 8-ounce jars

INGREDIENTS:
4 lbs. crab apples or other tart apples, such as Granny Smith
4 C. water
Sugar

1. Wash crab apples and cut them in half. If crab apples are not available, use any tart apple, such as Granny Smiths, which should be cut into quarters. Do not peel or core.
2. Put the apples in a large saucepan with the water. The topmost crab apples should be just above the water.
3. Bring to a boil, then cover the pot and simmer slowly until the apples are quite soft, about an hour, depending on the firmness of the fruit at the start.

4. Purée everything through a food mill fitted with the medium plate to remove the seeds.

5. Strain the purée through a colander lined with several layers of damp cotton cheesecloth, a chinois, or a jelly bag for several hours and collect the free-run juice. Do not press down on the fruit. Measure. If you want to also make some Apple Butter (pages 22–24), save the purée.

6. Add 1 cup of sugar to every 1 cup of juice in a large Dutch oven. Work with only 4 to 6 cups of juice at a time.

7. Bring to a boil and cook to the jell point.

8. Fill and process prepared jars as described on page 6.

Apple Jelly with Scented Geranium

Apple jelly is a fundamental kind of jelly that can easily be flavored with herbs. These jellies are both particularly nice with a light cake. Make either of the jelly rolls in Chapter Twelve: Using Preserves (pages 182–183). Rather than rolling the cake up, cut out rounds about four inches in diameter and brush them with rose- or lemon-geranium apple jelly while they are still warm, then pile on some lightly sugared sliced strawberries.

Rating: Moderate
Special Instructions: Apple jelly is one of the easiest to make, but determining the jell point is a steeper learning curve.
Yield: Six to eight 8-ounce jars

INGREDIENTS:
4 lbs. or 7 to 8 large crab apples or other tart apples, such as Granny Smith
4 C. water
Sugar
Rose- or lemon-scented geranium leaves

1. Follow steps 1 through 7 for Apple Jelly (pages 73–74).
2. Place a leaf of rose- or lemon-scented geranium in each jar.
3. Fill and process prepared jars as described on page 6.

Mint–Apple Jelly

Peppermint or spearmint both work well for this. For a moderately flavorful mint jelly, quickly simmer a bunch of fresh mint leaves in the apple juice for about five minutes, then strain, add the sugar, and proceed. A more intensely flavored jelly uses an infusion of mint.

Rating: Moderate
Special Instructions: This recipe takes two days to prepare.
Yield: Six to eight 8-ounce jars

INGREDIENTS:
2 C. fresh spearmint or peppermint leaves and tender tips (approximately 1 large bunch)
4 C. water, plus additional for mint extract
4 lbs. or 7 to 8 large crab apples or tart apples, such as Granny Smith
Sugar

Day 1

1.   Prepare the mint extract: Rinse a large bunch of fresh mint and pat it dry. Coarsely chop the mint until you have 2 cups of leaves and tender tips. Pack the leaves into a pint jar and add boiling water to cover.
     Note: If you are concerned that the jar might crack, stand a silver spoon in the jar before pouring in the boiling water. Silver quickly conducts away enough heat to protect against breaking the glass.
2.   Cap and stand the jar in a dark place at room temperature for 24 hours.

Day 2

3.   Pour the mint infusion into a saucepan. Bring it just to a boil, remove from the heat, and strain.
4.   Follow steps 1 through 5 for Apple Jelly (pages 73–74).
5.   Taste your infusion to see how intense the mint flavor is. Usually I find that about 3 tablespoons of infusion to 4 cups of apple juice extract is sufficient. However, you might like a more intense or a more subtle flavor. Add the mint infusion to the apple juice extract. Start will less; you can always add more.
6.   Add 1 cup of sugar to every 1 cup of juice in a large Dutch oven. Work with only 4 to 6 cups of juice at a time.
7.   Bring to a boil and cook to the jell point.
8.   Fill and process prepared jars as described on page 6.

Quince

Quince Jelly

Early each March, my friend Delilah (also an avid gardener) invites me to visit her in Center Valley, Pennsylvania. I stay overnight, and we spend the next day at the Philadelphia Flower Show. My usual hostess gift is a small basket with a jar or two of my preserves. They're always welcome. However, quince jelly seems to top the list for Delilah: "I just opened the jar of quince jelly you left. It's so flavorful, it shoots off the scale. I've never had anything so unique and delicious." This is another easy jelly to make, by which I mean that quince has good levels of pectin and acid. My Quince Jelly is usually made as a by-product of Quince Butter, using the liquid that is strained off the pulp. There is no reason, however, why it cannot be purposely made.

Rating: Moderate
Yield: Six to eight 8-ounce jars

INGREDIENTS:
3 or 4 quinces, depending on size
Water
Juice of 1 large lemon
Red food coloring (optional)
Sugar

1. Peel the quinces and cut them in half. Scoop out the cores and seeds with a melon baller. Measure the peels and cores and set aside. Drop the fruit into a bowl of water with a squeeze of lemon juice as they are prepared. This will keep them from discoloring.

2. Put the quince peels and cores into a saucepan with 1 cup of water to every cup of peels and cores. Bring to a boil, cover the pan, and reduce the heat to a simmer, cooking for 30 minutes.

3. Strain, reserving the liquid and discarding the peel and cores.

4. Coarsely chop the fruit into chunks and put it in a separate saucepan with additional water, if necessary, to barely cover the pieces.

5. Bring to a boil, cover, and reduce the heat to a simmer. Cook for 30 minutes, or until the fruit is soft and may easily be pierced with a skewer or toothpick.

6. Purée the quinces using the coarse plate on a food mill. Strain them through a colander lined with damp cotton cheesecloth, a chinois, or a jelly bag and collect the free-run juice. Do not press down on the fruit. If you would like to make Quince Butter (pages 25–26), save the purée that remains after straining the juice.

7. Combine the peel/seed liquid with the free-run liquid and measure.
8. Add 1 tablespoon of fresh lemon juice for every 3 cups of liquid.
9. Put the liquid, but not more than 4 to 6 cups, in a large Dutch oven and begin heating. As it approaches a boil (small bubbles appear on the bottom of the pan), add 1 cup of sugar for every cup of liquid and stir well until the sugar dissolves.
10. Bring to a boil and cook to the jell point. You may, if desired, tint the jelly with food coloring before bottling and processing.
11. Fill and process prepared jars as described on page 6.

Quinces have the potential to turn a lovely glowing Venetian red. Sometimes quince jelly and jam does this for me, other times it does not. I cannot figure out why it will or why it won't. I just go with the flow; sometimes I have golden greenish quince jelly rather than ruby red jelly. As mentioned above, the jelly can be tinted with some red food coloring just before bottling. Another choice would be to add some cranberry juice before the sugar is put into the quince extract. I hasten to add that by cranberry juice, I do not mean the commercial stuff you buy in a bottle, but something you would prepare yourself from cranberries cooked in water until they burst, then strain through a colander lined with several layers of damp cotton cheesecloth. In fact, here is a recipe for jelly prepared from a combination of quinces, cranberries, and apple.

Paradise Jelly

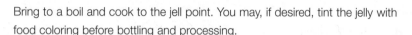

When I got married, my mother gave me her elderly edition of *The Settlement Cook Book*, compiled by Mrs. Simon Kander. Originally published in 1901, it is a compilation of German Jewish recipes used at the Milwaukee Settlement House for cooking classes taught to recent German immigrant women. Clearly popular, mine is the enlarged and revised thirtieth edition, published in 1951. It is easy to tell my mother's favorite recipes: the book naturally falls open to certain pages, which are often stained as well. I had it rebound once and have spilt on and stained pages of my own choosing.

Clearly Mrs. Kander made no assumptions about what her readers might or might not know. Her book has everything: household rules, how to make soap, how to start a wood or coal fire, electric and nonelectric kitchen equipment, food placement for both mechanical refrigerators and iceboxes. There are directions for serving and feeding the family from infants to invalids, as well as various recipes low in starch and sugar and for wheat-, egg-, or milk-free diets. And that is just what's up front, before it really gets cooking. Toward the back, 551 pages into the book, there is a section on making jelly, followed by another about preserving and pickling fruits, which covers marmalades, jams, and conserves. Her directions throughout the cookbook are, for that time, sound, practical, and thorough.

One of Mrs. Kander's jelly recipes that's been popular with my family and friends is Paradise Jelly, an amalgam of quinces, sweet apples, and cranberries. The original recipe calls for ten quinces, twenty apples, and a quart of cranberries. I've reduced the quantities and modified it.

Rating: Easy

Special Instructions: The combination of easy-to-jell apples, quinces, and cranberries makes this a reliable recipe. Even if it doesn't set when cool, it frequently sets up in a few weeks.

Yield: Six to eight 8-ounce jars

INGREDIENTS:

2 quinces

Water

1 Tbs. fresh lemon juice

4 Granny Smith apples

2 cups fresh cranberries

Sugar

1. Peel the quinces, quarter them and remove the cores, then slice. Set aside the peels and cores in water to cover. Drop the quince slices into water acidulated with the fresh lemon juice to keep the fruit from browning.

2. Peel and core four Granny Smith apples. Add the apple peels and cores to the quince peel and cores and the apple slices to the quince slices. If necessary, use a small plate to keep the fruit slices below the surface of the acidulated water.

3. Bring the saucepan of peels, cores, and water to a boil, then simmer briskly for 15 to 20 minutes. Strain, pressing down on the residue.

4. Drain the quince and apple slices and put them in a large Dutch oven. Rinse and pick over the cranberries and add them to the other fruit. Mix. Add the liquid from the peels and cores and sufficient water to peek through the top layer of fruit.

5. Bring this mixture to a boil and simmer it briskly until all the fruit is very soft, about 20 to 30 minutes. Strain through a fine mesh sieve lined with damp cotton cheesecloth, a chinois, or a jelly bag and collect the free-run juice. Do not press down on the fruit. If you would like to make Paradise Butter (page 26), set the residue aside.

6. Measure the liquid. Work with only 4 to 6 cups of liquid at a time. Return it to saucepan, bring it to a boil, and boil for about 10 minutes. Skim away any foam.

7. Add 1 cup of sugar for each cup of juice.

8. Bring to a boil and cook to the jell point.

9. Fill and process prepared jars as described on page 6.

Lemon

Lemon Jelly

For whatever reason, I really like Lemon Jelly but find Orange Jelly boring. So here's a recipe for the first, which is easily altered to create the second by substituting sliced oranges for the sliced lemons. If you do this, I'd recommend Valencia oranges over navel oranges. This Lemon Jelly recipe uses lemons and lemon juice, a different technique than the lemon pectin extract used to improve the jelling properties of fruits that are low in pectin. I developed the herb-flavored lemon jelly recipes in the next chapter using citrus pectin extract, with the intention of emphasizing the herbal flavors. There is certainly no reason why the Lemon Jelly given here could not be infused with herbs.

Rating: Moderately easy

Special Instructions: The recipe takes two days to prepare.

Yield: Six to eight 8-ounce jars

INGREDIENTS:

10 to 12 lemons

3³/₄ C. water

Sugar

Day 1

1. Juice enough lemons to make 1¹/₄ cups of juice. Put the juice in a large glass jar or stainless-steel container. Add water.

2. Slice 6 lemons—peel, pits, and all—and put them into the water and lemon juice mixture. Let it stand in the refrigerator for 12 hours.

Day 2

3. The next day, place the juice mixture in a nonreactive saucepan. Bring it to a boil, then simmer, covered, until the lemons are quite soft, anywhere from 30 to 45 minutes.

4. Strain the liquid through a colander lined with damp cotton cheesecloth, a chinois, or a jelly bag and collect the free-run liquid. Measure. Working with only 4 to 6 cups of liquid at a time, add the sugar, using a minimum of 1³/₄ cups of sugar for each 2 cups of liquid, to a maximum of 1 cup for each cup.

5. Bring to a boil in a large saucepan and boil rapidly until it jells.

6. Fill and process prepared jars as described on page 6.

Cactus

Cactus Jelly

One summer a local supermarket that caters to a Hispanic clientele in their produce section (which includes plantains, yautia lilas, malanga, ñame, sugarcane, and more) featured lots of *tuna*, fruit of *Opuntia* cactus, also known as cactus pears. From curiosity, I decided to make jelly from them, just to see what it was like. The supermarket cactus pears were, fortunately, prepared for market by the removal of the fine little spines, or *glochids*, that cover the surface of the plant. These can get painfully embedded into your skin and fester. Cactus pears are also very popular in Israel, where they are called *sabra*, after the native-born populace. The local saying is that both fruit and people are prickly on the outside, sweet on the inside. In the outdoor produce market, or *shuk*, Arab women have baskets of the fruit available for sale, deftly peeling them for customers.

Rating: Tedious
Yield: Four to five 8-ounce jars

INGREDIENTS:
20 cactus fruits
Water
1 C. Homemade Lemon Pectin extract (see recipe on page 11)
4 Tbs. fresh lemon juice
Sugar

1. Peel and seed cactus fruits, setting aside the peels.
2. Barely cover the peels with water, then simmer them until the peels are very soft, about 20 or 30 minutes.
3. Let the liquid cool, strain it, and measure. You should have about 2 cups of ruby red liquid.
4. Pour the liquid into a large Dutch oven and add the lemon rind pectin extract and lemon juice.
    Note: I also added 1 cup of slivered cactus pulp to intensify the flavor, then later removed it.
5. Bring the mixture to a boil and add $2/3$ cup of sugar for each cup of liquid.
6. Boil it fast and furiously to the jell point.
7. Quickly and carefully (this stuff is hot!) sieve off the cactus shreds, if you have added them.
8. Fill and process prepared jars as described on page 6.

Note: I decided that cactus jelly is nice, but not especially memorable, of more interest for what it was made from than for what it was.

SAVORY JELLIES and CONSERVES

Savory jellies are an aspect of preserves that I have explored more or less on my own rather than following in my mother's footsteps. She was more of a traditionalist in this area. To her, as to most of us, jelly has certain connotations, primarily as a sweetened fruit-based product. Perhaps if savory jellies had a name of their own, we wouldn't have this perplexity. Though not widely used even "across the pond," *tracklement* is a lovely British English word that designates a savory condiment served as an accompaniment to meat. It was first used by Dorothy Hartley in 1954 in her book *Food in England*. Her use of it in this sense was, she claimed, a special application of a dialectal word. But it seems to me that a chapter heading of "Tracklement" would mystify just about everybody. "Savory Jellies" is a less obscure option, with its connotation of seasoning and perhaps a hint of sharp as well as sweet tastes. And it is a type of preserve with which we are all familiar—after all, just think of the obligatory cranberry sauce that accompanies the Thanksgiving turkey on tables all across the United States. Savory jellies have wider applications in England and elsewhere abroad. Mint jelly is de riguer with lamb, while currant and rowan jellies are especially popular with game birds such as pheasant, duck, and grouse, and also venison and wild boar. Savory jellies' use can be as simple as a spoonful of preserves swirled in the pan to deglaze it after briskly sautéing, or thinned with a little wine and spooned over the meat. More elaborate recipes for sauces can be found in Chapter Twelve: Using Preserves.

Herb-infused jelly is an option that is subordinate to fruit-based jelly, if not completely ignored. The one exception that I've already mentioned is mint jelly. It may regularly be served with roast lamb in England, but that is not the way Americans tend to think of jelly. In my opinion, herb jellies are neglected in large part due to their method of production. Let's face it—herbs are entirely lacking in pectin and acid. Make herb jellies with standard commercial pectin, and you're jelling tea, an herb-infused water with so much sugar added that the first flavor is sugar-sweet. That is not what I want with my entrée, and I doubt you'd like it either. If, however, you use an apple jelly recipe as your starting place and flavor that with herbs, it is a different story.

I prefer to use fresh herbs rather than dried ones. Their flavor is brighter and sprightlier. Fortunately, these days many supermarkets have fresh herbs available in their produce section. Of course, the best way is to grow them yourself. Or, perhaps you have a friend with herbs to share. I had the advantage, while working on these recipes, of having a friend who was head gardener for the certified organic garden of a nearby, very upmarket, elegant restaurant. If you've ever had a garden, you know the fine line between just enough, an abundance, and a glut. By late summer, he was well into the last situation. For example, I'd be presented with a shopping bag of basil. After the freezer held all the pesto I could envision using, it was time to play around with recipes for preserves.

Savory herb jellies are the only type of preserve with which I'm willing to use commercial pectin—but only the Sure-Jell low-sugar type. The assist that they give to reaching the jell point means a shorter cooking time and stronger herb "presence" in the finished product. This is an "off label" use, but I've never had any difficulty with the modifications I suggest here.

Cranberries

Cranberries are a much-abused fruit. Most of the annual harvest is used for juice. Some of the remainder is turned into commercial preserves, typically a gloppy "jelly" that in households across America is, on the last Thursday in November, pushed out of a can, sliced into rounds, put out on the table for the Thanksgiving dinner, and then scraped into the garbage as the table is cleared for dessert. Cranberry relish is so easy: fresh cranberries are chopped up in a food processor with an orange and a little sugar, either left raw, or cooked. Here's an elaboration I think is really worth the effort. Just remember to make it early in the month so the flavors have sufficient time to marry.

Cranberry–Muscat Raisin Relish

While this is definitely not a jelly, it is a good starting place for savory preserves to serve with meat.

Rating: Easy

Special Instructions: This recipe takes two days to prepare. It is best to allow it at least two weeks to mellow before serving.

Yield: Four to five 8-ounce jars

INGREDIENTS:

2 C. muscat raisins* (you may substitute dark raisins)

1¹/₂ C. red wine vinegar

3 C. fresh cranberries

1¹/₂ C. red vermouth

³/₄ C. water

1 C. sugar

Day 1

1. Combine the muscat raisins and red wine vinegar. Allow the raisins to macerate (a fancy word that means soak and soften) in the vinegar for 24 hours.

Day 2

2. Rinse and pick over the fresh cranberries. Prick each one with a darning needle or cake tester. (It's tedious, but it keeps them from bursting.)

3. Drain the raisins, catching the liquid. Combine the soaking vinegar, red vermouth, water, and sugar. Bring to boil, then reduce the heat and simmer until the sugar is dissolved.

4. Add the raisins to the liquid and stir gently to separate.

5. Add the cranberries to the liquid and simmer the mixture until tender. Do *not* stir, or the cranberries will turn to mush, lessening the attractive appearance of the preserve. Instead, occasionally agitate the pan to keep the berries moving and to prevent scorching.

6. Strain the mixture over a bowl to catch the liquid. Return the liquid to the pan and bring it to a boil. Keep hot.

7. Use a wide-mouthed canning funnel to pack the raisins and cranberries into hot, sterilized 1-cup canning jars. Rap each jar on a wooden board to settle the contents, then spoon in more if necessary.

8. Process prepared jars as described on page 6.

This is a superb tart relish to serve as an accompaniment to rich fatty meats, such as duck, goose, or pork, and it is excellent with venison. An elegant presentation makes use of an inner, cupped radicchio leaf as a holder for an individual serving. The contrast between the cranberry relish and the white-veined burgundy red leaf is very attractive.

Note: Muscat raisins used to be readily available, found on supermarket shelves in a blue foil–wrapped box. For some unknown reason, they have become more of a specialty item. Lately I can only buy them in bulk five-pound boxes, directly from Sun-Maid Growers in California. Fortunately, raisins may be frozen. I repack them into one-cup portions first. You can also substitute dark raisins. The soaking time may then be reduced to eight or twelve hours, since these raisins are not as robust and sturdy as muscats.

Cranberry-Rosemary Jelly

This is the first herb jelly I made, if you discount the scented geranium leaf in the Apple Jelly that I describe in Chapter Six. It is straightforward and, with the combination of oranges and cranberries, jells easily.

Rating: Easy
Special Instructions: This recipe takes two days to prepare.
Yield: Three 8-ounce jars

INGREDIENTS:
2 medium-sized oranges
3 1/2 C. water
2 C. fresh cranberries (frozen cranberries may be substituted)
1/4 C. fresh rosemary leaves
4 whole cloves
2 to 3 1/2 C. sugar

Day 1

1. Wash the oranges and chop them coarsely, including the peel. Collect the seeds and tie them in cotton cheesecloth. Place everything in a nonreactive bowl. Cover with water and allow the mixture to sit, refrigerated, overnight.

Day 2

2. Put the oranges, seeds, and water in a nonreactive saucepan and bring it to a boil. Reduce the heat, cover the pot, and simmer gently for 15 minutes.

3. Rinse and pick over the cranberries and add them to the orange mixture. If you use frozen cranberries, first allow them to thaw.

4. Add the fresh rosemary leaves and cloves. Stir and mash the mixture gently with a wooden spoon. Cover the pot again, bring it just to a boil, reduce the heat,

and simmer for 20 minutes. The oranges and cranberries should be quite soft.

5. Line a colander with several layers of damp cotton cheesecloth and place it over a large bowl to collect the free-run juice. You may also use a chinois or a jelly bag.

6. Ladle the pulp and liquid into the lined colander and allow the flavored orange-cranberry infusion to drip for 2 or 3 hours. Do not press down on the fruit.

7. Measure the liquid. There should be $2^{1}/_{2}$ to 3 cups. Measure and set aside an equal amount of sugar.

8. Place the liquid in a large saucepan and bring it to a boil. Add the sugar, stirring well, and return the mixture to a boil.

9. Fill and process prepared jars as described on page 6.

Other cranberry recipes are in Chapter Nine: Native Harvest.

Grapes

I am fortunate that I have friends who hunt and who occasionally give me gifts of venison, pheasant, or wild duck. Sometimes the game is table ready. Other times, I assist in its preparation. While it is illegal to sell wild game, some is being farm raised, much like cattle and other animals. Venison, for example, is shipped here from New Zealand. Supermarkets in England offer Scottish venison. While track-lements are traditional accompaniments to game, they are also superb with pork, lamb, and poultry.

Grape Jelly with Thyme and Balsamic Vinegar

This is a great savory tracklement to serve with pork chops or roast, roast chicken, pheasant, or duck. The balsamic vinegar provides a tart sharpness that is a good foil for the meat or poultry.

Rating: Easy

Yield: Seven 8-ounce jars

INGREDIENTS:

1 tart apple, such as Granny Smith

1 lemon

3 C. water

6 C. Concord grapes

1 C. Homemade Lemon Pectin extract (recipe on page 11)

$^1/_2$ C. fresh thyme

1 to 1$^1/_2$ C. balsamic vinegar

1 box Sure-Jell for Lower Sugar Recipes pectin

4 C. sugar

1. Wash the apple and cut it into coarse pieces, peel, core, and all. Rinse the lemon, cut it into quarters, then cut the quarters into thin slices. Place everything in a large, nonreactive pot, adding 1 cup of water. Bring the mixture to a boil, then simmer, covered, for 10 minutes, or until the lemon is tender and the apple pieces are getting soft.

2. Rinse the Concord grapes and remove the stems. Add them and 2 additional cups of water to the softened apple/lemon ingredients. Bring the mixture to a boil, reduce heat, and simmer for 15 minutes. Turn off the heat and allow the ingredients to sit, covered, for another 15 minutes. Strain through a colander lined with several layers of damp cotton cheesecloth, a chinois, or a jelly bag and collect the free-run juice (a chinois is preferred). Do not press down on the fruit. Collect the free-run juice and measure out 4$^1/_2$ cups.

3. Combine the grape-apple juice with the homemade lemon pectin extract and fresh thyme. Bring the mixture to a boil, then cover it and simmer for 15 minutes. Let sit for 30 minutes, then strain, pressing on the thyme leaves with the back of a spoon to extract as much liquid as possible.

4. Add the balsamic vinegar.

5. Proceed using the Sure-Jell low-sugar grape jelly recipe.

6. Fill and process prepared jars as described on page 6.

Grape-Elderberry Jelly with Thyme and Juniper

Here is a nice variation that is excellent with venison, duck, or roast goose. To the best of my knowledge, elderberries are only available as a homegrown fruit harvested from this attractive flowering shrub or as a fruit you might gather in the wild. I haven't seen them in specialty stores or farmers' markets. The blend of grape and elderberry has a "gathered from the wild" flavor.

Rating: Moderate

Yield: Eight 8-ounce jars

INGREDIENTS:

1 tart apple, such as Granny Smith

1 lemon

3 C. water

6 C. Concord grapes

2 C. water

6 to 8 C. elderberries, measured after stripping off the clusters

$^1/_2$ C. thyme shoots

7 juniper berries

$^1/_2$ C. balsamic vinegar

1 to $1^1/_2$ C. Homemade Apple Pectin extract (recipe on page 10)

1 box Sure-Jell for Lower Sugar Recipes pectin

4 C. sugar

1. Follow steps 1 and 2 for Grape Jelly with Thyme and Balsamic Vinegar (page 86).
2. Wash the elderberries. Use a fork to strip the berries off their stems and into a suitably sized saucepan. Mash and crush them with the bottom of a clean glass jar, just to start some juices flowing. Heat gently for 15 minutes, then strain in a colander lined with several layers of damp cheesecloth, a chinois, or a jelly bag, collecting the free-run juice. Do not press down on the fruit.
3. Bruise the juniper berries in mortar. Combine 2 cups of grape extract juice and 2 cups of elderberry extract juice with the thyme shoots (use only the tender leafy tips) and juniper berries in a nonreactive saucepan.
4. Bring the mixture to a boil, then simmer, covered, for 15 minutes.
5. Turn off the heat and let sit, covered, for 30 minutes.
6. Strain the mixture through a colander lined with several layers of damp cotton cheesecloth, a chinois, or a jelly bag and collect the free-run juice. Do not press down on the fruit. Measure the juice. Add the balsamic vinegar and sufficient apple pectin extract to make $5^1/_2$ cups of liquid.
7. Proceed using the Sure-Jell low-sugar grape jelly recipe.
8. Fill and process prepared jars as described on page 6.

Lemons

Whatever the reason, one summer I wanted a lighter, paler tracklement to serve with cold roast chicken. It was primarily the taste I was after, but also the visual effect of a pale translucent Lemon Jelly that I envisioned as more summery than a dark autumnal Grape Jelly.

Lemon Jelly with Lemon Basil and White Wine Vinegar

Rating: Moderate

Yield: Four 8-ounce jars

INGREDIENTS:

1¹/₂ to 2 C. Homemade Lemon Pectin extract (recipe on page 11)*

1 C. Homemade Apple Pectin extract (recipe on page 10)*

2 C. lemon basil leaves, packed

¹/₂ C. white wine vinegar

¹/₂ package Sure-Jell for Lower Sugar Recipes pectin

2 C. sugar

1. Measure 1 cup of homemade lemon pectin extract and 1 cup of homemade apple pectin extract into a large, nonreactive pot.
2. Rinse the lemon basil and pick the leaves off the stems. Add them to the liquid.
3. Bring the mixture just to a boil, turn down heat to maintain a low simmer, and cover the pot.
4. Let simmer for 15 minutes. Turn off the heat and allow the leaves to steep, pot still covered, for an additional 15 minutes. Strain through a colander lined with several layers of damp cotton cheesecloth, a chinois, or a jelly bag while still warm and collect the free-run juice. Press down on the leaves with the back of a spoon to extract as much liquid as possible.
5. Measure. Add enough Homemade Lemon Pectin extract to equal 3 cups. Add white wine vinegar.
   Note: Check the label to find out the acidity of your vinegar. Most vinegar is 5 percent. If the one you are using is stronger, adjust by using ¹/₃ or even ¹/₄ cup of vinegar.
6. Proceed using the Sure-Jell lower sugar recipe for apple jelly, using 2 cups of sugar.
7. Fill and process prepared jars as described on page 6.

Note: If you want to go ahead with this recipe but do not have the time or inclination to prepare the pectin extracts, you can make Apple Jelly with Lemon Basil and White Wine Vinegar by substituting 2 cups of apple juice extract, prepared as follows:

Apple Extract

INGREDIENTS:

4 lbs. or 7 to 8 large crab apples or tart apples, such as Granny Smith

4 C. water

1. Wash crab apples and cut them in half. If crab apples are not available, use any tart apple, such as Granny Smiths, which should be cut into quarters. Do not peel or core.

2. Put the apples in a large saucepan with the water. The topmost crab apples should be just above the water.

3. Bring to a boil, then cover the pot and simmer slowly until the apples are quite soft, about an hour, depending on the firmness of the fruit at the start.

4. Purée everything through a food mill fitted with the medium plate to remove the seeds.

5. Strain the purée through a colander lined with several layers of damp cotton cheesecloth, a chinois, or a jelly bag for several hours and collect the free-run juice. Do not press down on the fruit. Measure. If you want to also make some Apple Butter (pages 22–23), save the purée.

6. Measure 2 cups of the apple juice extract, add lemon basil, and proceed with the recipe.

Lemon-Tarragon Jelly

This makes a wonderful finishing glaze for chicken, pork, or fish. Just thin slightly with the pan juices.

Rating: Moderate
Yield: Six 6-ounce jars

INGREDIENTS:
3 C. Homemade Lemon Pectin extract (recipe on page 11)*
1¹/₂ C. Homemade Apple Pectin extract (recipe on page 10)*
2 C. coarsely snipped and loosely packed fresh tarragon leaves
¹/₂ tsp. butter
3 C. sugar
1 box Sure-Jell for Lower Sugar Recipes pectin

1. Combine homemade lemon pectin extract and 1 cup of homemade apple pectin extract in a large saucepan. Add the fresh tarragon. Bring to a boil and simmer for 3 minutes.
2. Turn off the heat, cover, and let stand for 20 minutes. Strain and measure the liquid. Add enough additional apple pectin to make 4¹/₂ cups.
3. Add ¹/₂ teaspoon of butter to the liquid to prevent foaming.
4. Mix ¹/₄ cup of sugar with Sure-Jell pectin.
5. Stir the sugar and pectin mixture into the hot liquid; bring to a boil while stirring constantly.
6. Add the remaining sugar; bring back to a full rolling boil for 1 minute.
7. Fill and process prepared jars as described on page 6.

Note: If you want to go ahead with this recipe but do not have the time or inclination to prepare the pectin extracts, you can make Apple Tarragon Jelly, substituting 4¹/₂ cups of apple juice extract, prepared as follows:

Apple Extract

INGREDIENTS:

4 lbs. or 7 to 8 large crab apples or tart apples, such as Granny Smith

4 C. water

1. Wash crab apples and cut them in half. If crab apples are not available, use any tart apple, such as Granny Smiths, which should be cut into quarters. Do not peel or core.

2. Put the apples in a large saucepan with the water. The topmost crab apples should be just above the water.

3. Bring to a boil, then cover the pot and simmer slowly until the apples are quite soft, about an hour, depending on the firmness of the fruit at the start.

4. Purée everything through a food mill fitted with the medium plate to remove the seeds.

5. Strain the purée through a colander lined with several layers of damp cotton cheesecloth, a chinois, or jelly bag for several hours and collect the free-run juice. Do not press down on the fruit. Measure. If you want to also make some Apple Butter (pages 22–23), save the purée.

6. Measure $4^{1}/_{2}$ cups of the apple juice extract, add tarragon, and proceed with the recipe.

Apples

Caramelized Apple–Sage Relish

This is a somewhat more complicated recipe, but I think you'll agree it is worth the effort. Serve with pork, Rock Cornish game hen, pheasant, or roast chicken.

Rating: Moderate
Yield: Four 8-ounce jars

INGREDIENTS:
6 large Granny Smith apples
$1/4$ C. fresh lemon juice
2 lemons
Water
2 C. sugar
$1^1/2$ C. Homemade Apple Pectin extract (recipe on page 10)
$1/4$ C. apple cider vinegar
1 fresh bay leaf
3 4-inch sprigs of sage plus 4 additional sage leaves for jars
$1/4$ C. Calvados (apple brandy)

1. Peel and core the apples, setting aside the peels and cores. Cut the fruit into small cubes. Toss with the lemon juice. Cover the bowl with plastic wrap and set it aside.
2. Coarsely chop the rind from two lemons. Place it, together with the apple peels and cores, into a pot with water barely to cover.
3. Bring to a boil, then simmer until cores, peel, and rinds are tender. Drain through a fine-mesh sieve, saving the liquid.
4. Combine the sugar with $1/2$ cup of homemade apple pectin extract. Bring to a boil, then cook over medium heat without stirring until the syrup turns medium amber. Pay attention! It turns dark very quickly, so watch it.
5. Combine the cider vinegar with the remaining cup of homemade apple pectin extract. Prepare a bouquet garni by bundling the fresh bay leaf and sprigs of sage in a piece of washed all-cotton cheesecloth, tying it closed with a string.
6. Combine the apple/lemon liquid, bouquet garni, and diced apples with the caramelized sugar/pectin mixture. The caramelized sugar will stiffen up as it cools, so stir and scrape the bottom and sides of the pan with a wooden spoon until it liquefies again and blends with the other ingredients.
7. Cook the mixture over low to moderate heat until the apple dice turn translucent, the liquid begins to cook away, and the mass of apples and liquid thickens.

When a spoon leaves a track as you drag it through the relish, take the pot off the heat.

8. Add 1 tablespoon of Calvados (apple brandy) to each jar. Alternatively, add all the Calvados to the apple relish and stir well.

9. Add 1 sage leaf to the bottom of each jar.

10. Fill and process prepared jars as described on page 6.

There are recipes for Currant Jelly in Chapter Eight: Delectable Berries (page 107), and for Highbush Cranberry and Rowan Jelly in Chapter Ten: Backyard Harvest (pages 146–147 and 148). These, and other tart jellies, are all well suited to use as a savory jelly.

CHAPTER EIGHT
DELECTABLE BERRIES

Berries were very much a part of our summers on Carmen Hill Road #2. We picked blackberries and dewberries—which looked like blackberries but whose thorny stems trail on the ground—and the small black-cap raspberries. Blueberries were a delicious treat, picked ripe and warm from the summer sun. The best blackberries came from the meadow down the road, where someone pastured a herd of huge black-and-white Holstein cows. The thorny square canes grew in a huge tangle. At that time, I was relatively immune to poison ivy, so if there was a really good lot of glistening berries intermingled with the itchy stuff, I was the one sent in with a bucket to harvest them. The cows were relatively uninterested in our activities. Mostly they reclined in a rather graceful manner and watched, chewing their cuds, as Grandma Gussie, Aunt Gert, my mother, my older sister, Carol, my younger brother, Ben, and I climbed over the gate and went about our foraging. (My father had to work during the week and took the train up from New York City on the weekends. As I recall, he was not particularly skilled as a berry picker. This was women's work, and we were very good at it.) My brother, Ben, remembers the berry picking, and also the necessity of watching where you walked!

Now this was not land any of us owned. But just like any other tribe of hunter-gatherers, we felt that this was our territory. I still remember the indignation expressed by the grown-ups the one time it was obvious that someone else had been berry picking before we got there.

Most of the berries were eaten fresh. In the years when there were extra, my mother would make preserves. And in the winter months, back in the city, we'd take a spoonful of blackberry jam on toast and inevitably someone would say, "Do you remember … ?" The sunny summer days and blue sky with puffy white clouds were recalled with perfect pleasure, along with the rich clusters of underripe red and luscious black berries dangling from canes more than head high on a little girl, fingers and mouth stained purple with juice and the taste of the sun-warmed berries that demanded sampling as we picked.

More than any other fruit, berries are perishable. We never picked soon after a rain, as the berries' flavor is weaker then. Blackberries, dewberries, and raspberries are especially soft, so they easily crush and then become moldy. No wonder that they cost so much in the grocery store, frequently several dollars for a tiny half-pint of raspberries or blackberries. They also stain: even as a small child I found that I should not put a few berries in my pocket to be eaten later. Not only are the berries smooshed to a pulp, as my mother pointed out, the purple stain cannot be removed.

These very same bramble berries are often vigorous inhabitants of wild places. In Oregon, blackberries are a veritable scourge, thorny tangles invading ill-tended gardens as well as filling roadsides and waste places. They have square canes and thorns that are reluctant to let go, pinching into your skin and pulling it up when you back off. Raspberries have rounded, white canes and, while thorny, are not so aggressive as blackberries.

Timing is everything in berry picking. Berries, I have learned, must be picked ripe, as they are one fruit that does not continue to mature after harvesting. The season requires sufficient rain for juicy berries, enough sunny weather to ripen them, and a dry spell for a couple of days before picking. Wet berries have an insipid flavor and, I swear, once picked they can get moldy before I get home. The best time for berry picking is relatively early in the morning, late enough that the dew has dried off the berries, but before the heat of the day affects the flavor. I have a wide, shallow ash-splint basket that I use for berry picking, either picking directly into the basket or using it to hold eight pint-sized pressed-paper baskets and putting the berries in those.

Finding a place to pick wild berries adds another dimension to the experience of making preserves. I recall that my favorite bunk along Route 7 in Wilton, Connecticut, was replaced by a commuter parking lot even before we moved away in 1995. One morning I was there, gingerly working my way into a tangle of blackberries, when I noticed a hen pheasant crouched on the ground with her wings somewhat outspread. I froze into place, and we looked at each other. I expect pheasants to take off when I disturb them, with a heart-stopping reverberation from their wing strokes as they rocket up from concealment. This bird just stayed there, hunkered down. Perhaps, I thought, she was injured. Taking one more step was enough to send her off and reveal the dozen or more fuzzy, brown, and honey-striped golf ball–sized chicks she'd been sheltering. I again froze into place until I felt sure the babies had regrouped with their mother and would no longer be underfoot, then went on my way with an enchanting memory.

I've found a couple of places for blackberrying in Hunterdon County, New Jersey, where we now live. Occasionally in spring, there are reports of black bears in the area, bachelor males wandering over from Pennsylvania looking for a lady friend. Any bear that wants a berry patch where I intended to go picking, well, no contest, it's all his. And one woman told me of berry picking on a sunny, rocky hillside in Bucks County, Pennsylvania, when she heard a raspy, vibrating, rattling sound. Looking around she indeed saw a rattlesnake coiled up and indicating its displeasure with her intrusion. She also decided that retreat was the most prudent option. But berry picking is rarely so exciting, generally it's a serene affair, enjoyable solo or in company—of the human kind, that is!

Berries are referred to as "soft fruits," which, I suppose, distinguishes them from "stone fruits" such as cherries, peaches, plums, and apricots. Should you decide to grow blackberries, there's the advantage that berries produce a harvest very quickly, in just a year or two. The disadvantage is that bramble berries have territorial ambitions. They sucker like crazy and require vigilant efforts to keep them within their allotted boundaries. In a way, that makes it easy to share the plants.

A neighbor grows thornless blackberries, vigorous plants with large, tasty fruit and absolutely, positively no thorns. You can lean right into the canes and emerge unscathed, never looking like the losing combatant in a grudge match with a wildcat. In the past, after the neighbor picked all the berries, I'd be invited to come help myself. The first time I showed up with a single pint basket in my hand I got laughed at—production is such that, even picked-over, there were sufficient berries to fill a quart or two. Like other blackberries, these would sneak off underground runners that would pop up in the adjacent turf, to be cut off the next time the lawn was mown. I dug half a dozen suckers and passed them on to my daughter, Mira, who now has her own patch of thornless blackberries.

Blackberries

Hedgerow plants. I remember a September visit to friends in England. One evening we had dinner at Simon's cousin's rambling Georgian house, where dessert was an apple and blackberry cobbler made from berries picked that afternoon by my hostess and her daughter, the girl barely awake at midday after a round of debutante balls the night before. Well-grown blackberries can have fruit as thick around as my thumb and as long as the last joint. They grow in clusters, each berry made up of individual drupelets that change from green to wine red to glossy black when ripe and bursting with juice. Blackberries come off the stem still attached to the greenish center. Another distinguishing characteristic, as has been mentioned, is that blackberries have square canes.

Blackberry Butter

The big drawback to blackberries (after you get past their thorniness) is the number of small seeds just the right size for getting stuck between your teeth. That's nuisance enough if you're eating a handful fresh, but it becomes even more irritating in jam, where fruit is not strained. So Katzy would make blackberry butter, where the fruit was put through a food mill with the fine plate in place. Since there is pulp together with the juice, it is not properly called a jelly.

Rating: Easy
Yield: Six 8-ounce jars

INGREDIENTS:
8 C. blackberries
Sugar

1. Quickly rinse the blackberries: Fill the sink with water, put about half the berries into a large colander, and swish them up and down a couple of times. Drain well. Repeat with the remaining berries. Any water that clings to the berries is acceptable (if you process them right away), but on no account let them sit in water or wait more than a few minutes before starting the cooking process.
2. Put the berries into a large Dutch oven. Use a potato masher or the bottom of a clean glass jar to crush some berries and get their juices flowing.
3. Heat gently for a few minutes, until the berries are cooked.
4. Put the cooked berries, still hot, through a food mill fitted with the fine plate to remove the seeds, then measure the purée.*
5. Taste the purée for sweetness. If there were (as there should be) some underripe berries and the purée has a hint of tartness, mix it with an equal amount of sugar. If this seems too sweet for your taste, reduce the sugar to $3/4$ cup per cup of purée. I use the same measuring cup for blackberry purée and sugar, allowing the sugar to become stained with the berry pulp and scraping out the last little bit.
6. Cook the mixture gently over low heat until the purée has thickened and a spoon dragged through the mass leaves a track.
7. Fill and process prepared jars as described on page 6.

Note: Carole Nagy makes her blackberry or raspberry butter by mixing the crushed fruit with sugar and putting it through the Squeezo to remove the seeds before she cooks it.

Blackberry Jelly

Blackberry Jelly is a tricky preserve—it's not easy to get a good set. When everything works just right (the stars are perfectly aligned, perhaps), you have a delicious accomplishment to be deservedly proud of.

Rating: Difficult

Special Instructions: Blackberry Jelly will have a softer set than other jellies, such as apple or grape, and using the Homemade Apple Pectin (page 10) helps achieve a firmer set.

Yield: Three to four 8-ounce jars

INGREDIENTS:

8 C. blackberries

2 C. Homemade Apple Pectin extract (recipe on page 10)

2 Tbs. fresh lemon juice

Sugar

1. Measure, rinse, and cook blackberries as described in steps 1 through 3 of the Blackberry Butter recipe (page 98).
2. Strain them through a colander lined with several layers of damp cotton cheesecloth or use a chinois or a jelly bag, collecting the free-run juice. Do not press down on the fruit. Measure the juice.
3. To each 3 cups of blackberry juice, add 2 cups of Homemade Apple Pectin and 2 tablespoons of lemon juice. Measure the combined juice and pectin.
4. Bring the liquid to a boil.
5. Add an equal amount of sugar and bring the mixture back to a boil. Cook rapidly to the jell point.
6. Fill and process prepared jars as described on page 6.

Raspberries

My husband may favor blackberries, but I'll take raspberries any day. Once, years ago, when we were having dinner at The Boxing Cat in Darien, Connecticut, I was feeling comfortably full after a tasty meal and nothing on the dessert menu caught my fancy. I casually told the attentive waiter, "Only raspberries, that's all I could possibly want." The waiter came back, big smile on his face, and on his tray was a fat-bowled wineglass full of red raspberries with a little light cream poured over them. Heavenly. My husband swore he could see the canary feathers around my mouth as this satisfied kitty finished every luscious berry and drop of cream.

Wild raspberries are black in color, small fruited, and ripen in late June in New Jersey and Connecticut. Given the right combination of sufficient rain (so berries are not small and dry) and enough sun to develop their essence, they have an intense

flavor. It is easy to tell raspberries from blackberries: when you pick raspberries, the drupelets come away as a small cup, leaving behind the hard, white, inedible receptacle. Cultivated raspberries can also be a soft rosy red when ripe—or even amber gold. Red varieties make a good preserve, but I find the yellow ones, while good for eating fresh, lack the concentration of flavor necessary for a good preserve.

Raspberry Butter

Raspberry Butter and Raspberry Jelly are made in much the same way as blackberry preserves, with red raspberries more popular than black raspberries because of the latter's intense, somewhat heavy flavor. Using two parts black raspberry juice and one part, or even equal parts, apple pectin extract results in a jelly of excellent flavor and quality.

Rating: Easy
Yield: Six 8-ounce jars

INGREDIENTS:
8 C. raspberries
Sugar

1. Measure the raspberries and quickly rinse them by swishing the berries in a colander, 4 cups at a time, in a sink filled with cool water. Drain and repeat with the remaining fruit. Process the berries right after rinsing, or they are apt to quickly become moldy.
2. Put all the berries in a large Dutch oven. Use a potato masher or the bottom of a clean glass jar to crush some of the berries and get their juices flowing.
3. Heat the fruit gently for a few minutes until the berries are cooked through and the juices run freely.
4. Put the cooked, still hot berries through the fine plate of a food mill. Measure the purée.
5. Taste for sweetness. If there is just a hint of tartness, mix the berries with an equal amount of sugar. If this is too sweet for your taste, reduce the sugar to $3/4$ cup per cup of raspberry purée.
6. Cook gently until the raspberry purée has thickened and a spoon leaves a track when dragged through the mass.
7. Fill and process prepared jars as described on page 6.

Raspberry Jelly

Raspberry Jelly is the stuff that dreams are made of. When, that is, it comes out just right. A translucent ruby red with a quivering texture, not gummy, not too sweet … opening the jar is like smelling the perfume of paradise.

Rating: Difficult

Yield: Three to four 8-ounce jars

INGREDIENTS:

8 C. raspberries

2 C. Homemade Apple Pectin extract (recipe on page 10)

2 Tbs. fresh lemon juice

Sugar

1. Measure the raspberries and quickly rinse them by swishing the berries in a colander, 4 cups at a time, in a sink filled with cool water. Drain and repeat with the remaining fruit. Process the berries right after rinsing, or they are apt to quickly become moldy.
2. Dump all the berries (except the few you just have to sample) into a large Dutch oven. Crush them with a potato masher or the bottom of a clean glass jar to get their juices flowing.
3. Cook the berries over moderate heat for a few minutes until they are quite soft and the juices are flowing freely.
4. Strain them through a colander lined with several layers of damp cotton cheese-cloth or a chinois or a jelly bag, collecting the free-run juice. Do not press down on the fruit. Measure.
5. To each 3 cups of raspberry juice, add 2 cups of homemade apple pectin and 2 tablespoons lemon juice.
6. Bring the mixture to a boil.
7. Add an equal amount of sugar, stirring thoroughly.
8. Bring the mixture back to a boil and cook it rapidly to the jell point.
   Note: If it doesn't jell, you have fabulous raspberry sauce for cakes and ice cream.)
9. Fill and process prepared jars as described on page 6.

Strawberries

One of the first memories I have is connected with food. My parents, sister, and I are visiting my father, Robby's, friend Carl Psentsik for the weekend. He, his sister, Mitzi, and their auntie lived together—in winter in their New York City apartment and in summer in a vacation house that Carl built himself on property loaned to him by a friend. It is sometime in the early 1940s, and we'd come for the weekend. As I recall,

everyone else was asleep except for me and Carl, so it must have been early Sunday morning. I am wearing denim rompers and a cotton jersey. We go into the field by the house, looking for little wild strawberries in the dew-wet grass. That is, Carl did most of the finding and picking, and I did most of the eating. We didn't say much, but in anamnesis (a wonderful word that means the recollection or remembrance of the past), each intense burst of flavor from the tiny scarlet fruits, cool from the night, has a language all its own.

When my husband and I and our children first lived in Fairfield County, Connecticut—we moved there in 1968—there was a pick-your-own strawberry farm in Westport. The berries were sold by weight, and I used to joke with the owner that he should weigh me when I arrived and again when I was ready to weigh out with the green pressed-paper quart-sized baskets of fruit. He'd laugh and wave that thought away, both of us agreeing that his strawberries were too tantalizing to just pick and take home without sampling some. Strawberries today are often large, bloated, bland things shipped in from California. As with much else, size has replaced savor. They have good color, but only a vestige of the flavor these berries were once renowned for. This sad state of affairs makes me think of Izaak Walton's 1655 comment, "We may say of Angling as Dr. Boteler said of Strawberries; Doubtless God could have made a better berry, but doubtless God never did … "

Strawberry jam is the preserve that has the strongest memories for Monika Nicholson of Virginia Berry Farm. In her own words, "I remember my mom making jars and jars of strawberry jam. I always thought it was so neat! When I was a teenager, I decided to try making some of my own. I think I called my mom at work fifty times to ask questions. Now it is my seven-year-old daughter who thinks it is so neat that she can eat jam on her toast that was made by her mommy. This always makes me feel like all of the work I put into making the jam is worth it."

That's jam. I think that strawberry jelly lacks the oomph, the burst of flavor of the fresh berry, and a typical strawberry jam has the flavor, but too smooth a texture for my taste. A rather elaborate two-stage jam keeps some of the fruit intact and produces the most intense taste and aroma. Should you be so fortunate, small *fraises des bois* or the little alpine strawberries are best for the second-stage whole fruit, while any flavorful strawberry will do for the start. Don't guess at the timing; use a kitchen timer for the various cooking stages.

Strawberries are great to eat fresh. Some people like to guild the lily by dipping them in chocolate. Turn them into preserves, though, and you have to be careful that the results are not an insipidly sweet goo. That's one reason why I like combinations such as the Rhubarb-Strawberry Jam in Chapter Three: Jams (page 41). In case you prefer your strawberries "straight up," here are two recipes for unadulterated, nothing (well, almost nothing) but strawberries. The first one, for Strawberry Jam, is easy, and the other, for Strawberries in Strawberry Purée, takes it up a notch. While simple, it requires some time here and there over a couple of days.

Strawberry Jam

Rating: Easy

Special Instructions: This recipe takes two days to prepare.

Yield: Approximately six 8-ounce jars

INGREDIENTS:

6 to 8 C. first-quality, just-ripe but not soft strawberries

2 C. sugar

Day 1

1. Quickly rinse the strawberries by placing them in a colander, then swishing them up and down in a sink filled with cool water.
2. Hull the berries (that means use your fingers or a tweezerlike strawberry huller to pinch off the leaflike small green calyx, or cap, at the top of each berry).
3. Purée the strawberries through the coarse plate of a food mill.
4. Mix the strawberry purée with the sugar in a Dutch oven and let it sit in a cool place, covered, overnight.

Day 2

5. Juices should be flowing by morning. Put the pot over low heat. Once the strawberry and sugar purée has warmed up, raise the heat to moderate. Cook for about 15 to 20 minutes, stirring all the while.
6. The purée is ready to bottle when it has thickened somewhat and a spoon dragged through the mass leaves a track (which fills in again, fairly promptly).
7. Fill and process prepared jars as described on page 6.

Strawberries in Strawberry Purée

Rating: Moderate

Special Instructions: This recipe takes two days to prepare.

Yield: Four 8-ounce jars

INGREDIENTS:

2 C. strawberries

4 C. sugar

2 C. *fraises des bois*, or any other small, flavorful strawberry

$^1/_2$ C. fresh lemon juice

Day 1

1. Quickly rinse the strawberries and hull them. A strawberry huller, a pair of thin, flat, metal tweezers, is useful for this. Crush the strawberries and mix them with 2 cups of sugar. Let sit, refrigerated, for a couple of hours or longer.

2. Heat the strawberries and sugar, and bring the mixture just to a boil. Let it simmer for 5 minutes, then purée.

3. While the strawberries and sugar are cooking, mix the *fraises des bois* with 1 cup of sugar. Heat gently for 5 minutes, but do not boil.

4. Sieve out the *fraises des bois* and set aside. Add the sugar and any liquid to the sweetened strawberry purée, bring it to the boiling point, and slow boil for 3 minutes.

5. Return the little strawberries to the purée and simmer for an additional 2 minutes.

6. Take off heat, cover, and set aside overnight.

Day 2

7. The next day, again sieve out the strawberries and set them aside.

8. Add the remaining cup of sugar to the purée, bring it to a boil, and boil hard for 3 minutes.

9. Add the reserved berries and the lemon juice. Bring the mixture to a boil and boil for 3 minutes.

10. Fill and process prepared jars as described on page 6.

Strawberry-Pineapple Jam

Pineapple used as a minor amendment to strawberry jam makes a very pleasing addition. It is easy enough to prepare fresh pineapple, and the availability of peeled and cored fresh pineapple at the supermarket simplifies things even more.

Rating: Moderate

Yield: Approximately six 8-ounce jars

INGREDIENTS:

1 C. aromatically ripe fresh pineapple

6 C. strawberries

3 C. sugar

1. Cut the pineapple lengthwise into quarters. Peel, and remove the fibrous core. Cut a quarter section in half, lengthwise. Prepare 1 cup of pineapple by shredding the yellow flesh with two forks: stab the pineapple with one fork to hold it in place and use the other to scrape.
   Note: Use stainless-steel forks, as silver will quickly tarnish from the pineapple's acidity.
   Collect the juice as you shred the pineapple into a shallow soup plate.
2. Place the shredded pineapple and ¹/₄ cup of pineapple juice (water will serve if there isn't enough juice) in a nonreactive saucepan, cover, and simmer for 20 minutes, or until tender.
3. Meanwhile, prepare the strawberries: rinse and hull. Small strawberries may be left whole, while large berries should be cut in half or thirds.
4. Mix the strawberries with the sugar in a large Dutch oven and let them sit to start the juices flowing.
5. When the pineapple is soft, add it to the strawberries and stir well. Bring the fruit and sugar to a boil and reduce the heat so the mixture is at a gentle boil, stirring occasionally.
6. When the mixture begins to thicken, raise the heat and stir frequently. When a spoon leaves a track at the bottom of the pan, the jam is ready.
7. Fill and process prepared jars as described on page 6.

See also Rhubarb-Strawberry Jam in Chapter Three: Jams (page 41).

Currants

There was an abandoned farmstead on Carmen Hill that had a few red currant bushes in the former dooryard. When the grown-ups thought it was about time, we'd start checking on the bushes, walking in from the dirt road on our way to the lake. It was a race of sorts—when the berries ripened, would the birds get them first, or would we? As a child, I didn't much care. The trailing clusters of transparent, ruby red berries were very pretty, but one taste and I spat out the tart, sour fragment.

Currants are clearly an adult sophisticated taste—while I still don't eat them raw, I love preserves made from currants. Popular in England, once popular over here, currants are now difficult to obtain. One reason is a plant disease called white pine blister rust, which alternates between all five-needle pines and currant or gooseberry bushes.

Beginning in the early 1900s, cultivation of currants and gooseberries, indeed any *Ribes* species, was prohibited by federal law. The ban was abolished on the federal level in 1966, but their cultivation continues to be banned in several states. I assume New Jersey is not among them, since there is one pick-your-own place not far from where I live that offers red and white currants as well as raspberries. I prefer to go in the morning, when things are still cool and the succulent berries, ripe and swollen with flavor, have not yet been overheated by the more intense summer sun of late day.

There are three types of currants. Black currants, with astonishingly high levels of vitamin C, are vital for making crème de cassis, an alcoholic cordial made in Burgundy. They are also popular for making jam and syrup. Red currants are even more of a favorite for preserves, such as the well-liked red currant jelly used in England as an accompaniment for lamb or puddings. White currants, least common of the three and with a pearl-like pink blush to their translucent perfection, are also admirable for making preserves. Less tart than the others, white currants may be eaten fresh.

Currant Jelly

Currants are among the fruits high in both pectin and acid that result in ease of making jelly. In fact, a very delicate jelly may be made by dissolving the requisite amount of sugar in warm currant juice, bottling it in hot sterilized glasses, and sealing. The resulting jelly (it takes several days to set) is less firm, and of course it does not keep as well. As currants also have small seeds, making them into jelly means that the seeds are removed from the finished product.

Rating: Easy
Yield: Three to four 8-ounce jars

INGREDIENTS:
8 C. red currants
4 C. water
Sugar

1.   Rinse the currants by placing them, 3 to 4 cups at a time, in a colander and swishing them around in a sink filled with cool water. Drain. Pick over to remove any overripe fruit, but do not bother removing the stems.
2.   Put the currants in a large saucepan and crush some with a potato masher or the bottom of a clean glass jar. Add 2 cups of water.
3.   Bring the mixture to a boil, then reduce the heat to a slow boil and cook for 15 to 20 minutes, until the currants have lost their color.
4.   Strain the fruit through a colander lined with several layers of damp cotton cheesecloth, a chinois, or a jelly bag and collect the free-run juice. Do not press down on the fruit. If the currants are very flavorful, take a second extraction: After straining off the juice, return the currants to the saucepan. Add another 2 cups of water and heat at a simmer for 15 minutes, let sit for 15 minutes, then strain. Combine the two extractions. This is something I do only for very flavorful, difficult-to-obtain fruit, such as currants.
5.   Measure the juice. Measure an equal amount of sugar and set aside.
6.   Put the juice in a large Dutch oven and bring it to a rapid boil.
7.   Boil for 5 minutes, then add the sugar, stirring well.
8.   Bring the mixture back to a boil and cook it to the jell point.
9.   Fill and process prepared jars as described on page 6.

Currant-Elderflower Jelly

Elderberries are in bloom when currants are ripe. Their flowers add a wonderful wild taste to the jelly. I remember that Katzy made this once and tied the elderflowers in a piece of cotton cheesecloth to keep little bits of petals from the small flowers coming loose into the jelly. So that's what I now do.

Rating: Easy

Special Instructions: Elderberry bushes are in bloom in late July.

Yield: Three to four 8-ounce jars

INGREDIENTS:

8 C. red currants

4 C. water

2 trusses (full clusters) of elderflowers

Sugar

1. Follow steps 1 through 5 for Currant Jelly (page 107).
2. Rinse elderflowers by swishing them in water. Shake off any water that clings to them, but it is unnecessary to pat the flowers dry.
3. Tie the elderflowers loosely in a single or double layer of cotton cheesecloth.
4. Bring the currant juice to a strong simmer. Holding the elderflower clusters by their stems, swish them around in the hot juice for 5 minutes or so, depending on how strong a flavor you prefer.
5. Remove and discard elderflowers.
6. Bring the flavored currant juice up to a boil and add the sugar, stirring well.
7. Bring the mixture back to boil and cook to the jell point.
8. Fill and process prepared jars as described on page 6.

Currant–Raspberry Jelly

Currants pair up very well with raspberries. Not only do their flavors harmonize, the currant juice help "set" that of the raspberries.

Rating: Easy

Special Instructions: If you use red raspberries, the color of the finished jelly will be a lovely red, while if you use blackcap raspberries, it will be darker.

Yield: Approximately four to five 8-ounce jars

INGREDIENTS:

8 C. currants

1¹/₂ C. water

4 C. raspberries

Sugar

1. Rinse the currants by placing them, 3 to 4 cups at a time, in a colander and swishing them around in a sink filled with cool water. Drain. Pick over to remove any overripe fruit, but do not bother removing the stems.

2. Place them in a large saucepan and crush with a potato masher or the bottom of a clean glass jar. Add 1 cup of water.

3. Bring the mixture to a boil, then reduce the heat to a slow boil and cook for 15 to 20 minutes, until the currants have lost their color.

4. Strain the fruit through a colander lined with several layers of damp cotton cheesecloth, a chinois, or a jelly bag and collect the free-run juice. Do not press down on the fruit. Measure and set aside.

5. Place the raspberries in the same saucepan you cooked the currents in and crush them lightly. Add ¹/₂ cup of water, less if the raspberries are very juicy. Cook slowly until the juices are flowing easily.

6. Strain the raspberries through dampened cotton cheesecloth, a chinois, or a jelly bag and collect the free-run juice. Do not press down on the fruit. Measure the juice and combine with the currant juice in a large Dutch oven.

7. Measure an equal amount of sugar.

8. Bring the juices to a boil and cook for 5 minutes. Add the sugar and stir to dissolve. Bring back to a boil and cook for about 3 minutes, or until it reaches the jell point.

9. Fill and process prepared jars as described on page 6.

Bar-le-Duc Preserves

This recipe is more than just a nuisance to make; it helps if you are obsessive-compulsive. It only works if you can obtain good-sized red currents. When you read the recipe, it becomes clear why the real stuff retails at $30 for a tiny little three-ounce jar. I've made Bar-le-Duc Preserves, but, I confess, only once. It is a classy, delicious adjunct to roast duck or goose or game, such as venison or pheasant. Is it good enough to be worth the effort? Cumberland Sauce (pages 203 and 204), made with currant jelly, is a whole lot easier.

Rating: Tedious

Special Instructions: This recipe takes three days to prepare.

Yield: Three 4-ounce jars (I thought it made sense to use the smallest jars I could find.)

INGREDIENTS:

2 C. large, ripe red currants

1¹/₂ C. sugar

Day 1

1.   Rinse the currants. Gently remove them from the stem. With a tiny pair of embroidery or manicure scissors, make a little slit in one side of each currant. Use a sewing needle to tease out the seeds. Try to avoid mangling the currants.

2.   Place the seeded currants in a large saucepan and toss with the sugar. (In my case, it was taking so long to seed the currants that I stopped partway into the process, measured out the sugar, and began tossing berries with the sugar as I went along. Also, I just agitated the pan rather than stirring with a spoon.)

3.   Cover and let sit overnight.

Day 2

4.   The next day, skim out the fruit. Bring the syrup slowly to the boiling point and immediately turn down the heat. Return the currants to the syrup and simmer for just 3 minutes.

5.   Remove from heat, cover, and let stand for 24 hours.

Day 3

6.   The next day, bring the mixture just to a boil.

7.   Fill and process prepared jars as described on page 6.

Pineapple in White Currant Jelly

One year, having obtained some white currants, I came up with this elegant recipe, transparently pale with shreds of pineapple suspended in the currant jelly.

Rating: Moderately Easy
Yield: Six 8-ounce jars

INGREDIENTS:
6 C. white currants
1 C. aromatically ripe pineapple
Sugar

1. Cut the pineapple lengthwise into quarters. Peel, and remove the fibrous core. Cut a quarter section in half, lengthwise. Prepare 1 cup of pineapple by shredding the yellow flesh with two forks: stab the pineapple with one fork to hold it in place and use the other to scrape.
   Note: Use stainless-steel forks, as silver will quickly tarnish from the pineapple's acidity.

2. Rinse the white currants by placing them, 3 cups at a time, in a colander and swishing them around in a sink filled with cool water. Drain. Pick over to remove any overripe fruit, but do not bother removing the stems.

3. Put the currants in a large saucepan and crush some with a potato masher or the bottom of a clean glass jar. Add 2 cups of water.

4. Bring the mixture to a boil, then reduce the heat to a slow boil and cook for 15 to 20 minutes, until the currants have lost their color.

5. Strain the fruit through a colander lined with several layers of damp cotton cheesecloth, a chinois, or a jelly bag and collect the free-run juice. Do not press down on the fruit.

6. Measure the currant juice and shredded pineapple. For every 3 cups combined, measure out 2 cups of sugar.

7. Put juice and pineapple in a large Dutch oven and bring to a boil. Reduce the heat to keep things at a slow boil for 5 minutes.

8. Add sugar, stir well, return to a full boil, and cook to the jell point.

9. Take off the heat and stir for a couple of minutes to distribute the pineapple shreds.

10. Fill and process prepared jars as described on page 6.

Gooseberries

Gooseberries are even harder to find in the market than currants, and when you do, they are expensive. They make an excellent jam. For the best jam, you want not green but ripe gooseberries, showing a rosy color. The round, translucent berries have observable veins and a few large seeds. Gooseberries are a nuisance to prepare, as each berry must be "topped and tailed," that is, the little stem at the top and the dried remains of the flower must be tediously removed before you begin. But it is nowhere near as fussy work as preparing currants for Bar-le-Duc.

Gooseberry Jam

Rating: Easy, if somewhat time-consuming
Yield: Four 8-ounce jars

INGREDIENTS:
4 C. gooseberries
1 C. water
2 to 2¼ C. sugar

1. Rinse and prepare the gooseberries by removing any remnants of the flower and little stems that held the fruit to the branch. Larger than a blueberry, smaller than a grape, gooseberries are best used whole. Alternatively, you can pulse/chop the prepared gooseberries in a food processor. Do avoid overprocessing and turning them into a purée.
2. Put the gooseberries, together with a scant cup of water, into a large Dutch oven. Cover, bring to a boil, and turn down the heat to simmer the fruit for 10 or 15 minutes until it is tender.
3. Add 2 cups of sugar if the gooseberries are ripe, an additional ¼ cup if they are somewhat underripe and a little sour.
4. Cook at a rapid boil, stirring frequently, until the jell point has been reached.
5. Fill and process prepared jars as described on page 6.

Blueberry and elderberry recipes may be found in Chapter Nine: Native Harvest.

NATIVE HARVEST

Fruit for preserves, as I've mentioned previously, is easy to obtain. Supermarkets generally have quality produce, with some year-round variations. Farmers' markets are no longer just roadside stands. In 2002, the New York Botanical Garden in the Bronx began hosting a Wednesday farmers' market, with vendors driving in from New Paltz, New York, and orchards along the Hudson River Valley. What you do need to be in the country for, though, is the pleasure of foraging and picking fruit growing wild.

The year I was six or seven, my mother's sister Gert bought a cottage in Brookfield, Connecticut. For somewhat more than the next decade, this was where we spent our summers. The little house was an odd combination of a few refined details and extremely basic conditions. Originally, I think it had been two down, two up, with various additions before we came on the scene. Downstairs there was a living room and an all-purpose cooking-dining-activities room, with a pair of glass-paned French doors separating the two rooms. We ate there occasionally and played Monopoly, Parcheesi, and canasta at the big table. The fireplace in the living room had an elegant keystone arch surround made of rough-textured granite blocks, but the house had no indoor plumbing to speak of. Next to the sink in the all-purpose room was a long-handled cast-iron well pump on the counter. Originally there was a kerosene-fueled stove in there too, and the icebox (later replaced by a refrigerator, the kind with a cylindrical coil on top) was located in the enclosed back porch, which is where we always had breakfast and lunch, and supper was mostly eaten out there, too. The common wall with the all-purpose room was clapboard, and there was a sturdy door and a window, so I think the porch was added later, as was the tiny room we called the kitchen, with a few cupboards above and a couple of counters with open shelves beneath them. The two-seater outhouse was back behind the cottage and off to one side. The only other room downstairs was my aunt's tiny bedroom. The stairs to the two attic bedrooms where the rest of us slept were on the back wall of her bedroom, so at night anyone needing the honey bucket on the back porch had to transit her bedroom coming and going. (As for me, even a flashlight was not sufficient to coax me into the dark of night for a trip to the outhouse.) The two upstairs bedrooms each had just about enough space for three wood-framed army cots against the walls, painted olive-drab, and a very small bureau. The sloping ceilings were decorated with travel posters, of Switzerland, as I recall.

Even in the summer, mornings on Carmen Hill Road #2 were always quite cool, with dew-soaked grass. The sunny summer days were much warmer, and the small bedrooms up under the roof were always hot and stuffy when, as a little girl, I was indignantly, mutinously, sent upstairs to bed while it was still daylight outdoors.

There are so many memories from the time that we spent on Carmen Hill Road #2. It was summertime, and summers are always golden, even though I remember one string of rainy days and a marathon Monopoly game to keep us occupied. The first couple of years we were there, the only electricity came from some glass-tank acid batteries in the basement, so we didn't even have a radio.

The Dugan's bakery truck came by a couple of times a week, as did the milkman. The iceman came three times a week, delivering huge blocks of ice. If I were polite, he'd give me a sliver of ice chipped off one of the blocks to lick and suck on. The family next door, who lived on Carmen Hill Road #2 year-round, had a vegetable patch, a potato field, and another field of corn. This was back when hybrid corn was just introduced. The neighbor, Ed Knapp, told us, and we all agreed, that 'Country Gentleman' and 'Golden Bantam' were terrific improvements. He also kept hens, so we bought eggs as well as our vegetables from him. In addition, he kept half a dozen nanny goats (and a rather ill-tempered billy), but we stayed with cows' milk delivered in tidy glass bottles. We were never there late enough into the autumn when he slaughtered the few shoats that were raised for meat each year. But in summer, after our dinner, I'd go next door on the little dirt track worn through the woods between the houses to slop the pigs with whatever scraps were left from our meal. Ed Knapp gave us a lift into town every other week, to New Milford. The grown-ups went grocery shopping, and the children were deposited at the library to find enough books to check out to last us until the next trip.

Grapes

Aunt Gert was the head of a high-school physical-education department and later a high-school principal. While my brother, Ben, was born after the cottage was purchased, my sister and I were of school age. So our family's arrival and departure were controlled by the academic year. Thus wild grapes were an end-of-season largesse on Carmen Hill. These were Concord grapes, wine-dark purple grapes, somewhat tough-skinned and with lots of seeds, so they were not especially good for eating out of hand but were wonderful for making grape jelly. Ben, recalls, "It seems to me that there was the question of whether the grapes would be ripe enough before the end of summer (was Labor Day our last weekend?) so that we could make jelly. I think they were ripe some years, not others. I remember picking grapes. Mostly along the road, you could walk into the woods (probably fairly spindly second growth, though at the time it seemed quite wild to me), but there were some more-tangled spots with vines, where there were grapes, or other spots ('bunks' we used to call them) for blackberries. The grapes had skins that slipped off; they, too, were fragrant."

And my sister, Haya, remembers, "My only real memories of Katzy making jam are in the summers up on Carmen Hill Road, when she 'hated to see the grapes go to waste' and put up many jars of jam and jelly. I believe the grapes were Concords and that the vines had been planted by early settlers on the hill, whose houses no longer existed but where lilac bushes and daylilies still bloomed, giving clues to where their dooryard gardens had been located."

Grapes are an ingredient of my childhood memories. The wrist-thick vines with their peeling brown bark wove through the trees around my Aunt Gert's summer cottage. They were sturdy enough for screaming children playing at Tarzan of the Apes to swing on, provided, that is, you could find one that had let sufficiently loose of its stranglehold on a tree. Toward the end of summer, late in August, we'd begin searching for grapes to harvest. There were several good spots that would be checked out.

First, the grapes had to be reasonably ripe. A mix of mostly ripe and some underripe grapes is better for making jelly than all ripe fruit. Second, the grapes had to be reachable. Many of the vines were so old that they'd hoisted their way so far up into the trees that the clusters of grapes were inaccessible. Inaccessible by people, that is, for birds, raccoons, and other critters were our competitors for the sweet and juicy fruit. Harvests were variable from year to year, dependent on sunshine and rainfall. Concord grapes are available at the supermarket in autumn, so even if you cannot go gathering, it is still possible to make your own grape jelly.

There's one thing that is different about grapes from any other fruit you might use for making preserves: grapes naturally contain tartaric acid. When promptly made from freshly processed juice, tiny crystals are apt to form in the finished jelly. While not in the least harmful, the crunchy little crystals are undesirable. There are two very simple methods to avoid this situation. The first is to pour the cooled juice into glass jars and refrigerate it for forty-eight hours. The tartrate crystals will settle out onto the glass, and the juice can be poured off and processed into jelly. The crystals easily wash off the glass. Another method, which my mother taught me, is to add some apple to the grapes when you process them for juice. This is a good technique to follow if you want to make jelly from the grape juice the very same day. Add one cup of peeled, chopped apple for every quart of grape berries before processing into juice. This somehow inhibits the formation of tartrate crystals, but does not affect the taste.

Grape Jelly

The best-flavored grape preserves are made from a mix of two-thirds ripe and one-third underripe red grapes. Underrripe grapes are higher in pectin and acid than ripe grapes. Pectin and acid are both necessary for the jell, or set, and a certain amount of acid makes a better-tasting jelly. If you have grapes that must be processed now and no time for jelly making, remember that the prepared juice can be frozen for processing into jelly whenever it is most convenient.

Rating: Easy

Special Instructions: Do not use reactive, that is, aluminum or unlined copper, pots for this recipe, as they will affect the flavor.

Yield: The total from two batches will be eight to ten 8-ounce jars.

INGREDIENTS:

10 C. or more Concord grapes (approximately 8 lbs.)

1 apple (optional)*

2 C. water

Sugar

1. Wash the Concord grapes.
2. Cut the apple into quarters, peel, core, and all, then chop coarsely. Set aside.
3. Put a couple of cups of grapes into a large stainless-steel pot, then crush them with a potato masher or the bottom of a clean glass jar. This provides a small amount of juice and prevents scorching.
4. Add the water.
5. Add the cut-up apple.
6. Heat the fruit mixture slowly to the boiling point, reduce the heat, and simmer until the seeds come free from the pulp.
7. Line a large colander with several layers of damp cotton cheesecloth. Set the colander over a large pot or bowl and carefully pour the grapes and liquid into it. Allow the free-run juice to drip through the cheesecloth. You may also use a chinois or a jelly bag. Do not press down on the fruit.
8. If you desire, set the pulp aside for later use in making Grape Butter (page 117).
9. Measure the free-run juice. Process into jelly 4 cups of juice at a time— a smaller batch means the jell point is reached more quickly, resulting in better flavor.

10. Taste a little bit of the juice. For every 1 cup of reasonably sweet grape juice, measure out $^2/_3$ cup of sugar. If you used a greater percentage of underripe grapes and the juice is on the tart side, you can use 3 or $3^1/_2$ cups of sugar to 4 cups of juice.

11. Bring juice to a boil, then add the sugar. Boil to the jell point.

12. Fill and process prepared jars as described on page 6.

Note: If apple was added to the grapes before processing, you can go ahead and make jelly right away. Otherwise, allow the juice to cool, pour it into jars, and refrigerate for two days. If you have grapes that must be processed now and no time for jelly making, remember that the prepared juice can be frozen for processing into jelly whenever is more convenient. Set the pulp aside for later use.

Herb-infused grape jelly recipes can be found in Chapter Seven: Savory Jellies and Conserves.

Grape Butter

Our mother, well versed in the thrifty mode of "use what's available," not only made Grape Jelly, she made use of the leftover pulp to make Grape Butter.

Rating: Easy
Yield: Variable, depending on how much grape pulp you have to start with.

INGREDIENTS:
Grape pulp leftover from making Grape Jelly (above)
Sugar
Cinnamon (optional)
Ground cloves (optional)

1. Purée the grape pulp through a food mill, using the medium blade. This removes the seeds.

2. Measure the pulp. Add $^2/_3$ as much sugar and heat to a simmer.

3. If you would like spiced grape butter, add $^1/_2$ teaspoon of cinnamon and $^1/_4$ teaspoon of cloves for every 4 cups of purée.

4. Heat the mixture slowly over medium-low heat until thickened, up to 30 minutes or longer, depending on how much juice is left in the pulp. Stir frequently to prevent burning.

5. Alternatively, heat in a slow oven, 225° Fahrenheit, stirring occasionally. This takes longer but eliminates the risk of scorching.

6. Grape butter is ready when a spoon dragged through the mass leaves a track.

7. Fill and process prepared jars as described on page 6.

About Grapes

"As American as apple pie." That's an oxymoron, because the center of dispersal for wild apples, their point of origin, is eastern Turkey and the southwestern region of Asia Minor in what is now Russia. Apples were dispersed throughout Europe, and centuries later were one of the comforting, familiar crop plants that European settlers brought with them to the New World, along with horses, honeybees, and clover. But these settlers found that their new homeland had bounty of its own to offer, from wild turkeys and corn to delicious fruits. New kinds of grapes, cranberries, blueberries, and elderberries were at once reminiscent of and different from soft fruits the settlers had left behind. For example, while grapes is grapes, the species the settlers found growing were not quite the same as those they had cultivated in the Old World. The European species, or common grape, *Vitis vinifera*, is believed to be native to Asia Minor, in the region near the Caspian Sea.

Whether as fresh fruit or fermented into wine that "maketh glad the heart of man" (women too), grapes have been associated with people as far back as the Bronze Age. Archaeologists have found grape seeds that date as far back as 3500 B.C. in their excavations of dwellings in south central Europe. By 2440 B.C., Egyptians were using hieroglyphics to describe how to grow grapes. Prior to 600 B.C., Phoenician traders introduced wine grapes to Greece, Rome, and southern France, from whence the Roman Empire brought them to Europe and spread them throughout that continent. When the Vikings sailed to North America, arriving on the Atlantic shores of what is now Canada, they were astonished by the profusion of wild grapes. Whether it was Leif Ericson or Bjarni Herjulfson who got here first, he found the vines so abundant that the country was named Vineland. These would have been the fox grape, *Vitis labrusca*, which is found growing from Maine to the Piedmont of South Carolina and as far west as the mountains of Tennessee. The dark-red to almost-black fruits have a wonderful aromatic fragrance when ripe.

Since European grapes failed to thrive in cold climates, European settlers in the northeastern regions domesticated this new species, even crossing the native grape with its European cousin. The resulting cultigen, *Vitis labruscana*, is hardier and has larger fruits than its European ancestor and a less foxy taste than its American parent. The Concord grape, mainstay of the grape juice and jelly industry, was developed by Ephraim Wales Bull, who was born in Boston in 1806, and as an adult purchased land in Concord, Massachusetts. Finding that late frost in spring or early frost in autumn ruined many grape harvests, he determined to develop a hardy, tasty grape from native stock. After years of raising grapevines from seed, growing the plants to maturity and fruiting, then choosing the best and most flavorful, he exhibited his best selection to the Massachusetts Horticultural Society in 1853 and introduced it to the market the following year.

There is another native grape, the southern muscadine and scuppernong, *Vitis rotundifolia*, which is a tender species growing south of the Mason-Dixon Line. Native from Virginia southward into central Florida and westward to eastern Texas, this is a thick-skinned, wonderfully flavorful grape with an aromatic scent that has been popular since antebellum times in the South and is little known outside the region.

Back in January 1524, Giovanni de Verrazano set sail from France for North America. Italian by birth, Verrazano had entered the French maritime service, making several notable voyages of discovery. Arriving in what is now Cape Fear in North Carolina more than two months after sailing from France, he continued northward up the coast, exploring the eastern seaboard as far as today's Nova Scotia and becoming the first European to enter New York Bay. As recorded in his journals, he made landfall several times, interacting with the Native Americans. Verrazano found muscadines growing in the Cape Fear River Valley of North Carolina. Another early account, this time by Sir Walter Raleigh, sixty years later, in 1584, describes the grapevines he found growing on coastal North Carolina as follows: "The coast of North Carolina is so full of grapes that the very beating and surge of the sea overflowed with them." They were "on the sand and on the green soil, on the hills as on the plains, as well as every little shrub … also climbing towards the tops of tall cedars. … In all the world the like abundance is not found."

Scuppernongs and Muscadines

Scuppernong refers to the original greenish bronze–skinned grape and its cultivars. Muscadine grapes have dark-purple skins. While some muscadine and scuppernong cultivars are self-fertile, they will produce a better crop if planted near other, different, self-fertile varieties. These grapes don't grow in bunches in the manner of more-familiar grapes, but are more scattered on the vines, growing individually or in small clusters of a dozen or so grapes.

Scuppernong and Muscadine Grape Jam

One September I was lecturing in Georgia. I saw scuppernong grapes on an arbor at the home of noted garden designer Ryan Gainey's house in Decatur, Georgia. Sitting on a glider in the leafy green shade, reaching up to pick aromatic grapes, I was smitten. I quickly learned the technique of squishing a grape between my tongue and the roof of my mouth, spitting out the tough skin and seeds, and enjoying the succulent sweet pulp. I mentioned my fascination with these grapes to the garden club member who was driving me from garden visit to garden visit. She passed the message on to her husband, who graciously went to a local farm stand and bought me some of each kind, both scuppernongs and muscadines. I traveled home to Connecticut with an aromatic bag of grapes at my feet, concerned lest they be prematurely crushed in the overhead compartment. The jelly I made carried with it memories of my trip and the kindness of the people I'd just met.

Rating: Easy

Special Instructions: Scuppernong and muscadine grapes are handled somewhat differently from Concord-type grapes. Because they have rather thick skins, skin and pulp are processed separately.

Yield: Eight to ten 8-ounce jars

INGREDIENTS:

10 C. scuppernong or muscadine grapes, or a mixture of the two

Water

Sugar

1. Rinse the grapes and pick off their stems.
2. Squeeze the pulp free from the skins, setting them aside in separate containers.
3. Coarsely chop the skins and put them in a saucepan with a little water, about 1/2 cup.
4. Cover and simmer over low heat until tender, about 15 minutes. Remember to stir occasionally to prevent sticking. Add a little more water only if needed.
5. Place the pulp in a separate pot. Add only enough water to prevent scorching, about 1/2 to 1 cup.
6. Simmer over medium-low heat until the pulp has softened and the seeds have separated from the pulp. Use a food mill to separate the seeds from the pulp.
7. Combine the sieved pulp and softened, chopped skins and measure. Use 1/2 to 3/4 cup of sugar for every cup of grape pulp.
8. Bring the mixture slowly to a boil, reduce the heat, and simmer until thickened. Stir frequently to prevent scorching. Alternatively, heat in a slow oven, 225° Fahrenheit, stirring occasionally. This takes longer but eliminates the risk of scorching.
9. Fill and process prepared jars as described on page 6.

Scuppernong and Muscadine Grape Jelly

Rating: Easy
Yield: Four to five 8-ounce jars for each batch

INGREDIENTS:
8 to 10 C. scuppernong or muscadine grapes, or a mixture of the two
Water
1 apple (optional)*
Sugar

1. Rinse the grapes and pick off their stems.
2. Squeeze the pulp free from the skins, setting them aside in separate containers.
3. Cut the apple into quarters, peel, core, and all, then chop coarsely. Set aside.
4. Coarsely chop the grape skins and put them in a saucepan with a little water, about $1/2$ cup, and simmer until soft.
5. Place pulp in a large, nonreactive saucepan. Crush lightly with a potato masher or the bottom of a clean glass jar and add the softened skins, their cooking liquid, the apple, and just enough water to be visible beneath the top of the grapes.
6. Simmer for 20 to 30 minutes.
7. Line a large colander with several layers of damp cotton cheesecloth. Set the colander over a large pot or bowl and carefully pour the grapes and liquid into it. Allow the free-run juice to drip through the cheesecloth. You may also use a chinois or jelly bag. Do not press down on the fruit.
8. Measure the free-run juice. Process into jelly 4 cups of juice at a time—a smaller batch means the jell point is reached more quickly, resulting in better flavor.
9. To every 4 cups of juice, measure $2^2/3$ cups of sugar. Bring juice to a boil and add sugar, stirring all the while.
10. Boil until the jell point is reached.
11. Skim off any foam.
12. Fill and process prepared jars as described on page 6.

Note: If apple was added to the grapes before processing, you can go ahead and make jelly right away. Otherwise, allow the juice to cool, pour it into jars, and refrigerate for two days. If you have grapes that must be processed now and no time for jelly making, remember that the prepared juice can be frozen for processing into jelly whenever is more convenient.

Lingonberries and Cranberries

My father, Robert Solomon Orlove, was born in 1904 in the village of Konoptop, which was then in the Russian Ukraine. The month and date were more uncertain, as the Julian calendar was in use in Russia when he was born, and he never did figure out the conversion to the Gregorian calendar employed elsewhere. Those were turbulent times, and he was still an infant when the family moved to Germany and not yet a teenager when they left for Scandinavia, living for several years in Sweden before the family immigrated piecemeal to the United States. My father loved to reminisce, and his stories would begin not with "Once upon a time … " but with "There was a boy in my class … " referring to fellow students in his Swedish gymnasium. Many of these stories had to do with food, for though he did not cook, my father enjoyed a good meal.

After I grew up and married and eventually settled first in Norwalk, then in Wilton, Connecticut, I would occasionally take the train to New York City and meet Robby, as my father was called, for a day of visiting art galleries, food stores, and for a pleasant meal at some restaurant of his choosing. One autumn day it was Luchow's, near Union Square in Manhattan. My venison came garnished with a red pickled crab apple, and with the leap mind and memory is capable of, my father waxed nostalgic for Seckel pears in lingonberry jelly that he remembered from his Swedish boyhood. I knew what Seckel pears were, small brown-skinned pears that arrive in the market each fall. But what were lingonberries? They are a small, red-skinned berry, he said, that was kept for winter use simply by storing them in a barrel and covering the berries with water. (Cranberries, a closely related berry, are harvested in September and October and can be kept for up to a year under proper conditions.)

After some sleuthing, I discovered that lingonberry, *Vaccinium vitis-idaea*, is a diminutive relative of our native American cranberry, *Vaccinium macrocarpon*. Lingonberry grows on open heaths in the more northerly regions of Europe and at higher elevations. The little plants, less than a foot high, bear small, oval, red berries, about one-third inch across. Their tart flavor makes tasty preserves, and they are also popular for piquant sauces to accompany game.

Berry picking is very much a part of the Swedish culture, especially since the public land is open to all. Wild-harvested berries and mushrooms that are sold rather than used by the family are tax-exempt up to 550 Euros, a significant factor in Sweden's highly taxed economy.

Inez Fungard Horscroft was born in Finland. Her first husband, "Willy" Fungard, was a Swedish diplomat, and they lived in Sweden and Norway. They had a summer cottage in Sweden, and Inez told me of picking lingonberries in the 1940s, 1950s, and into the 1960s. In fact, she said, if she still lived in Sweden, she'd still be picking lingonberries. She and Willy would go for walks in the countryside, enjoying the colors, scenery, and scents of woodland and meadow. While her husband would sit on a convenient nearby tree stump, smoking his pipe and reading the newspaper, Inez would go berry picking. She used a berry rake, called a *tyttebaer plukker* or a *lingonplocker*. Imagine a shallow wooden box with a handle. The side opposite the handle is cut away and there is a set of rounded metal fingerlike prongs attached to the bottom that extend beyond it. She would scoop the rake over the low-growing, berry-laden plants. Mostly berries would be scooped into the box, along with some leaves and twigs. She would gently pour the berries into a bucket or basket, and scoop again. To clean the berries, when she got home, Inez would pour the berries into a large basin or a bucket filled with water. The leaves, twigs, and other debris could then be scooped off as they floated to the surface.

In Scandinavia, lingonberry preserves are traditionally served with meatballs and boiled potatoes, and also with pan-fried Baltic herring and mashed potatoes. For a more piquant taste, one can combine approximately a half cup of lingonberry jam with a tablespoon of preserved ginger in syrup that has been finely grated.

On another trip, Robby happily took me to a store in Manhattan that specialized in Swedish food, both fresh and packaged. I remember being fascinated by a crate of live crayfish, but what interested us both was the barrel of fresh lingonberries in water. They were sold by volume, and the quart I purchased was dipped, dripping, from the barrel. They were a goodly price, more expensive than the cranberries available in every neighborhood grocery store. But for the first try, I wanted lingonberries as the benchmark against which subsequent attempts could be measured. Rather than a jelly, my first attempt was Seckel Pears in Lingonberry Syrup.

Seckel Pears in Lingonberry or Cranberry Syrup

You have the option of eating the pears, dyed burgundy red from the syrup, on the third day, after they have cooled off, instead of canning them. They make a wonderful winter dessert when served in a shallow bowl atop a slice of pound cake with some of the ruby red syrup drizzled over them. The pears will keep, refrigerated, for a week or two. If you want to keep them longer, they need to be canned. Any extra syrup can be cooked to the jell point, and you'll have a red jelly, transparent and quivering, to spoon over the little pears. Lingonberries are seasonally available at a specialty stores offering Scandinavian food products. If not available, substitute cranberries. After all, the two berries are cousins. The lingonberries are just a smidgen more tart. A spoonful of lemon juice will easily adjust the flavor balance.

Rating: Easy

Special Instructions: The pears will be poached in ever-sweeter syrup over the course of three days. Fruit is apt to shrivel if plunged directly into a heavy syrup made from equal amounts of sugar and juice.

Yield: Three 16-ounce jars

INGREDIENTS:

4 C. lingonberries or cranberries

3 C. water

3 C. sugar

24 Seckel pears

Juice of 2 lemons

Day 1

1. Combine the lingonberries or cranberries with the water. Bring the mixture to a boil and simmer, uncovered, until the berries have burst and are quite soft.

2. Strain the fruit through a fine sieve, without squeezing the pulp. This should yield about 3 cups of lingonberry or cranberry juice. Set the pulp aside to use for lingonberry or cranberry butter.

3. In a large, heavy saucepan, combine 1 cup of sugar with the juice and heat, stirring occasionally, until the sugar is dissolved.

4. Next, rinse the pears, peel the skin, but leave the little stem still attached. (It makes a prettier presentation.) As each pear is prepared, put it in a bowl of water acidulated with the juice of 1 lemon to keep them from turning brown.

5. When all the pears are peeled, drain and put them into the saucepan with the syrup. Simmer, covered, for 5 minutes. Then take pan off the heat and allow the pears to sit in the syrup overnight.

Day 2

6. The next day, remove the pears from the syrup with a slotted spoon and set them aside in a bowl. Add 1 cup of sugar to the syrup and heat, stirring, until the sugar is dissolved.

7. Return the pears to the saucepan, simmer for 5 minutes, and again allow them to sit overnight.

Day 3

8. On the third day, once again repeat the process: Remove the pears from the syrup, add another cup of sugar to the syrup, heat to dissolve the sugar, and then simmer the pears for 5 minutes.

9. Pack the pears into prepared jars with their necks to the center (usually 8 small pears will fit neatly into a pint jar). Keep the pear-filled jars warm in a pan of hot water.

10. Measure the syrup. If using cranberries, add 1 tablespoon of lemon juice to every 2 cups of syrup.

11. Bring the syrup to a boil and cook to the jell point. Pour it over the pears to fill the jars, leaving a half-inch headspace. If you wish, set aside any remaining syrup to make Lingonberry-Pear or Cranberry-Pear Jelly (below).

12. Process the jars as described on page 6.

Lingonberry-Pear or Cranberry-Pear Jelly

One of my father's stories was about a boy in his class who was eating soup with crackers. First he had too much soup, so he added another few crackers. But the crackers soaked up all the soup, so he added more broth. Perhaps what my father was trying to explain with this story is that life doesn't always come out even. So it is with Seckel Pears in Cranberry or Lingonberry Syrup. There always seems to be syrup left over. Rather than start again with more pears, I made jelly from the syrup.

Rating: Easy

INGREDIENTS:
Leftover syrup from Seckel Pears in Lingonberry or Cranberry Syrup
1 to 2 lemons

1. Measure the leftover syrup from the recipe for Seckel Pears in Lingonberry or Cranberry Syrup (above). For each cup of liquid, add the juice of $^1/_2$ lemon.

2. Bring the mixture to a boil and heat it to the jell point.

3. Fill and process prepared jars as described on page 6.

Cranberries

Bog Berries

The genus *Vaccinium* offers us a number of edible berries: lingonberries and cranberries, highbush and lowbush blueberries, huckleberries, bearberries, and more. Other common names include bilberry, blaeberry, and grouseberry, craneberry, deerberry, foxberry, and whortleberry; several of these names suggest that people are not the only ones with a fondness for these fruits. Anthropologists mention that plants with lots of common names are those that are important to people.

While lingonberries are most often collected from wild-growing plants, cranberries are a cultivated specialty crop. Since cranberries thrive in acid soil topped with a layer of sand and with ample fresh water, they're suitable for growing in places where other crops cannot be grown. Wild cranberries were gathered by Native Americans and utilized by English colonists since the 1600s. Deliberate cultivation began around 1816, when Henry Hall of Dennis, on Cape Cod in Massachusetts, began farming cranberries. Supposedly, colonists used to roll them down stairs to select the best, firmest berries for winter storage, and a similar technique used commercially today bounces the berries on a conveyor belt. Today most of the tangy red berries are grown in marshland regions of Wisconsin. Massachusetts and southern and coastal New Jersey (especially down in the Pine Barrens) used to be big producers, but urbanization has put housing where cranberries once grew, and conversion to blueberry production has also played a role. Other states that grow cranberries on a commercial scale include Oregon and Washington, in wetlands along their coasts. In 2001, the total cranberry production from these five states was a whopping 4,793,480 barrels. Since each barrel weighs 100 pounds, that's close to half a billion pounds of cranberries.

Native from southern Canada and northeastern United States, Newfoundland to Minnesota, southward to North Carolina, cranberry is a creeping, mat-forming plant that grows in sunny, acid, boggy areas. At three-quarters of an inch in diameter, its glossy red fruits are twice as big as lingonberries. I've seen cranberries growing in Massachusetts. Today the bogs are manufactured, scooped out and recessed to lie somewhat below the ground, with a more geometrically precise perimeter than natural ponds and bogs. Cranberry bogs are crisscrossed by a few narrow dikes and surrounded by ditches, with the inflow of water from adjacent ponds controlled by flumes or specialized gates. In early September, before the harvest begins, when the plants' leaves have turned a ruddy color and just before the berries are harvested, the bogs are a wonderful, glowing red.

Most of us are familiar with cranberries as a stiff jelly dumped out of a can and sliced into rounds, a once-a-year appearance quivering on a plate and waiting for the Thanksgiving turkey. While it is true that four-fifths of the annual cranberry crop is processed into juice, sauce, or relish, that still leaves sufficient fresh cranberries for home cooks to easily make something better tasting. One year, my son, Seth, and his wife, Kim, gave me a wooden box of fresh cranberries from a local grower. Stamped "$1/20^{th}$ of a standard barrel," that five pounds of cranberries gave me an ample amount to experiment with.

Since cranberries start off on the tart and tangy side of the taste spectrum, it is simple to tip the flavor balance of a preserve in that direction. Or, instead make a sweet purée, and the result is a wonderful sauce for desserts such as cheesecake, pound cake, ice cream, or custard.

DeeDee's Cranberry Chutney

Cranberries are a nostalgic treat for my sister who now lives in Jerusalem, Israel. The crimson berries are as unusual there as they are commonplace here in the United States. While shipping fresh cranberries to her would be problematic, a jar of chutney is another, much simpler matter. And here is her response: "I opened the jar of your pear-cranberry chutney and spread some on a slice of fresh bread, to top the other slice that had been covered with thin slices of cheddar cheese—a perfect combination! Your chutney is so good that only a small amount was needed. The fruit tastes fresh, the spicing perfect, and the color a delight to the eye. I plan to prepare a meal of some sort of curry for my dinner this Friday evening, with some of this chutney as a garnish."

DeeDee Stevens, who graciously shared this recipe, lives in Vista, California. She and my daughter, Mira, became friends when my son-in-law, Steve, was a student pilot and DeeDee's husband was his Marine Corps flight instructor. It was DeeDee's mother-in-law who taught her how to make jam and chutney. Since there aren't very many people in suburban Southern California who make preserves (perhaps, DeeDee notes, because great produce is available year-round in the supermarkets, though I find great produce makes superb preserves) her efforts are well received. So well, in fact, that she always has to make extra batches of strawberry, peach, and apricot jam before the season is over because she gives so much away. She gives jams and chutneys to neighbors or as hostess gifts or as a "thank-you" for volunteers who help on a committee with her. One neighbor has the only peach tree in the neighborhood, so they share: the neighbor provides the peaches, and DeeDee makes the jam.

The directions she uses are the Sure-Jell Low Sugar recipes. The low-sugar pectin allows DeeDee to taste more of the fruit, and the preserves made with it have a more pure color. One of her favorite recipes is the following for Cranberry Chutney, which she makes every fall to serve with turkey or ham. It's also good, she points out, to dress up plain baked chicken breast, in after-Thanksgiving sandwiches, and on pork chops or with pork loin roast.

Rating: Easy
Yield: Variable, depending on the size of the pears

INGREDIENTS:
2 tsp. pickling spice
6 whole cloves
5 whole allspice
$^1/_2$ C. water
4 C. fresh cranberries
3 or 4 firm-ripe winter pears
$^3/_4$ C. dark raisins
$^3/_4$ C. golden raisins
$2^1/_2$ C. firmly packed dark brown sugar

1. Place the pickling spice, cloves, and allspice in a large tea ball or tie the spices in cotton cheesecloth. Set aside.

2. Put the water in a large, nonreactive saucepan.

3. Rinse and pick over the cranberries and add them to the saucepan.

4. Add the raisins.

5. Peel, core, and coarsely chop the pears and add them to the saucepan.

6. Add the dark brown sugar. Stir to mix the ingredients.

7. Add the spices in the tea ball to the saucepan, burying it in the other ingredients.

8. Bring the mixture to a boil over high heat. Reduce the heat to low and simmer for 20 minutes, stirring occasionally. Cook until thickened. Remove the spices.

9. Allow the chutney to cool.

10. Fill and process prepared jars as described on page 6.

Blueberries

We were afoot when we spent our summers on Carmen Hill Road #2. Neither my mother nor grandmother could drive. Aunt Gert had gotten a license and a car after buying the property, but she was a timid driver. A minor accident that ended up with the car in a ditch convinced her that that this was not for her. We walked or, if only some of us were going somewhere, might hitchhike. (Three adult women and three children make rather a large crowd to fit into a car along with the driver and whoever else was there to begin with.) Our mailbox was two miles away from the house in one direction, while Candlewood Lake, where we'd go swimming, was two miles away in the opposite direction. The pace was necessarily slow, since my brother was born the year after the cottage was bought and had to be carried the first summer. After that, he walked with the rest of us. Our young legs got tired, and it was unfortunately downhill to the lake, uphill as we went back. I did a lot of whining. I don't remember habitually taking any buckets with us, but we sauntered slowly enough to check out our favorite foraging spots.

There was a sunny sloping meadow where blueberries grew, and by early July, that would be closely watched. The little green berries would swell, turn red, a darker purplish color, then ripen into a wonderful blue with a whitish bloom on their skins that rubbed off with handling. Each of us had a white enamel pail to pick into (much of my picking went straight into my mouth). I can recall the "plink, plink, plink" as the first berries hit the bottom of a pail, a sound that quieted as soon as the bottom was covered by a layer of berries. Most years, we ate the berries fresh or my mother would bake a blueberry cake. One year there was a fire that swept through the meadow. Grass fires are not very hot, and the blueberry bushes weren't harmed. I don't know whether it was additional nutrients that became available in the ashy residue or if the soil warmed more from the sooty black layer, but the following year the berries were larger, sweeter, and more plentiful.

We distinguished between tall blueberry bushes, low blueberry bushes, and huckleberries. Highbush blueberry, *Vaccinium corymbosum*, grew on tall shrubby

bushes even higher than we could reach to pick. Since birds tended to go after blueberries on the upper branches, this worked out well for all of us.

Decades later, a friend of mine in Georgetown, Connecticut, planted highbush blueberries. At least two different cultivars should be planted, as each by itself sets fruit poorly. Ellie planted around six or eight shrubs, two or more of three different cultivars. She got her harvest within the first couple of years. Then the birds found them. Fortunately for her, blueberries are handsome shrubs. As well as delicious fruits, they have pretty bell-like white flowers, a wonderful red leaf color in autumn, and the fine little twigs at the tips of the branches have attractive red bark, providing winter interest. Pruning the vase-shaped shrubs to remove the lower branches, Ellie made a copse, or thicket, underplanted with all sorts of wonderful, shade-tolerant woodland plants. Years later, a neighbor in New Jersey, more interested in blueberries than aesthetics, made a cage out of heavy-duty metal mesh hardware cloth over his bushes, high enough to stand up in with a screen door for entry. Even so, the occasional determined bird would find its way in and need to be shooed out.

Cultivating Blueberries

Upon reaching Lake Huron in 1615, Samuel de Champlain made mention in his journal of finding Native Americans gathering blueberries. By 1831, Henry Rowe Schoolcraft, an explorer, Indian agent, and authority on Indian customs, frequently mentioned the large patches of blueberries he saw on his travels and the manner in which the Native Americans made use of them. Yet it was not until the early 1900s that the blueberry found its way into cultivation. It is a fascinating story.

In the 1860s, Colonel James A. Fenwick had a cranberry plantation in the heart of the New Jersey Pine Barrens. His daughter, Mary Fenwick, married J. J. White. When Colonel Fenwick died in 1882, he left the cranberry farm to his wife but appointed White manager. And it was White who was the first to excavate the area, create bogs, and deliberately cultivate cranberries where they had not naturally been found growing. By 1912, his was the largest cranberry operation in New Jersey.

Elizabeth Coleman White, the oldest of his four daughters, became interested in the possibility of adding blueberry production to their cranberry crop. Blueberries naturally grew in the same general area, in the somewhat drier land between the cranberry bogs. They ripened in July, which would nicely fit in with the September and October cranberry harvest season. However, at that time, efforts to cultivate blueberries were unsuccessful. And the wild fruit, which was picked by "Pineys" (as inhabitants of the Pine Barrens were known) was very variable in both size and flavor. In 1911, Elizabeth White read a 1910 USDA publication researched and written by Dr. Frederick Colville. Titled "Experiments in Blueberry Culture," it described his efforts to develop blueberries as a crop suitable for cultivation.

Supported by J. J. White, Dr. Colville agreed to conduct his research at Whitesbog while Elizabeth devised a clever scheme to identify the best of the wild plants as a foundation for their work. She hired local Pineys to find the best shrubs, those with large, tasty blueberries. She sent them out equipped with an aluminum gauge with a five-eighths-inch diameter hole, bottles of formalin (a preservative solution), and labels. Those shrubs with berries too large to fit through the gauge were identified, collected, and brought to Whitesbog to be grown. Cuttings were made, up to 100 from each shrub. Often only 10 percent would take and grow roots. At the time, cross-pollination, the need to plant two different clones for the best fruit set, was not clearly understood.

Elizabeth White and Dr. Colville persevered. They produced the first crop of cultivated blueberries in 1916. By 1927, not only were blueberries available for sale, Whitesbog had a brand-new business, that of selling propagated blueberry plants, not just locally, but shipping them across the country.

Blueberry–Crab Apple Jam

Because they are low in both pectin and acid, blueberries do not jell well and thus are poor for jelly making. One solution is to use commercial pectin. As explained previously, I prefer not to use it but instead blend low-pectin, low-acid fruits with others that provide the missing ingredients. With blueberries, the two options use tart crab apple or citrus in the form of lemon or orange. And blueberries make excellent jam and conserve.

Rating: Easy
Yield: Approximately six 8-ounce jars

INGREDIENTS:
2 lbs. or about 4 large crab apples or other tart apples, such as Granny Smith
3 C. blueberries
5 C. sugar, or to taste

1. Rinse and peel the crab apples. Quarter them, remove the cores, and cut the apples into approximately blueberry-sized dice. They will yield about 4 cups.
2. Put the apples in a saucepan and add just enough water to barely cover them.
3. Bring the mixture to a boil, then simmer briskly for 10 minutes.
4. Add the blueberries, rinsed and picked over, together with the sugar.
5. Cook until the mixture thickens and the juice is clear, gently stirring all the time.
6. Fill and process prepared jars as described on page 6.

Cranberry-Blueberry Conserve

Winter is a great season for making marmalade, but sometimes I feel like something different. Fortunately, both blueberries and cranberries freeze beautifully. So if I have stockpiled the fruit in their appropriate (and different) seasons, I can easily make a batch of this delicious conserve. To freeze blueberries or cranberries, tip the fruit out of its box or bag onto a shallow, rimmed jelly roll pan. Inspect it for any soft, bruised, or moldy berries, undersized, bulletlike green blueberries, bits of leaves, and so on, which need to be removed. Freeze the berries, loose, until they are as hard as little BBs. I usually leave them overnight. Then pour the berries into heavy-duty plastic storage bags. I find that the two-cup size is most useful—as well as making preserves, there are always muffins to bake.

Rating: Easy

Yield: Four or five 8-ounce jars

INGREDIENTS:

1/2 orange

1 small lemon

1/2 C. water

2 C. cranberries, fresh or thawed

2 C. frozen blueberries

4 C. sugar

1. If the cranberries are frozen, thaw them out.
2. Cut half an orange into quarters or sixths, depending on how fine you want the pieces. Crosscut each strip into eighths.
3. Cut the lemon in half from top to bottom. Then cut each half into thirds and each strip into pieces of the same size as the orange.
4. Put the citrus into a small saucepan, add water, and simmer the mixture gently for 20 to 30 minutes or until the peel is quite soft.
5. Transfer the citrus and any liquid to a Dutch oven and add the cranberries.
6. Cook the mixture over low heat until the cranberries are soft, about 15 minutes. Don't stir, or the cranberries will break apart. Just agitate the pan, shaking it gently every now and then.
7. Add the blueberries, still frozen, to the pan and cover. Raise the heat to moderate and cook for 10 to 15 minutes.
8. When the blueberries are thawed and the liquid in the pan has reached a strong simmer, add the sugar. Now gently stir the contents.
9. Bring the mixture to a boil and cook it until the conserve is thick.
10. Fill and process prepared jars as described on page 6.

Maine Blueberry Jam with Grand Marnier

Highbush blueberries were not the only kind we found growing wild on Carmen Hill #2. Lowbush blueberry, *Vaccinium angustifolium*, was more common in the occasional field that was let go, no longer used for pasture or as a hayfield. Some of the little bushes would even grow along the roadsides, jostling their way in among black-eyed Susans, summer phlox, and ditch lilies, which today are more commonly known as daylilies. (Back then they were also called outhouse lilies, since folks used to plant them near that necessary structure.) When the lowbush blueberries, somewhat smaller than those of highbush blueberry, were ripe, the bushes would make a convenient stopping place for fretful children with tired legs. We'd all spread out onto the verges or into the edge of a field to pick and eat blueberries for an energizing snack before continuing down the dirt road.

When I was grown and married and making my own preserves, a friend who was vacationing in Maine brought me a couple of quarts of the tiny wild blueberries that grow there. What a special gift, better than a jar of preserves, since I could play with recipes and make up my own.

Rating: Easy

Special Instructions: For best results, let the jars stand for two weeks before sampling the jam.

Yield: Approximately four 8-ounce jars

INGREDIENTS:

5 C. wild blueberries

¹/₄ C. water

3 C. sugar

5 Tbs. Grand Marnier

1. Place the blueberries in a large nonreactive saucepan with the water. Start heating gently.
2. As the berries begin to release their juice, turn up the heat and add the sugar.
3. Boil the mixture, stirring frequently, until thick.
4. Spoon 1 tablespoon of Grand Marnier into each prepared jar.
5. Fill and process the jars as described on page 6.

See also Blueberry-Orange Conserve in Chapter Four: Conserves (pages 46–47).

Elderberries

Elderberries, *Sambucus canadensis*, were always easy to find on Carmen Hill, great big bushes with feathery leaves and large lacelike flat heads of little off-white flowers. They bloomed in early summer, followed by enormous clusters of glistening, small, black berries. They grew in damp sunny places, such as the edge of the pond in the cow pasture. I didn't think much of them as a child. The little berries are juicy, all right, but the flavor of the fresh berries isn't all that great, being rather tart. Besides, elderberries also have little seeds just the right size for getting stuck between your teeth. So they were not something to eat out of hand or have for lunch. But they did make a fine jelly, which also took care of their seediness.

We knew the elderberries were ripe and ready to pick when the clusters of dark purple-black berries would turn and hang downward. The entire cluster would be cut loose from the stems, easy enough with a pair of clippers. Elderberry has weak wood, easily damaged in heavy winds or from other stress. No matter, because elderberry easily comes back from the roots. My father used to make us little flutes from the brown-barked canes, pushing out the soft pith in the center and using his pocketknife to cut a notch close to one end.

It is easy enough to strip grapes from their stems. Elderberries are so small and soft that trying to strip them off by hand leaves you with lots of squashed berries and purple fingers. We used to use forks, sitting around the back porch picnic table with its oilcloth tablecloth and stripping berries into an enamel *schissel*, or basin. Here's how to do it. Rinse the clusters in a basin of water, then slide the tines of a fork behind the berries and just pop them loose into a separate container. It goes quite quickly, and soon the large green-stemmed clusters are bare of berries. Then it is easy to make the jelly, with its wonderful, unique, piquant flavor.

Elderberry Jelly

You'll need to forage or grow these berries in your garden. Elderberries don't seem to appear in grocery stores or even in farmers' markets.

Rating: Easy

Special Instructions: On its own, Elderberry Jelly is somewhat soft and quivery and will not set up firm. One option to thicken it is to use equal parts elderberry juice and apple juice prepared from underripe tart green apples, such as Granny Smith. Or, use $2^1/2$ cups of elderberry juice to $1^1/2$ cups of grape juice for a pleasant, flavorful blend that will also jell more readily. See also the recipe for Grape-Elderberry Jelly with Thyme and Juniper in Chapter Seven: Savory Jellies and Conserves (page 87).

Yield: Three or four 8-ounce jars from each batch

INGREDIENTS:

8 C. elderberries

Water

Fresh lemon juice

Sugar

1. Rinse the elderberries and strip them from their stems using the tines of a fork, as described on page 134. Measure 8 cups.
2. Put half the elderberries in a large nonreactive saucepan with just a little water and crush them with a potato masher or the bottom of a clean glass jar to start the juices flowing.
3. Add the remaining elderberries. Bring the fruit and water slowly to a boil, then reduce the heat to a simmer.
4. Cover and simmer for about 15 minutes.
5. Pour the mixture through a colander lined with several layers of damp cotton cheesecloth, a chinois, or a jelly bag. Do not press down on the fruit. Let it drip for a couple of hours, collecting the free-run juice.
6. Measure the juice. To 4 cups of elderberry juice, add $1/4$ cup of fresh lemon juice to provide the necessary acidity.
7. Add 3 cups of sugar for each 4 cups of elderberry juice. Stir thoroughly.
8. Bring to a boil and cook to the jell point.
9. Fill and process prepared jars as described on page 6.

Elderberry-Apple Butter

I prefer makeing elderberry butter to making an unstrained jam, which would be full of the little seeds.

Rating: Easy
Yield: Approximately four or five 8-ounce jars

INGREDIENTS:

3 C. elderberries
1¹/₂ lbs. or about 3 large crab apples or other tart apples, such as Granny Smith
¹/₄ to ¹/₂ C. water
4¹/₂ C. sugar
1 lemon

1. Rinse the elderberries and strip them from their stems using the tines of a fork, as described above. Measure 3 cups.
2. Peel, core, and coarsely chop the apples until you have 3 cups.
3. Put the elderberries in a large nonreactive saucepan and mash them a bit with a potato masher or the bottom of a clean glass jar to start the juices flowing. Start heating gently. Add ¹/₄ to ¹/₂ cup of water, if necessary, to prevent scorching.
4. When the juice begins to flow, add the apples.
5. Bring the mixture to a boil, reduce the heat to a simmer, and cook until the apples are soft.
6. Purée through the fine grate of a food mill to remove the seeds.
7. Grate the rind of the lemon and juice it.
8. Return the pulp to the pan with the sugar, the lemon rind, and its juice.
9. Cook slowly until the fruit butter is thick, stirring frequently to avoid scorching. Or, process in a 225° Fahrenheit oven, stirring occasionally, until a spoon dragged through the mass leaves a track.
10. Fill and process prepared jars as described on page 6.

CHAPTER TEN

BACKYARD HARVEST

My friends and neighbors John Clarke and Carol Thompson Clarke have a large vegetable garden and a small orchard where they grow a couple of apple trees, some peaches, pears, plums, and cherries, and soft fruit, such as red currants and blueberries. Carol cans and freezes produce throughout the summer and also makes preserves. That's great for folks who live in the country or the suburbs and have the space to do so. City dwellers frequently believe that they don't have room for that sort of amenity. Perhaps they grow a couple of tomato plants and a pot of basil in their small backyards, but the special pleasure that comes from harvesting homegrown fruit is something they see as denied to them.

There are two things to think about. One is the choice of trees and shrubs you plant. Consider small flowering trees. Should you plant a flowering crab apple that has tiny, unusable fruit, or would a fruiting crab apple with beautiful flowers and fruit of a size and taste to use for preserves be a better choice? Why plant a Bradford pear, with its froth of white flowers, inedible fruit, and habit of splitting apart under a winter load of snow, when you could plant a functional pear tree with equally beautiful white flowers and a crop of tasty pears?

Another option is fruit that grows on something other than a tree. Monika Nicholson is well aware of the options and possibilities that ornamental shrubs with edible fruit have to offer. After all, she's connected with Virginia Berry Farm, a wholesale nursery that grows a wide range of fruiting plants, from blueberries, raspberries, blackberries, and grapes to figs, currants, and more. She makes strawberry jam, damson plum jam, and sour-cherry preserves. The preserves usually come out a little runny (cherries being low in both pectin and acid), and she likes them best on ice cream.

Like the man who suddenly discovered he was speaking in prose (unlike poetry, it's something we all do without being aware of it until it's pointed out to us, as M. Jourdain discovers in Molière's play *Le Bourgeois Gentilhomme*), you may find out that you are already growing trees and shrubs that bear fruit that can be used to make delicious preserves, but you simply didn't know it. Serviceberry, elderberry, and highbush cranberry bushes are some of the shrubs you might find growing in your yard or that you could easily acquire from a local nursery or garden center. These shrubs are not only attractive, their fruit is a good source of food for birds. In addition, they're also suitable for making preserves that people can enjoy. Some, like elderberry, make up into a sweet jelly that's tasty on toast. Others, such as highbush cranberry, result in a tart jelly that is a good accompaniment for meats such as pork, lamb, or game.

Most of us limit ourselves to eating commercially available kinds of fruits: apples, pears, plums, grapes, blueberries, and so on. Expand your horizons. Sure, it would be lovely to have a small orchard, perhaps a grape arbor and a hedgerow of soft fruits. But even if you live in the city, a backyard garden can offer the opportunity to gather fruit for making preserves. And these are fruits that are simply not available at the supermarket. Shrubs such as cornelian cherry, highbush cranberry, and rugosa roses are all possibilities for backyard harvests. Now that's something Katzy would certainly approve of!

Roses

My parents' house in the Midwood section of Brooklyn was on a street lined with trees, and it even had a median down the center that was green with trees and shrubs. There were two large maples in front of the house, so as you can imagine, the street side of the property was very shady. There was a small, narrow side yard, and the concrete driveway in back didn't leave much room for plants. Just off the little two-by-nothing wooden porch in back were two rose bushes. To my regret, I have no idea what they might have been. The roses were classic tea rose form, with tightly furled buds that opened into full-blown fragrant roses. However, unlike most tea roses, these never seemed to be affected by any pests or diseases. It certainly could not have been due to the care they received, as this consisted of Katzy dumping the coffee grounds on them every day. A thick layer of grounds served as mulch; if I poked around there were lots of pink worms, and the roses flowered beautifully. Recently I came across a modern cultivar, a David Austin rose named 'Brother Cadfael,' which has the rich pink color, form, and a lovely fragrance similar to that of the roses I remember.

My brother, Ben, remembers our mother making rose-petal jelly, something that made such an impression on his young mind that he recalls it more than forty years later. "I definitely remember Katzy making rose-petal jelly from the petals of the rose bushes behind the back porch on East 17th Street in Brooklyn. I realize that in my memory, the porch seems very high, almost dizzying to look off. I recall Katzy pouring coffee grounds on the bushes, in fact I recall the coffeepot—it was a drip, and the middle section that held the coffee had an interesting circular pattern of holes. I have dimmer memories of her cooking the petals, and the jelly itself was fragrant and a light pastel color."

Jelly made from roses sounds very romantic, and the translucent pale pink color is, as Ben remembers, usually appealing. I prefer rose petal jam, finding the flavor more interesting. Flowers lack pectin and acid, so either you must use commercial pectin or use an apple extract, made from crab apples or tart apples such Granny Smith as a base. How to do so is mentioned in the recipe. The roses must be organically grown, free of pesticides or other chemicals.

Rose Petal and Crab Apple Jelly

Rating: Moderate

Special Instructions: Finding organically grown rose petals is difficult. So is reaching the jell point. If this jelly remains a syrup, it's still delicious. This recipe takes two days to prepare.

Yield: Three or four 8-ounce jars

INGREDIENTS:

2 C. red or deep pink organically grown rose petals (see instructions below for gathering the petals)

Water

2 lbs. or about 4 large crab apples or other tart apples, such as Granny Smith

Sugar

Day 1

1. Gather the rose petals. The morning, when the roses are fresh and just after the dew has dried, is a better time to gather petals than in the middle of a hot summer day. Snip off the bitter white portion at the base of each petal, more easily done if you hold the partly opened flower with one hand wrapped around it and trim it all at once rather than tediously trimming the petals one by one. Red or deep pink, very fragrant roses are the best, and the buds should be only part-way, rather than fully, open. Rinse quickly two or three times in a bowl of water. Drain.

2. Push the petals gently into a jar. Do not pack them so tightly that the petals are bruised and leave little space for the water you'll pour over them.

3. Cover the rose petals with boiling water, cap the jar, and let it stand at room temperature in a dark place for 24 hours.

Day 2

4. When ready to proceed, wash, core, and quarter the just-ripe crab apples until you have 4 cups. Cook them in a small amount of water (below the level of the fruit) until very soft, about 15 minutes.

5. Purée the crab apples in a food mill, then strain them through several layers of damp cotton cheesecloth, a chinois, or a jelly bag and collect the free-run juice. Do not press down on the fruit.

6. Strain the rose infusion in a colander lined with damp cotton cheesecloth, a chinois, or a jelly bag. Combine the two liquids.

7. Measure the combined liquid and place it in a large Dutch oven.

8. Add 1 cup of sugar for every cup of liquid.

9. Bring the mixture to a boil and cook it rapidly to the jell point.

10. Fill and process prepared jars as described on page 6.

Rose Petal Jam

As with other jams and fruit butters, it is the bulk or mass of the fruit that creates the texture of the preserve. The proportion of rose petals to sugar is three to one. Even so, this jam will have a softer texture than many others.

Rose petal jam, called *rothozahari* in Greece and *marmellata di rosa* in Italy, is made from rose petals crushed with sugar and has a more concentrated flavor than rose petal jelly.

Rating: Moderate
Special Instructions: Finding organically grown rose petals is difficult.
Yield: Variable

INGREDIENTS:

12 C. of organically grown deep pink or red rose petals (see instructions below for gathering the petals)
4 C. sugar
2 tsp. fresh lemon juice
Water

1. Gather the rose petals. The morning, when the roses are fresh and just after the dew has dried, is a better time to gather petals than in the middle of a hot summer day. Snip off the bitter white portion at the base of each petal, more easily done if you hold the partly opened flower with one hand wrapped around it and trim it all at once rather than tediously trimming the petals one by one. Red or deep pink, very fragrant roses are the best, and the buds should be only partway, rather than fully, open. Rinse quickly two or three times in a bowl of water. Drain.
2. Pack the petals firmly as you measure them.
3. In a wide, shallow bowl sprinkle the rose petals with the sugar.
4. Knead the rose petals with your fingertips, vigorously pulverizing the sugar and petals together.
5. When the petals have wilted and formed a pulpy mass, cover them tightly with plastic wrap and refrigerate for 2 hours.
6. Put the rose petal and sugar pulp into a large Dutch oven.
7. Add the lemon juice and, if needed, just a little water. Cook over low heat, stirring constantly, for 10 to 15 minutes, until a thick syrup has formed.
8. Fill and process prepared jars as described on page 6.

Rose Hips

When growing roses, all too often the focus is on flowers. As each one fades, it is cut away in a process known as "dead-heading," to encourage further bloom. But flowers are only one part of the cycle of seasons for a rose bush: fruiting, the production of orange-red hips, is supposed to follow. Some roses have larger hips than do others. Clearly, a rose with large hips is better if you want to make jam. And none is better than the rugosa rose, *Rosa rugosa*. Tolerant of salt spray and able to grow in sandy soil, this rose is a great shrub for planting in seaside gardens. I find it naturalized and growing wild on Cape Cod and in gardens along the Connecticut shore as well as in inland gardens, as this adaptable shrub rose is equally happy with richer soil. The large single flowers are either magenta pink or white; the dark-green leaves have a wrinkled appearance; and large hips turn orange-red when ripe and should be picked after the first frost for best flavor. If the hips are deep red, they're overripe.

Early one fall, my friends John and Diane wanted to go away to Cape Cod for a vacation. Their son, Johnny, came to stay with me. When his parents got back to Connecticut, they brought me a basket of beach plums and a goodly amount of rose hips. What fun I had making preserves!

Rose Hip Butter

I can only describe the flavor as a very tasty cross between apricots and almonds. That I like it so well is interesting, because I don't like rose hip tea at all. As with other jams and fruit butters, the density is provided in large part by the mass of fruit pulp in the recipe.

Rating: Moderate

Special Instructions: You can add as much as an equal quantity of tart apples to stretch the rose hips if you have only a limited quantity.

Yield: Approximately four or five 8-ounce jars

INGREDIENTS:

4 to 6 C. orange-ripe rugosa rose hips

Water

2 to 3 Tbs. fresh lemon juice

Sugar

1. Remove any dried-up bits of old flowers, stems, and calyces from the rose hips and rinse.

2. Place the rose hips in a large saucepan and add water to just cover. Bring to a boil and simmer briskly until the rose hips are very soft.

3. Purée the rose hips and liquid through the medium plate of a food mill to remove the seeds and then again through the fine plate to remove the little hairs.

4. Measure the purée. If you prefer a hint of tartness, add 1 tablespoon of lemon juice for each 2 cups of purée.

5. Measure 1 cup of sugar for each cup of purée. Set aside.

6. Cook the purée rapidly in a large saucepan, stirring constantly, until it begins to thicken.

7. Add the sugar.

8. Cook the mixture over high heat, stirring constantly, until a spoon leaves a slowly filling track on the bottom of the pan.

9. Fill and process prepared jars as described on page 6.

143

BACKYARD
HARVEST

Cornelian Cherries

Cornelian cherry, *Cornus mas*, is a popular garden ornamental, grown as a large shrub or small tree that covers itself with little chartreuse flowers in early spring before the leaves appear. A kind of dogwood rather than truly a cherry, each cluster of small flowers is similar to those in the center of a flowering dogwood blossom. Preserves and syrup made from cornelian cherries are popular in Europe, but in the United States, the fruit is usually left for the birds to enjoy.

Cornelian Cherry Jelly

One year, I got permission from Dr. Hamilton and Patrick J. Cullina, who managed Rutgers Gardens, the botanical garden of Cook College, Rutgers University, in New Brunswick, to collect some fruit to experiment with for preserves. It worked out so well I went back another year. The first time I easily gathered two quarts of cornelian cherries in late July. They were hard ripe, too tart to eat out of hand, just shifting over from bright red to a darker burgundy color. That weekend, I extracted the juice. Since each fruit has a single large seed (rather the way a cherry has a pit), and they are not as juicy as cherries, I used a little water at the start of the process. The fruit is so intensely flavored I was able to make three extractions. Had I wanted to make cornelian cherry jam, I would have stopped after the first extraction, puréed the fruit to remove the seeds, and then strained the juice. Because cornelian cherry is high in pectin and acid, it jells easily. The color is a beautiful deep, very dark red, and the jelly has a fine, quivery consistency, together with an excellent flavor.

Rating: Easy

Special Instructions: If you extract more juice than you want to make into jelly immediately, the surplus can be put in a tightly capped jar and stored in the freezer for later use. Rather than have the jar only partly full, it is better to fill it, allowing just enough air space for expansion of the liquid when it freezes.

Yield: Eight 8-ounce jars

INGREDIENTS:

12 C. cornelian cherries

Water

2 to 3 C. Homemade Apple Pectin extract (recipe on page 10). If Homemade Apple Pectin extract is not available, use water as a substitute.

7 to 7^1/$_2$ C. sugar

1. Wash and pick over the cornelian cherries and remove any bits of leaf or stem.
2. Add sufficient water to be just barely visible below the cornelian cherries, bring to a boil, then simmer for approximately 40 minutes. Keep the heat on low and watch the mixture carefully to prevent scorching.
3. Strain through a colander lined with several layers of damp cotton cheesecloth, a chinois, or a jelly bag and collect the free-run juice. Do not press down on the fruit. Set aside.
4. Return the berries to the pot with more water, and again simmer, this time for 20 minutes.
5. Strain through a colander lined with several layers of damp cotton cheesecloth, a chinois, or a jelly bag and collect the free-run juice. Do not press down on the fruit. Set aside.
6. Return the fruit pulp to the pot for a third time, using apple pectin extract as the liquid, and simmer for 20 minutes.

7. Strain and combine all three extractions. There should be about 7 or 7$^1/_2$ cups of liquid.

8. Add the sugar (since the juice is rather tart, I decided to use equal parts juice and sugar).

9. Stir well until the sugar is dissolved, return to a boil, and cook rapidly to the jell point.

10. Fill and process prepared jars as described on page 6.

Highbush Cranberry

Highbush cranberry, also known as American cranberry bush, *Viburnum trilobum*, is a popular ornamental that also happens to be a native plant. Though the fruits are red and tart, it is not truly a cranberry, but instead is a viburnum. Cold tolerant, highbush cranberry thrives in sun to part shade and also grows well in moist situations. Just because all viburnums are not poisonous, it doesn't mean they are good—that is, tasty to eat. The bright-red fruits of American cranberry bush are edible but have somewhat of a musky, old-socks odor and taste when fresh (which explains why although they're great for making tasty preserves, they are rarely, if ever, eaten out of hand).

Cultivars that are most commonly available in garden centers are those selected for their ornamental qualities, and if you are truly interested in growing them at home, it is worthwhile to seek out certain cultivars selected for better taste rather than good looks. Three cultivars that bear especially well include mid-September-fruiting 'Wentworth,' midseason 'Hahs,' and late-October-fruiting 'Andrews.' 'Phillips' is a recent introduction from the University of New Hampshire, where it was selected for its fruiting quality: it is completely free of the musky flavor and yields jelly said to be as good as that from red currants in flavor and color. 'Ukraine' is a selection of the botanic garden of Kiev, with abundant crops of large, high-quality fruit and bright fall foliage.

European cranberrybush or guelder rose, *Viburnum opulus*, is very similar in appearance to American cranberry bush. It happily grows in gardens from North Dakota to Massachusetts. Thriving in damp, shady places such as streamside thickets, it grows anywhere from eight to fifteen feet high and wide. If you're shopping in a garden center, use some care in choosing cultivars: 'Compactum' is half the size of the typical shrub, which is fine where space is limited; 'Nanum' is even smaller, but is shy about flowering and, as a result, bears little fruit. The tart, acidic berries are unpalatable when raw, but when processed with sugar, the juice becomes a tasty jelly. Some people like to add thinly sliced orange or lemon peel, plus their juice, to make more of a conserve.

Highbush Cranberries

Make a first extraction in the manner suggested for cornelian cherries, then look at the color of the cooked berries and nibble on a couple to see if there is sufficient flavor so that a second extraction is worth the effort. This tart jelly is more suited to use as an accompaniment to poultry, pork, lamb, or game than as a sweet jelly served on an English muffin.

Highbush Cranberry Jelly

Rating: Easy
Yield: Three to four 8-ounce jars

INGREDIENTS:
8 to 12 C. highbush cranberries
Water
3 to 4 Tbs. fresh lemon juice
Sugar
4 lbs. or 7 to 8 large crab apples or other tart apples, such as Granny Smith (optional)
1 orange (optional)

1. Rinse and pick over the highbush cranberries. Place them in a large saucepan.
2. Add 1 cup of water for every 4 cups of highbush cranberries. Bring the liquid to a boil, then reduce the heat and simmer for 15 to 20 minutes, or until the berries are quite soft.
3. Purée the fruit through the medium plate of a food mill. Examine initial purée for seeds. If they are mixed in with the puréed pulp, use the fine plate of the food mill to purée the pulp a second time. Set aside the purée if you would like to make Highbush Cranberry Butter (page 147).
4. Strain through a colander lined with several layers of damp cotton cheesecloth, a chinois, or a jelly bag and collect the free-run juice. Do not press down on the fruit. Set aside.
5. Some people like the tart flavor of highbush cranberry, while others find it too strong. Taste a little of the extract, keeping in mind that it will be sweetened. If you find the flavor too strong, chop the optional crab apples or tart apples and cook them with a little water. Strain as you did the cranberries and use up to equal parts apple extract and highbush cranberry juice. Or, add the orange, cut into thin slices and simmered together with the highbush cranberry fruit. Of course, another option would be to use both apple and orange.
6. Measure the juice or juices and place them in a large Dutch oven.

7. Add 1 tablespoon of lemon juice to every 3 cups of highbush cranberry or high-bush cranberry-apple extract.

8. Bring the liquid to a boil. Add 1 cup of sugar for each cup of liquid, stirring constantly until the sugar is dissolved.

9. Boil to the jell point.

10. Fill and process prepared jars as described on page 6.

Highbush Cranberry Butter

Rating: Easy

Yield: Variable, depending on the volume of set-aside purée from Highbush Cranberry Jelly (above)

INGREDIENTS:

Set-aside purée from Highbush Cranberry Jelly

2 Tbs. fresh lemon juice

Sugar

4 lbs. or 7 to 8 large crab apples or other tart apples, such as Granny Smith (if not used in jelly)

1 orange (if not used in jelly)

1. Measure the set-aside purée from the Highbush Cranberry Jelly recipe.

2. Add 1 tablespoon of lemon juice for every 3 cups of purée. Stir to combine thoroughly.

3. Measure 1 cup of sugar for each cup of purée. Set aside.

4. Some people like the tart flavor of highbush cranberry, while others find it too strong. Taste a little of the purée, keeping in mind that it will be sweetened. If you find the flavor too strong, chop the optional crab apples or tart apples and cook them with a little water. Purée the apples through the medium plate of a food mill. Use up to equal parts apple purée and highbush cranberry purée. Or, add the orange, cut into thin slices and simmered together with the highbush cranberry fruit. Of course, another option would be to use both apple and orange.

5. Place the fruit in a large Dutch oven and begin heating. As it just begins to plop small volcanolike bubbles, quickly stir in the sugar.

6. Turn the heat to medium high and cook, stirring constantly, until a spoon dragged through the mass leaves a clear track.

7. Fill and process prepared jars as described on page 6.

Rowan or Mountain Ash

Rowan, also called mountain ash, *Sorbus* species, are often grown as ornamentals in the United States and are prized for their bright-orange clusters of berries. In Europe, they are used for making jam or jelly that is especially popular when served with game such as pheasant, grouse, or venison. While it is true that the fresh fruit has an astringent, puckery quality making it unsuitable for eating out of hand, it becomes an excellent, if slightly bitter, jelly that is very good when served with lamb, pork, poultry, or game. There are several German and Russian cultivars that are said to be sweet enough to eat fresh and also useful for making tasty preserves; however, I have not sampled them and cannot make a personal comparison.

Rowan Jelly

Rating: Easy

Special Instructions: Rowan berries are somewhat dry. Using a combination of rowan and apple is helpful.

Yield: Three to four 8-ounce jars for every 4 cups of extracted juice

INGREDIENTS:

4 to 6 C. rowan berries

1¹/₂ lbs. or 3 large crab apples or tart apples, such as Granny Smith

Water

Sugar

1. Clean and pick over the rowan berries, removing any remnants of the dried-up flowers and stems. Put them in a large saucepan.
2. Coarsely chop the crab apples or tart apples. Add them to the saucepan with the rowan berries. Stir to mix the two fruits. Add just enough water to barely cover the fruit.
3. Bring the mixture to a boil and promptly reduce the heat, cover the pot, and simmer for 15 minutes or until the fruit begins to soften.
4. Crush the fruit with a potato masher or the bottom of a clean glass jar. Continue to simmer it until the fruit is very soft, stirring occasionally.
5. Strain through a colander lined with several layers of damp cotton cheesecloth, a chinois, or a jelly bag and collect the free-run juice. Do not press down on the fruit. Measure the juice and place it in large Dutch oven.
6. Add an equal quantity of sugar. Bring the mixture to a slow boil and stir it constantly until the sugar is dissolved.
7. Raise the heat and cook the mixture rapidly to the jell point.
8. Fill and process prepared jars as described on page 6.

Hedgerow Jelly

This is a popular jelly in England made in the autumn from a combination of wild, gathered fruit. Since it is a mixture of whatever is available, it is never going to come out quite the same from one time to the next. Popular ingredients include rowan berries, wild crab apples, sloe or blackthorn (a kind of small, very astringent black plum used for making preserves or sloe gin), blackberries, elderberries, rose hips, or hawthorn fruit—you get the idea. You may also include commercially available substitutes, such as crab apples, Italian prune plums, and blackberries; however, the flavor will not be as unique as with the wild-gathered version.

Rating: Easy
Yield: Three to four 8-ounce jars for every 4 cups of extracted juice

INGREDIENTS:
12 C. or more of a diversity of hedgerow fruits, whatever you can forage
Water
Juice of 1 lemon
Sugar

1. Select a well-balanced assortment of fruit, keeping in mind that sloes are very strong and crab apples are a good modifier. Rinse, and pick over the firmer fruit.
2. Start the fruits—except for the blackberries—cooking, with water to just barely cover. Simmer until soft, anywhere from 30 to 45, even 60 minutes.
3. Strain through a colander lined with several thicknesses of damp cotton cheese-cloth, a chinois, or a jelly bag and collect the free-run juice. Set aside.
4. Rinse and pick over the blackberries or other soft fruit. Mash slightly with a potato masher or the bottom of a clean glass jar, add just a little water, and simmer until soft, about 15 to 20 minutes.
5. Strain. Combine the two juice extracts and measure.
6. Add 1 tablespoon of lemon juice for every 2 cups of juice.
7. Measure 1 cup of sugar for every cup of juice and set aside.
8. Put the juices in a large Dutch oven. Bring them to a slow boil and add the sugar. Stir constantly until the sugar has dissolved.
9. Bring to a rapid boil and cook to the jell point.
10. Fill and process prepared jars as described on page 6.

Seaberry or Sea Buckthorn

Seaberry, *Hippophae rhamnoides*, is a very thorny shrub from the colder regions of eastern Europe and Asia. Seaberry grows in Washington State, the Canadian prairies, and New Jersey, tolerating shady coastal dunes and salt spray as well as arid and dry conditions. It does not thrive where summers are hot and humid and does poorly in regions with high rainfall.

Tolerant of drought, sandy soil low in fertility, and salt spray, seaberry is a good choice for seaside gardens. I've seen it growing on the dunes in Holland, a country where it is even used for highway plantings. The somewhat sprawling, irregular, multistemmed shrub has inconspicuous yellowish flowers in March or April before the gray-green leaves appear. Seaberry is dioecious, which means that each shrub is either male or female. Only female plants will bear fruit, but a male is necessary for pollination (and can "service" as many as to eight female shrubs). Flowers appear on older wood, so the berries are somewhat concealed by the current year's growth and, due in large part to the thorns, are moderately awkward to harvest. They ripen in late August into early September. I've heard it said that if you wait until there is a frost, the frozen berries can be shaken onto a tarp or sheet spread on the ground, but that seems too long to wait; here in New Jersey, the first light frosts don't arrive until into October.

In eastern Europe and Russia, where seaberry is known as Siberian pineapple for its taste and juiciness, the berries are commercially harvested for juice, which is processed into jellies and liqueurs. Some people really like seaberry jelly, while others may not. Remember that the flavor of unfamiliar fruits can always be modified by blending it with juice extracted from crab apples or tart apples.

Two cultivars selected abroad for their fruit production are available through Eastern Shore Nursery of Virginia, a wholesale-only nursery. 'Botanica' is a Russian variety that produces an abundant crop of bright-orange fruit that ripens in mid-August, and 'Leikora' is a German variety with orange fruits that ripen in September and persist into fall and winter. One Green World, a mail-order nursery that is mentioned in Appendix B, offers many more cultivars. Seaberry is a more popular name than sea buckthorn, thereby avoiding confusion with buckthorn, *Rhamnus cathartica* or *Rhamnus frangula*, two aggressively invasive shrubs.

Seaberries

What I do in my kitchen and what a commercial company manufacturing preserves for sale by the thousands of jars does are two very different matters. I can work in small batches, spending a morning to produce half a dozen jars. It doesn't really matter to me if the ingredients for a particular preserve cost one dollar or two dollars a jar. Taste, delicious flavor, is the bottom line. I found it amusing, therefore, that a report by a German company that discussed the product development for seaberry preserves had an aside to the effect that "domestic production" may have a much higher fruit content than commercial products. Seems to me that this goes without saying.

My "research" focuses on how to tweak a recipe to the point where I feel it's as good as it gets. When playing around with certain fruits, using them in combination actually yields better, i.e., tastier, results than using them solo. Seaberry is one such fruit, giving a more pleasant, better-balanced flavor when combined with apples, pears, or quinces. And, when cultivars developed for their flavor are what I work with, rather than any old happenstance shrub used for landscaping, the results are even better.

Seaberry Jelly

Rating: Easy
Yield: Approximately three to four 8-ounce jars for every 4 cups of extracted juice

INGREDIENTS:
12 C. orange seaberries
Water
1¹/₂ to 3 lbs. of tart apples, such as Granny Smith, or firm-ripe winter pears such as Comice,
    or quinces
3 to 4 Tbs. fresh lemon juice
Sugar

1.   Rinse and pick over the seaberries. Put them in a large pot.
2.   Crush the fruit somewhat, using a potato masher or the bottom of a clean glass jar.
3.   Add 1 cup of water. Bring the fruit to a boil, cover the pot, and turn down the heat to a simmer. Cook for 10 to 15 minutes, until the juice flows freely.
4.   Strain through a colander lined with several thicknesses of damp cotton cheese-cloth, a chinois, or a jelly bag and collect the free-run juice. Do not press down on the fruit. Measure the juice, and if you would like to make Seaberry Butter (page 152), set aside the pulp.
5.   Decide if you want to make a blend of seaberry-apple, seaberry-pear, or seaberry-quince. Once the companion fruit has been selected, rinse and chop 4 to 8 cups, depending on the balance you want to produce—i.e., will the seaberry predominate or be more of an accent? Place the fruit in a pot with some water. Bring to a boil, then simmer until soft.
6.   Purée the fruit through a food mill using the medium plate to strain out the seeds.
7.   Place the pulp in a colander lined with several thicknesses of damp cotton cheesecloth, a chinois, or a jelly bag and allow the juice to drip for several hours, collecting it. Do not press down on the fruit. If you are making Seaberry Butter, reserve the strained pulp of this fruit as well.
8.   Combine equal amounts of seaberry juice and the companion fruit juice. Measure.
9.   Add 1 tablespoon of lemon juice for every 2 cups of juice.
10.   Measure 1 cup of sugar for each cup of juice. Set aside.
11.   Bring the liquid just to a boil and add the sugar. Stir constantly until the sugar is dissolved.
12.   Boil to the jell point.
13.   Fill and process prepared jars as described on page 6.

Seaberry Butter

Rating: Easy

Yield: Approximately two to three 8-ounce jars for every 4 cups of purée

INGREDIENTS:

Set-aside seaberry purée from Seaberry Jelly (page 151)

Set-aside apple, pear, or quince purée from Seaberry Jelly

2 or more Tbs. fresh lemon juice

1 orange or lemon (optional)

Sugar

1. Measure and combine the set-aside seaberry pulp from the Seaberry Jelly recipe with an equal amount of companion fruit pulp.

2. Place in large Dutch oven. Add 1 tablespoon of lemon juice for every 2 cups of pulp. Stir to mix well.

3. If desired, you can add the finely slivered peel of an orange or lemon to each 2 cups of pulp for additional flavor. Simmer the peel in a small amount of water in a covered pot until tender, then add the liquid along with the peel to the purée.

4. Add from ³/₄ to a full cup of sugar for each cup of pulp, depending on the tartness of the fruit pulp and your personal preference for sweetness.

5. Bring the mixture to a boil, then cook at a brisk simmer, stirring frequently, until a spoon leaves a track when dragged through the pulp.

6. Fill and process prepared jars as described on page 6.

Mahonia

Mahonia is a genus of ornamental evergreen shrubs with hollylike leaves. Our native American species, *Mahonia aquifolium*, has the common name "Oregon grape," suggesting its appeal to the westward settlers. Small, attractive berries are a deep blue covered with a white bloom that rubs off when they are handled. One year late in June (having first asked permission and making sure the shrub had not been sprayed with pesticide), I gathered berries from a plant of *Mahonia bealii*, an Asian species that was growing at a local garden center. They were absolutely ripe, to the point of falling off into my hand. The prickly, sharp leaves made me yelp and snatch my hand away every now and then, dropping a goodly number. However, within minutes, I'd filled a small paper bag. I had collected six cups of berries. The berries were so ripe that the brown paper bag was quickly stained red and getting soft from the juice. I carried my booty home and processed the berries right away. There is no commonly cultivated fruit that I can compare the flavor with, and of the wild fruits I gather for jelly making, it is elderberry that is closest in taste.

That year I had a young man helping me in the garden. My "head gardener," Chris Stout, happened to notice the jars sitting on the kitchen worktable. He also had mahonia growing in his garden but, like so many others, never thought of it as a plant with edible fruit. Of course you know what came next—a request for a sample. Reporting the results of his informal, at-home opinion poll to me, he said that Lila, his mother, and his *meme* (grandmother) Dorothy both liked it very much, mentioning that it reminded them of elderberry jelly. His mom remarked, "It was great on toast, with a tangy aftertaste." One brother did like it, and the other one did not. And his friend Doug said, "Whatever a mahonia is, it makes a great jelly."

On the other hand, in an e-mail, my brother, Ben, wrote, "About the jelly—I found it to be pleasant and agreeable, enjoyed on toast with cream cheese. But I also noted that it didn't strike me as unusual or memorable. Somehow I had high expectations for trying a jelly from a new sort of fruit." Perhaps what is needed is a blind taste test to avoid raising expectations. Regardless, mahonia does make a tasty, savory jelly.

Mahonia Jelly

Rating: Easy

Yield: One 8-ounce jar and five 4-ounce jars.

Note: I made many smaller jars because I wanted samples available for discerning friends to taste.

INGREDIENTS:

6 C. mahonia berries

1¹/₂ C. water

1 C. Homemade Apple Pectin extract (recipe on page 10)

3³/₄ C. sugar

1. Rinse and pick over the mahonia berries.
2. Put the berries in a pot with 1 cup of water, then heat until the juice begins to flow. The berries will turn a deep midnight blue-black as the bloom disappears.
3. Strain the pulp through a colander lined with damp cotton cheesecloth, a chinois, or a jelly bag and collect the free-run juice. Do not press down on the fruit. The yield will be about 2 cups of a very tart, dark-red juice. Set aside.
4. Return the drained pulp to the pot, add ¹/₂ cup of water, and heat again.
5. Strain the pulp again. The yield should be an additional ³/₄ cup of juice.
6. Combine the juice from both extractions with the apple pectin extract.
7. Add the sugar to the juice and bring it to a boil, stirring constantly, until the sugar is dissolved.
8. Boil the mixture quickly to the jell point.
9. Fill and process prepared jars as described on page 6.

Another backyard fruit that offers potential for jam and jelly making is ornamental quince, *Chanomeles japonica*, mentioned briefly in Chapter Two: Fruit Butters.

CHAPTER ELEVEN

WILD WEALTH

There is something special about gathering in the harvest, an event recognized in festivals and celebrated in hymns, songs, and poetry. My mother, Katzy, and my Aunt Gert certainly felt that the various blackcap raspberries, blackberries, dewberries, blueberries, and grapes that we picked on Carmen Hill were indeed "wild wealth," and a regular part of our summers there. It was a tradition that, having been learned in my childhood, I follow as an adult: keeping an eye out for berry patches in meadows, grapevines in trees, and fruit-bearing bushes and trees at the woodland's edge. I enjoy the peaceful time spent picking in a berry patch, mindful of the simple task at hand, fingertips and lips soon stained purple as I sample the harvest.

This is a common thread for many women where preserving was and is part of a family tradition. Faith Marcovecchio, her mother, grandmother, and great-grandmother always picked the berries that they used for preserves. In the Upper Peninsula of Michigan, where her grandmother and great-grandmother lived much, if not all, of their lives, there were lots of wild places with wild strawberries, thimbleberries, and chokecherries, and her family also grew raspberries in their own backyard. When Sandra Green was a little girl living in Orrington, Maine, it was her mother, Hilda Stewart, who made all the preserves, using anything that was available. The family lived in a rural area, surrounded by field strawberries, blueberries, raspberries, blackberries,

chokecherries, and crab apples. Each season, Hilda was able to make enough preserves to last the family for a year. Sandra recalls, "My childhood memories were of my brother, Leroy, and me sent to pick those oh-so-small strawberries. We left the house with our coffee cups and were sent to get enough for a pie. My mom knew we would never come home with enough. We ate more than we picked. Dad was then sent to help us. It was always a joke in our family, about earning our evening meal. Blueberry picking was the same, except my brother was better at it than I was. I don't make preserves myself, so I really don't have any information in the present. Mine is all past history and memories."

Joyce Carleston also has memories of learning all the basics of how to make jams and jellies from her mother, Meta Schkade. The ripples continue to spread, and a few friends helped Joyce learn to judge when the jelly or jam has cooked long enough to set. She's gotten some further hints from an old recipe book compiled by the ladies in her mother's church. And what preserves does she make today? Joyce told me, "I make jams and jellies from the wild fruits available in our area [Texas]. My basic recipe is for dewberries, wild yellow or red plums, and wild grapes. We prepare the fruit for the juice as follows: sort, wash, and cook the fruit in a little water until it is soft. Some of the fruit should not be completely ripe since I don't use pectin. For jelly, I strain the cooked fruit through cheesecloth. We like jam, so I use various colanders to get as much pulp in the juice as I can. I even put a few plum seeds on top of the jam in the jars. The men in our family like the dewberry and plum jam cooked with the seeds left in so there is no need to strain the cooked juice."

As cities sprawl outward, girdled by suburbs connected by highways, and farms sprout McMansions rather than crops, it is getting more and more difficult to find places where one can gather undomesticated fruit. Further, the fruit must be safe to eat, not necessarily raised organically but definitely free of toxic residues or any other harmful matter. I remember an elderly farmer in Fairfield County, Connecticut, from whom I was buying a peck of quinces decades ago. When I commented on the beauty of the fruit, he told me that when lead arsenate was taken off the market as an insecticide he made sure to stockpile enough in his toolshed to ensure he wouldn't run out. I drove away horrified that I'd been using the peels in making quince butter.

In *Wild Preserves*, published in 1977, when perhaps there was not as high a level of concern about food safety as there is today, the author, Joe Freitus, discusses mountain ash, *Sorbus* species. Freitus writes, "European Mountain Ash is easily located along highways and streets as it is not harmed by most automobile pollution." Some plants are. And while it's true that today gasoline is formulated lead-free, just because a plant may be unaffected in its growth by car emissions does not necessarily mean the fruit is safe to eat. So if you go foraging, try to find a peaceful site away from the rush of a highway and its traffic. And do keep in mind that all land belongs to someone. It is only proper and polite to request the landowner's consent—rarely has anyone from whom I've asked permission denied it.

For example, one summer's day I was at a winery on the North Fork of Long Island. At the edge of the parking lot was a huge tree just loaded down with smallish blue-purple plums so ripe that fruit was falling to the ground and cars were being heedlessly driven over it, crushing the fruit into the gravel. I asked permission to pick the fruit, and while the woman was clearly puzzled by the request, it was granted. I picked two paper bags (each of a size to hold two bottles of wine) full of plums from the lower branches of the tree, and when I got home, I made some delicious plum conserve. Every time I ate some, it reminded me of that summer day and all the good things that happened then.

Saskatoons

Joan and Bob Means used to spend some of their vacation time in Nova Scotia gathering saskatoons and making jam. If your only association with this fruit is the delightful little children's book *Under the Saskatoon Tree*, let me tell you more. Native to the United States and Canada, saskatoon, *Amelanchier canadensis*, grows as a large shrub or small tree with small, creamy white, fragrant flowers, followed by blueberrylike fruits. Other names for it are shadbush and shadblow, as it is said to flower when the shad swim upriver to spawn. Back when we lived in Connecticut, I found saskatoon growing near a cattail swamp and also in a wet meadow. In fact, there was one planted as an ornamental in the courtyard of the Wilton library. They'll grow just about anywhere—in sun or light shade—and seem to like a damp soil but not soggy. When I'd go picking in July, it was a good day if I got some saskatoon berries to bring home and eat fresh; birds like them as much as I do, and they're quicker at determining when the berries are ripe. More and more, I see this shrub used as an ornamental, popular for its attractive white springtime flowers, beautiful, with tasty fruit in summer and wonderful orange-rust fall leaf color. It would be an excellent choice for a backyard ornamental that has edible fruit. Any recipe using blueberry can be made with saskatoons.

Saskatoon Jelly

Each little saskatoon berry has ten little seeds, so jelly is a better option. My experience has been with more-modest quantities of fruit, whatever I could glean from an occasional tree in competition with the birds. (I'm sure raccoons and opossums would avail themselves of a nocturnal snack as well.) Therefore, saskatoons were used in combination with apples. While it was never a huge quantity, the jelly I did make was a special treat.

Rating: Easy
Yield: Approximately three 8-ounce jars

INGREDIENTS:
1 to 1¹/₂ lbs. or 3 large crab apples or other tart apples, such as Granny Smith
Water
2 or 3 C. saskatoons, or whatever you manage to gather
2 Tbs. fresh lemon juice
Sugar
¹/₂ tsp. butter (optional)

1. Cut up the apples, skin, core, and seeds, and measure 3 cups. Put them in a medium-sized saucepan with enough water to come just below the level of the apples.
2. Cook the apple and water mixture over high heat. When a boil is reached, turn down the heat and simmer, covered, until the apples are quite soft. This should take about 20 to 30 minutes.
3. Purée the fruit through the medium plate of a food mill to remove the seeds.
4. Strain the apples through a colander lined with damp cotton cheesecloth, a chinois, or a jelly bag and collect the free-run juice. Do not press down on the fruit. Set the pulp aside for future use in making fruit butter, either solo or in combination with another fruit, if you desire.
5. Rinse the saskatoon berries, place them in a saucepan, and add ¹/₂ cup of water.
6. Simmer the berries over moderate heat until they are quite soft and the juices are flowing.
7. Strain the fruit through a colander lined with damp cheesecloth, a chinois, or a jelly bag and collect the free-run juice. Do not press down on the fruit.
8. Combine the juices and measure them.
9. Add 1 tablespoon of fresh lemon juice for every 2 cups of juice.
10. Measure the sugar, 1 cup for each cup of juice, and set aside.
11. Pour the juices into a Dutch oven and bring them to a boil. If you are concerned about foam, add the butter to prevent it.
12. Add the sugar and stir the mixture thoroughly.
13. Boil to the jell point.
14. Fill and process prepared jars as described on page 6.

Chokecherries

Faith Marcovecchio recalls that the women in her family tended to make jams. That was mostly, she thinks, to avoid the messy business of having to strain the fruit to make jelly. Except, that is, for Chokecherry Jelly. Chokecherries are very tart, and the fruits are tiny, so you have to make jelly to avoid all the skins and pits. If you ever taste chokecherries right off the tree, I promise that you'll spit them right back out again. The astringent, puckery qualities of the fruit guarantee that everything that's picked will end up in the bucket. Faith mentioned that she had her grandmother's recipe box at home and would check to see if a recipe for chokecherry jelly was in it, but she suspected the recipe resided in her grandmother's head. Since that recipe was, alas, not forthcoming, here's a different one. The two are probably very similar. Jelly is, when you come right down to it, juice extracted from fruit by cooking, combined with sugar, and boiled to the jell point. Once you've made one, it is simple to extrapolate to some other kind of fruit.

A brief pause here. There are chokecherries and chokeberries. Both are edible in the sense of "good for making preserves." They are different genera, easy to tell apart by their habit of growth and appearance. At the most simple, chokecherries have a cherry pit inside the fruit, while chokeberries do not. Chokecherry, *Prunus virginiana*, grows in Canada from Newfoundland to Saskatchewan and southward to Kansas and North Carolina in the United States. It is a small tree growing about ten to twelve feet tall, sometimes more, with dense, bottle-brushlike clusters of white flowers followed by pea-sized dark-red to black fruit in summer. Chokeberry, *Aronia arbutifolia*, is found wild over most of the eastern United States. A multistemmed shrub, it grows about six to ten feet tall, also has white flowers, and produces dense clusters of bright- or dull-red berrylike fruits about one-quarter inch across. There is a cultivated variety, 'Brilliantissima,' which is grown as an ornamental for its unusually showy, shiny bright-red berries.

Interestingly enough, while chokeberry is grown primarily as an ornamental in the United States, it is cultivated in Czechoslovakia, Germany, Scandinavia, and the former Soviet Union for fruit production. It is closely related to black chokeberry, *Aronia melanocarpa*, another deciduous native shrub that is also found in eastern North America, thriving in damp places. The pea-sized purplish black berries have an astringent, tart flavor that makes them unpalatable for eating raw, but which make a delicious syrup or preserves. The shrub is commercially cultivated in Denmark, eastern Europe, Russia, and Siberia. In Poland, black chokeberry juice is used to make jelly or syrup in combination with black currant. 'Autumn Magic' is a clone recently introduced by the University of British Columbia, where it was selected for both edible and ornamental attributes. It has good-sized fruit and excellent fall color. 'Nero' and 'Viking' are two other black chokeberry cultivars that are popular as ornamental shrubs with edible fruit—let's make that "useable," as I find it too astringent to eat fresh.

Handle chokeberry or black chokeberry fruit like grapes: crush and begin cooking with just a little water. Freezing the fruit before cooking is said to release more juice, but I've always picked enough that squeezing out the last drop has not been a concern. Once the fruit is soft and juices are flowing freely, allow it to drip through a colander lined with damp cotton cheesecloth or through a chinois. Since the juice is somewhat low in acidity, add some lemon juice before processing it into jelly.

Chokecherry or Chokeberry Jelly

Rating: Moderately easy

Special Instructions: This recipe takes two days to prepare.

Yield: Four or five 8-ounce jars

INGREDIENTS:

8 C. chokecherries or chokeberries

4 C. water

2 to 4 Tbs. fresh lemon juice

2 lbs. or 4 large crab apples or other tart apple, such as Granny Smith (optional)

Sugar

Almond extract (optional)

Day 1

1. Rinse and pick over the chokecherries or chokeberries and remove any bits of leaves and twigs.

2. Put the fruit in a large saucepan with the water. Bring to a brisk simmer. Cover the pot, lower the heat, and simmer for 15 minutes, or until soft.

3. Strain through a colander lined with several layers of damp cotton cheesecloth, a chinois, or a jelly bag. Allow the cooked fruit to drip for several hours or overnight, collecting the free-run juice. Do not push down on the fruit.

Day 2

4. The next day, measure the extracted juice. There should be about 4 cups. If you would like to make Chokecherry or Chokeberry Butter (page 161), set aside the pulp.

5. If the chokecherries were mostly ripe, add 1 tablespoon of lemon juice for each cup of prepared juice. Use less lemon juice if $1/4$ of the fruit was underripe, as underripe fruit will give a good set without the need to add citrus.

6. Some people like the tart flavor of chokecherries, while others find it too strong. Taste a little of the extract, keeping in mind that it will be sweetened. If you find the flavor too strong, chop the optional crab apples or tart apples and cook them with a little water. Process them through the medium plate of a food mill and strain as you did the chokecherries. Use $1/4$ to $1/3$ cup of apple extract to every $3/4$ or $2/3$ cup of chokecherry juice. If you would like to make Chokecherry or Chokeberry Butter, set aside the pulp.

7. Measure $3/4$ cup of sugar for each cup of juice and set aside.

8. Heat the juice until it comes to a full rolling boil.
9. Add the sugar.
10. Boil hard, stirring constantly, to the jell point.
11. If you would like to intensify the flavor, add $1/4$ teaspoon of almond extract to each jar before filling with the hot jelly.
12. Fill and process prepared jars as described on page 6.

Chokecherry or Chokeberry Butter

Rating: Easy
Yield: Variable, depending on how much pulp you have

INGREDIENTS:
Set-aside chokecherry or chokeberry pulp from Chokecherry or Chokeberry Jelly (above)
Set-aside apple pulp left from Chokecherry or Chokeberry Jelly
Sugar

1. Measure the purée and put it in a large Dutch oven.
2. Add an equal quantity of sugar and, over moderate heat, stir until the sugar has dissolved.
3. Bring to a full rolling boil and cook, stirring constantly, until the mixture has thickened and a spoon dragged through the purée leaves a slowly disappearing track.
4. Fill and process prepared jars as described on page 6.

Beach Plums

As I described in Chapter Ten: Backyard Harvest, early one autumn some friends brought me a basket of beach plums that they had picked on Cape Cod. That is how most people find beach plums, growing on sand dunes in coastal areas along the eastern seaboard from Maine to Virginia. In spring, numerous small white flowers cover the black-barked branches like snow, to be followed in August and September by small, round plums that turn from red to a bloom-dusted blue when ripe. Beach plum, *Prunus maritima*, has been grown as an ornamental, provided its needs for a site with full sun and sandy, acidic soil can be met. And, as the name suggests, it is tolerant of salt spray.

Beach Plum Jelly

Rating: Easy
Yield: Variable

INGREDIENTS:
8 C. beach plums, mostly ripe and some underripe
Water
Crab apples or other tart apple, such as Granny Smith (optional; see note below)
Sugar

1. Rinse and pick over the beach plums. It is best if some are still red and underripe, since they will be higher in pectin.
2. Put the beach plums into a large pot, together with 2 cups of water for every 4 cups of fruit.
3. Bring to a boil, then turn the heat down to a brisk simmer and cook for 5 or 10 minutes, or until the beach plums have softened and their juices begin to flow.
4. Mash the fruit with a potato masher or the bottom of a clean glass jar, then continue cooking until they are quite soft and mushy.
5. Purée through a food mill with the medium plate to sieve out the seeds.
6. Put the pulp in a colander lined with several layers of damp cotton cheesecloth, a chinois, or a jelly bag and collect the free-run juice. Do not push down on the fruit. Set the pulp aside if you would like to make Beach Plum Butter (page 163). Measure the juice.
7. If you do not have enough beach plums and want to increase your yield of jelly, chop the optional crab apples or tart apples, no more than half the volume of the beach plums, and cook them with a little water. Process them through the medium plate of a food mill and strain as you did the beach plums. Add from $1/3$ to $1/2$ the volume of apple extract to the beach plum

extract. If you would like to make Beach Plum Butter, set aside the pulp.

8. Measure 1 cup of sugar for each cup of apple and/or beach plum extract.
9. Put the juice in a large Dutch oven. Bring it to a boil.
10. Stirring all the while, slowly add the sugar. Bring back to a boil and cook over high heat until it reaches the jell point.
11. Fill and process prepared jars as described on page 6.

Beach Plum Butter

Rating: Easy
Yield: Variable

INGREDIENTS:
Set-aside beach plum pulp from Beach Plum Jelly recipe (above)
Set-aside apple pulp from Beach Plum Jelly recipe or 1^1/$_2$ to 2 lbs. or about 4 crab apples or other tart apples, such as Granny Smith (optional)
Water
Sugar

1. Measure the set-aside pulp from the Beach Plum Jelly recipe.
2. If apples were used in the Beach Plum Jelly recipe, or to bulk up small amounts of beach plums, measure the apple pulp, and add 1 cup to every 2 cups of beach plum pulp. To make the pulp from scratch, chop the optional crab apples or tart apples and cook them with a little water. Purée the apples through the medium plate of a food mill.
3. Add ^{1}/$_2$ cup of sugar for each cup of purée.
4. Cook over moderate heat, stirring constantly, until a spoon dragged through the mass leaves a slowly filling track.
5. Fill and process prepared jars as described on page 6.

Buffalo Berries

Silver Buffalo Berry, *Shepherdia argentia*, is a six- to ten-foot-tall winter-hardy, drought-tolerant, sun-loving shrub found in open grassy areas, ravines, and along stream banks in the Plains States of the central United States and Canada. It thrives in poor soil. It has distinctive silvery leaves and stout one- to two-inch thorns at the tips of the branches, which usually make picking buffalo berry a painful experience. A simple method of harvesting involves laying a sheet under the shrub and shaking the branches until the berries fall off. Masses of sour, even bitter, red berries appear in late summer, becoming somewhat sweeter after they are kissed by frost. They make an excellent jelly or jam with a tart flavor that is especially good when served like cranberry sauce with poultry, pork, or game. Like seaberry, mentioned in Chapter Ten: Backyard Harvest (pages 150–152), silver buffalo berry is dioecious, and both a male and a female shrub are needed for fruit production.

Buffalo Berry Jelly

Rating: Easy
Yield: Variable

INGREDIENTS:
4 to 6 C. buffalo berries, mostly ripe and some underripe
Water
1^1/$_2$ to 2 lbs. or about 4 large crab apples or other tart apples, such as Granny Smith (optional)
Sugar

1. Rinse and pick over ripe buffalo berries, removing any leaves or small twigs. Stem the berries.
2. Put berries in a large saucepan together with ^{1}/$_2$ cup of water for each 4 cups of berries.
3. Bring to a boil, then turn down heat and simmer, covered, for 10 minutes.
4. Crush the berries with a potato masher or the bottom of a clean glass jar, then simmer for a few minutes longer.
5. Purée the berries and liquid through a food mill, then strain through several layers of damp cotton cheesecloth, a chinois, or a jelly bag to collect the free-run juice. Do not push down on the fruit. The juice will be cloudy in appearance. Measure.
6. Some people like the tart flavor of buffalo berries, while others find it too strong. Taste a little of the extract, keeping in mind that it will be sweetened. If you find the flavor too strong, chop the optional crab apples or tart apples and cook them with a little water. Process them through the medium plate of a food mill and strain as you did the buffalo berries. Measure.

7. Combine buffalo berry juice and apple extract juice, using 1 cup of apple extract for every 3 or 4 cups of buffalo berry extract.

8. Measure the combined juices and put no more than 4 or 5 cups of juice in a large Dutch oven.

9. Place over high heat. As the liquid approaches a boil, add 1 cup of sugar for each cup of juice. At this point, the juice will turn orange.

10. Boil rapidly to the jell point.

11. Fill and process prepared jars as described on page 6.

Additional Wild Fruit

In this chapter, my focus has been on wild fruits that my family and I gathered from meadows, roadsides, and woodland clearings, mostly in Connecticut, and those I seek out today in New Jersey. In addition to the fruits discussed in this chapter, this "wild wealth" includes various berries in Chapter Eight: Delectable Berries and cranberries, blueberries, grapes, and elderberries in Chapter Nine: Native Harvest. There are other wild fruits in other regions of the country that have at one time or another been used in making preserves and with which I am unfamiliar. As a sampling, I have compiled descriptions of some of these wild fruits. If you want to follow up on your own, check out the following.

Pin Cherry or **Bird Cherry**, *Prunus pennsylvanica*, is native in much of North America, from Newfoundland to British Columbia, southward to Colorado and the mountains of North Carolina. The shallow-rooted tree grows anywhere from twenty-five to forty feet tall, but it is usually smaller rather than taller. It has clusters of long-stemmed, pea-sized, tart, little light cherry–red cherries in late summer, which are good for making jelly. The pit, or stone, inside the fruit is rather large in proportion to the overall size of the fruit, so you'll need to gather more than you first think. Simmer the fruit with just a little water for five to ten minutes before straining the juice.

Sand Cherry, *Prunus pumila*, is native to dunes and sandy, rocky inland shores around the Great Lakes Region. It is a semi-prostrate, less-than-three-foot-tall shrub with astringent, half-inch, dark-red to purple-black fruits. Simmer the fruit with just a little water for ten to fifteen minutes before straining the juice.

Western Sand Cherry, *Prunus bessyi*, is a native of the northern Great Plains of both the United States and Canada. It grows about four feet tall and spreads out wider than that. Several cultivars—'Mando,' 'Manmoor,' and 'Brooks'—have been developed for commercial fruit production, as the short-stemmed red cherries can be nearly an inch in diameter and are sweet. If you decide to grow them in your garden, keep in mind that if you want a good fruit set, sand cherry is one of those plants that requires a partner for cross-pollination. This can be a different clone (genetically identical plants produced asexually from a single parent) of sand cherry or even a late-flowering plum, as long as both flower simultaneously. Since sand cherries are juicy, use just enough water to start the juices flowing. Simmer only until soft and the juices are flowing freely.

Chickasaw Plum, *Prunus angustifolia*, grows wild from New Jersey westward to Kansas and southward to Florida and Texas. The thorny small trees, about fifteen feet tall, grow in dense thickets. The white flowers appear before leaves do, and the small red or yellow plums, which are about an inch long (more or less), ripen in July and make a delicious jelly or jam. I would wager that this is the one Joyce Carleston gathers. Less common, the wild goose plum, *Prunus hortulana*, is easy to distinguish: the trees are thornless and usually do not sucker. Its flowers open when the leaves are half grown, and the aromatic, tart, red-to-yellow plums dusted with a whitish bloom, which ripen in late summer, make excellent preserves.

Blue Elderberry, *Sambucus caerulea*, is a native plant on the western side of North America, growing from British Columbia in Canada south to California and eastward into Montana and Utah. It's been said that this is the best of the different species of elderberries. Where it grows well, the large shrubs can reach tree-sized proportions and grow thirty feet tall. To reach the berry clusters, you need a long pole with a hook at the end to pull them into reach. Two people make it easier, one to snag the branches and the other to clip the berry clusters into a basket or pail.

Lowbush Cranberry, *Viburnum edule*, is a native viburnum found in the forests of British Columbia, northern Oregon, Washington, Idaho, and Montana, where it grows along moist woods, along stream banks, and at the edge of ponds and bogs. Flowering in late May or early June, the tart, bright-red berries ripen in mid- to late August. Similar to cranberries in flavor, they are too tart to enjoy fresh but make a tasty, tart jelly, jam, or conserve.

The vitally important thing when gathering wild fruit is to know what you are gathering. Blackberries, raspberries, and wild grapes are pretty easy to recognize. There are many other suitable but unfamiliar fruits. If it is a family tradition, you'll have learned by observation. If you are starting the tradition, try to find someone with experience in local wild foods and accompany them. Go to a botanic garden or nature center and see what plants they have growing, helpfully labeled. Don't go once and think you know it well. Look at the plants in bloom, go back and see them in fruit, check them out in their autumn foliage display, and examine them again in winter, when outline and bark are clearly revealed. Safety first should be your motto.

CHAPTER TWELVE
USING PRESERVES

Jellies sweet and savory, jams and conserves and marmalades, fruit butters—now that you've made them, what will you do with them? Jack Lenzo recalls the "steady supply of homemade jams and jellies that were eaten with everything from toast and peanut-butter-and-jelly to more elaborate things, like crepes. We even had a German holiday cookie that used raspberry jam as 'glue' between two almond cookie parts."

My brother, Ben, remembers Grandma Gussie "drinking tea with cherry preserves in it. I liked the image and, just a year or two ago, got some nice cherry preserves. I found that I didn't like them at all in tea. So it goes. I remember Robby loving the older northern Europe preserves: gooseberry and lingonberry, pastries filled with jam and preserves from the eastern and central European-style bakeries, Black Forest cake, and hamantaschen filled with prune jam."

I remember those bakeries, too. Sometimes I would accompany my father on a Sunday visit to cousin Adolph and his wife, Carola. Robby would stop at the bakery down the street from their Manhattan apartment: display cases were fronted and topped with glass, so even when I was still too small to peer in the top, I could see the delectable treats within. Little tarts glazed with currant or apricot jelly, sponge drops in pairs with jelly between them, sugar cookies with jewel-bright preserves showing through the hole in the top. The staff behind the counters were enveloped

in white aprons, straps wrapped around the waist and tied in front. Once our choices had been made, they'd be placed in a white cardboard box, its pseudo-origami shape created from folding and bending the flat sheet, fitting tabs into slots. It would be tied with thin string, red and white threads spiraling around each other, which hung down from a spool on a ceiling hook. The string would be wrapped around and around the box and tied with a flourish into a small bow. Once in the apartment, the adults would talk in German while I would be expected to entertain myself, reading a book or something equally quiet. Later, later, it would be time for tea and pastries.

The four tastes are sour, salty, bitter, and sweet. Preserves can add their sweetness in a diversity of ways. Spreading preserves on toast is one—rather commonplace; using them with cakes and cookies, puddings and custards is another. Using preserves on their own or as an ingredient to glaze a ham, brush on barbecue, add sweetness to a marinade, or even in combination with vegetables such as carrots, winter squash, or sweet potatoes are other possibilities. When used with meat, keep in mind that marmalade, jam, and fruit butters marry well with other categories of taste, especially salty and savory. A dash of Worcestershire sauce, a splash of soy sauce, a spoonful of marmalade—you're on your way.

Fools, Parfaits, and Frozen Sweets

Quince Fool

A fool is the easiest of desserts. Just about any fruit is cooked with a little water and then puréed. The pulp is sugared and kept cool. At the last minute, whipped cream is added to the pulp in the proportions of two to one, mixed gently, and served in sherbet glasses. Those are the directions in the *Larousse Gastronomique*. One day I thought to myself that fruit butter is really nothing more than a cooked-down, sweetened purée. So I tried it and discovered that fruit butters work quite nicely in fools. Quince remains my favorite, with pear butter a close second and plum following right behind. Fool, by the way, comes from *fouler*, a French verb meaning "to crush."

INGREDIENTS:

1 C. whipping cream

1 tsp. vanilla extract

2 Tbs. extra-fine granulated sugar

1 C. of fruit butter

1.   Place a metal bowl and beaters in the freezer for an hour or more to chill. Make sure the cream is also very cold.

2.   Beat the heavy cream until lightly set.

3.   Add vanilla extract and sugar.

4. Continue beating a few seconds more until the cream makes a soft peak when the beater is lifted from the bowl.
5. Place the fruit butter in a separate bowl and break it up with a fork.
6. Gently fold the fruit butter and whipped cream together with a spatula. They need not be homogenous; in fact, I like the two in swirls.

Frozen Raspberry Jam Parfait

This is a delicious summertime dessert and delightful in the winter, also. In fact, if you like raspberries as much as I do, any time of year is fine.

INGREDIENTS:
4 egg yolks
$^1/_3$ C. sugar
2 Tbs. vodka
2 tsp. vanilla extract
$^1/_2$ C. raspberry jam or fruit butter
1 C. whipping cream
2 Tbs. sugar
Fresh raspberries for garnish

1. Beat egg yolks with $^1/_3$ cup of granulated sugar until the mixture is pale yellow. The mixture is ready when it falls from a spoon in a ribbon that slowly disappears back into the mass.
   Note: If you are using commercially produced eggs from battery-raised hens, they may carry the risk of salmonella. Look for pasteurized eggs to avoid any concerns when using raw eggs.
2. Beat in vodka and vanilla extract.
3. Break up the raspberry jam or fruit butter with a fork. Use a spatula to fold the jam into the egg yolk and sugar mixture until everything is well blended.
4. Take a generous cup of whipping cream. Whip until it begins to thicken, then sprinkle with the remaining 2 tablespoons of sugar. Continue beating until soft peaks have formed.
5. Gently fold the whipped cream into the jam, sugar, and egg yolk mixture.
6. Spoon into a plastic-lined metal bowl. Put the bowl in the freezer until the mixture is well frozen, at least 4 to 6 hours.
7. Unmold the parfait onto a serving plate, remove the plastic, and let it soften in the refrigerator for 20 minutes before serving. Decorate with fresh raspberries.

170

PRESERVING
MEMORIES

Frozen Marmalade and Yogurt

INGREDIENTS:

1 C. marmalade, jam, or fruit butter

2 C. whole-milk yogurt

2 or 3 pieces of candied ginger for garnish (optional)

1. Stir the preserves with a fork
2. Combine them with the yogurt. Mix more or less well, depending on your preference.
3. Spoon the mixture into a plastic container and put it in the freezer overnight.
4. If desired, garnish with chopped candied ginger before serving.

Baked Goods

Preserves have two roles to play in tandem with baked goods: as an ingredient added to the batter before baking or incorporated into a filling or frosting afterward. And for that, you can even use them straight out of the jar. Runny jam or jelly that did not quite set can be used as a syrup or sauce for desserts from ice cream to plain cake or over fruit compote. If the jam or jelly did properly jell and firm up, dilute it with a little water or enhance it with a liqueur such as kirsch, Cointreau, or Grand Marnier. Here are a few other suggestions.

Bread Pudding with Marmalade I

Bread pudding is one of those nostalgic comfort foods. A good bread pudding is succulent and delectable; a poor one is a soggy mess.

INGREDIENTS:

6 slices day-old good quality white bakery bread

4 to 6 Tbs. butter

4 to 6 Tbs. orange marmalade

2/3 C. whole milk

1/4 C. heavy cream

3 large eggs

5 Tbs. sugar

1 oz. candied orange peel

1 Tbs. sugar

Grated zest of one orange

1. Preheat the oven to 350° Fahrenheit.

2. Lightly butter a baking dish, 9 inches in diameter if round, 7 inches by 9 inches if rectangular, and 2 inches deep in either case.

3. Butter all the bread on one side. Softened butter (room temperature) makes this easier. Don't skimp on quality; packaged white bread that can be squished into spitball pellets is useless. Leave the crusts on or cut them off, whichever you prefer.

4. Spread three slices of bread with orange marmalade. Sandwich them together with the other three slices of buttered bread.

5. Spread just a little butter on the top side of each butter-and-marmalade sandwich.

6. Cut the sandwiches into triangles.

7. Place the triangles in the baking dish, butter side up, somewhat overlapping and standing nearly upright.

8. Beat together the milk, heavy cream, eggs, and 5 tablespoons of sugar.

9. Pour this mixture gently over the triangles of bread, trying not to disarrange them any more than you can help. Let stand until the bread gets soggy.

10. Pulse/chop the candied orange peel and remaining tablespoon of sugar in a small food processor. Add the grated zest of 1 large orange and scatter this mixture over the top of the pudding.

11. Bake for 20 to 30 minutes until puffy and golden with a crunchy top. Serve warm.

Bread Pudding with Marmalade II

INGREDIENTS:

1 loaf stale white bakery bread (enough to make 4 C. cubed)

2 C. milk

¹/₂ C. sugar

3 eggs

1 tsp. vanilla extract

¹/₂ tsp. nutmeg and/or 1 tsp. cinnamon (optional)

¹/₄ C. raisins

1 C. marmalade, fruit butter, or jelly

3 Tbs. sugar

¹/₄ tsp. vanilla extract

Cream to pass (optional)

1. Preheat the oven to 325° Fahrenheit.
2. Butter a pudding bowl.
3. Cut the bread into cubes.
4. Separate the eggs.
5. Beat together the milk, ¹/₂ cup of sugar, and the egg yolks with 1 teaspoon of vanilla extract. If you like, add some grated nutmeg or cinnamon.
6. Toss the bread with the raisins and put it in the buttered pudding bowl.
7. Pour the milk mixture over the bread and let stand to get soggy.
8. Bake for 30 minutes, or until firm.
9. Cover the pudding with marmalade, fruit butter, or jelly broken up with a fork.
10. Make a meringue of the egg whites by beating them until stiff peaks form. Add the remaining 3 tablespoons of sugar and a few drops of vanilla extract to the whites.
11. Spread the meringue over the marmalade and put the bread pudding back in the oven until the meringue is lightly browned on the peaks.
12. Serve hot, with cream or not, as you prefer.

Elderberry Fritters

It's a toss-up: do you want to leave the clusters of elderberry flowers on the bush to mature into little berries for jelly making, will you use a couple of clusters to provide a wild-harvest flavor to a jelly, or do you want to make Elderberry Fritters for a delicious and uncommon treat for a special summertime brunch?

Special Instructions: You want to coat the elderberry flower clusters with as little batter as possible. And, naturally enough, the size of the flower cluster will influence how much batter it requires.

INGREDIENTS:

1 egg

1 Tbs. melted sweet butter

$^1/_8$ tsp. salt

$^1/_4$ C. water or milk

$^1/_2$ C. flour

1 elderberry flower cluster per person, with one or two extra for hearty appetites

Oil for frying

Elderberry jelly to pass (optional)

1. Separate the egg. Set the white aside in a clean, dry bowl.
2. Beat the egg yolk.
3. Add butter and salt and half the liquid.
4. Stir in the flour to make a smooth batter.
5. Gradually add the remaining liquid. The batter should have the consistency of cream and should coat a spoon.
6. Whip the egg white until stiff.
7. Gently fold it into the batter.
8. Quickly rinse the elderberry flower clusters in a bowl of water and shake off any excess.
9. Dip the clusters into the batter, one at a time, just to coat. Allow any extra batter to drain back into the bowl.
10. Deep fry the clusters in hot oil until golden brown. Drain the Elderberry Fritters on a brown paper bag and serve hot, perhaps with some Elderberry Jelly (page 135) on the side.

Stuffed French Toast

I love French toast, dipped in eggy batter, fried until brown-laced golden brown, and eaten with a dollop of jam. Sunday brunch at its best. This version kicks it up a notch, as Emeril would say.

INGREDIENTS:

8 thick slices day-old French bread or any good white bread

4 oz. softened cream cheese

$1/4$ C. orange marmalade

3 eggs

$3/4$ C. whole milk

$1/2$ tsp. vanilla extract

$1/4$ tsp. nutmeg

Orange marmalade butter (recipe below)

1. Cut a pocket into each slice of bread from the top, using a serrated knife.
2. In a small bowl, mix together the cream cheese and orange marmalade. It is important that this mixture not be too sloppy, so avoid using syrupy marmalades.
3. Fill the pocket in each slice with about a rounded tablespoon of the blended cream cheese and marmalade.
4. In a larger, shallow bowl, whisk together the eggs, milk, vanilla extract, and nutmeg.
5. Dip the stuffed bread into the batter, making sure that both sides are well moistened.
6. Brush a griddle or heavy frying pan with butter and fry the bread pockets, turning once so that both sides become golden brown.
7. Serve at once with Orange Marmalade Butter (below).

Orange Marmalade Butter

INGREDIENTS:

8 Tbs. softened sweet butter

2 Tbs. sugar

2 Tbs. orange marmalade

1 Tbs. Grand Marnier, Cointreau, or rum

Grated zest of one large orange

1. Beat together all ingredients.

Note: Since this keeps well if refrigerated in a tightly closed jar, you might want to consider doubling the recipe just to keep some on hand.

Croissants à l'Orange

This upmarket version of French toast uses croissants instead of bread and bakes them in the oven for a more relaxed undertaking for the cook.

Special Instructions: The croissants need to be prepared one day in advance so they can soak up all the good flavor in the refrigerator overnight.

INGREDIENTS FOR TWO CROISSANTS:

3 Tbs. orange marmalade

1 Tbs. orange juice

$1/4$ C. half-and-half

$1/8$ tsp. vanilla or almond extract

1 egg

2 croissants

1. Generously butter an attractive ovenproof casserole dish. For even more elegance, use individual serving dishes.

2. In one small bowl, mix together 3 tablespoons of orange marmalade and 1 table-spoon of orange juice for each pair of small croissants. Set aside.

3. In another small bowl, mix together $1/4$ cup of half-and-half, $1/8$ teaspoon of vanilla or almond extract, and 1 egg. Set aside.

4. Cut each croissant in half lengthwise. Spread 1 tablespoon of the marmalade mixture over the bottom of a croissant and place it in the buttered casserole dish. Repeat with the remaining croissants.
   Note: There should be some marmalade mixture remaining. Refrigerate it in a closed container.

5. Put the croissant tops back into place and gently pour the egg mixture over them.

6. Cover the casserole dish with plastic wrap and refrigerate it overnight.

7. In the morning, remove the plastic wrap and bake the croissants in a preheated 325° Fahrenheit oven for 15 or 20 minutes.
   Note: If you take the casserole dish out of the refrigerator about 45 minutes to an hour before baking, the croissants will require less time, about 10 minutes, in the oven.

8. Remove them from the oven and glaze with the leftover marmalade mixture. If it is too stiff to brush over the croissants, warm it gently in a small saucepan or briefly in a microwave oven.

Muffins and Scones

My daughter, Mira, loves to bake. She used to make all the bread for her family, and she turns out muffins with ease. Here's a recipe that she shared with me. She mentioned that "The muffins don't seem to last more than a day or two before getting hard, so you need to eat them all pretty quickly—we had two left over that had to be crumbled and fed to the birds."

Apple Butter Muffins

Special Instructions: If you would prefer Apple Butter Bread to Apple Butter Muffins, spoon the batter into two well-greased loaf pans, and bake at 325° Fahrenheit for one hour, or until done. Both the muffins and the bread should freeze well.

INGREDIENTS:

3 C. flour

1 tsp. salt

1 Tbs. cinnamon

$^1/_2$ tsp. baking powder

1 tsp. baking soda

2 eggs

1 C. oil

1 C. sugar

1 C. apple butter

1 C. raisins

1 tsp. vanilla extract

1 C. coarsely chopped walnuts (optional)

1. Preheat the oven to 375° Fahrenheit.
2. Sift together the flour, salt, cinnamon, baking powder, and baking soda. Set aside.
3. In a separate bowl, beat together the eggs, oil, and sugar.
4. Stir in apple butter, raisins, and vanilla extract.
5. Add the dry ingredients and mix well.
6. If you desire, stir in the chopped walnuts.
7. Spoon the batter into muffin tins lined with paper muffin cups and bake for 15 minutes, or until done.

Scones with Clotted Cream and Strawberry Jam

This is the quintessential treat for a "proper" English cream tea. The combination of a warm scone split in the middle, slathered with ruby red jam that is lumpy with strawberries, and slathered with clotted cream is positively over the top. Of course, it really should be consumed in the garden of a thatched cottage on a warm summer afternoon, with bees buzzing around the roses. Here are full directions for trying this at home.

Scones

INGREDIENTS:

4 C. flour

1 tsp. baking soda

2 tsp. cream of tartar

1 tsp. salt

6 Tbs. cold butter

1 egg

1 C. buttermilk

1. Preheat the oven to 425° Fahrenheit.
2. Sift together the flour, baking soda, cream of tartar, and salt. Sift again.
3. Using a fork, a pastry blender, or your fingers, cut in the butter until the mixture resembles cornmeal. You want small lumps rather than a uniform mass.
4. Beat the egg into the buttermilk.
5. Make a well in the center of the dry ingredients and pour in the buttermilk and egg mixture.
6. Stir until a uniform dough has formed.
7. Lightly flour your work surface, turn the dough out onto it, and knead it until smooth, for less than a minute.
8. Grease a baking sheet. Tear off pieces of dough and flatten them, just a little, into an approximately round shape with the fingers of your closed fist. Prick the rounds with a fork.
9. Bake the scones for 8 to 10 minutes, until they are a light golden brown on top.
10. Wrap them in a tea towel to keep them warm and soft, and serve promptly.

Clotted Cream

There's clotted cream and there's clotted cream. One comes from Cornwall, and the other is from Devonshire. If you intend to make your own, homogenized milk simply won't work. For the best results, you need about two gallons of raw, unpasteurized, nonhomogenized milk. Some small local milk producers may keep tuberculin-tested herds and sell raw milk. Real purists want high-fat milk from Jersey or Guernsey cows. And the yield is low. One pint of cream makes about a half cup of clotted cream, with the texture of soft butter.

Cornish Clotted Cream

Special Instructions: The milk will need to stand overnight before cooking, and for a full day after cooking, so give yourself plenty of time to prepare this recipe.

INGREDIENTS:

4 C. nonhomogenized, unpasteurized raw milk

1. Allow milk, fresh from the cow, to stand overnight in a wide, shallow, scrupulously clean metal pan so the cream can rise to the top.
2. Early in the morning, scald the milk by heating it slowly for about an hour. Do not boil. A thick, slightly yellowish, softly firm crust will form over the milk.
3. Take the pan off the heat. Carrying it carefully to avoid breaking the crust, put the pan in a cool place.
4. In early evening, 12 hours later, skim off the clotted cream.

Devonshire Clotted Cream

INGREDIENTS:

4 C. nonhomogenized, unpasturized raw milk

1. Allow the milk to stand overnight, as described above.
2. In the morning, skim the cream off the milk and put it into the top half of a broad, shallow double boiler.
3. Cook the cream slowly. It will thicken and develop a yellowish crust as it scalds. This is Devonshire Clotted Cream.

It is now 4:00 P.M., and you are ready to enjoy a cream tea. Take a warm scone and split it open. Dollop some clotted cream on each half. Don't be stingy, but don't overdo it. Add some strawberry preserves (and only strawberry preserves will do). Serve with hot, unsweetened tea. That's the Devonshire way. In Cornwall, they reverse the order of strawberry preserves and clotted cream, first buttering the warm scone, spreading some strawberry preserves on top, and then adding a large dollop of Cornish-style clotted cream. Yummy!

Filling and Frostings for Cakes and Cookies

Using preserves to "dress up" a plain cake is extremely simple. Slice a pound cake in half lengthwise. Spread it with jam, fruit butter, or jelly that has first been broken up with a fork. Replace the other half of cake. Dust the top with confectioners' sugar before serving. Or, after they are baked, cupcakes made with plain yellow batter can be dipped into stirred currant or raspberry jelly, then rolled in coconut.

Apricot Glaze

INGREDIENTS:

1 C. apricot jam

2 Tbs. Grand Marnier, rum, or other liqueur

1. Purée the apricot jam in a food processor until smooth.
2. Scrape the jam into a small saucepan.
3. Add Grand Marnier, rum, or liqueur of your choice.
4. Heat just to a boil.
5. Serve the glaze spooned over pound cake or ice cream, or brush it over a fruit tart.

Whipped Jam Filling

I get my eggs locally, from a friend who keeps pastured hens and feeds them organically. I don't, therefore, have any concerns about eating raw eggs. Commercially produced eggs from battery-raised hens are a different story. If that's all that is available to you, look for pasteurized eggs, but keep in mind that the whites won't whip as high.

INGREDIENTS:

1 C. jam or jelly

1 egg white

1. Place jam or jelly in a bowl and break it up with a fork.
2. Add the egg white and whip both together until the mixture is stiff enough to spread.

Marmalade Cream Cheese Frosting or Filling

This easy, uncooked frosting is a yummy choice for the Jam Cake described later in this chapter (page 184), or carrot cake, or any other rich, moist, flavorful cake. As well, Orange Marmalade, Apricot or Peach Jam may be used instead.

Special Instructions: If the frosting becomes too soft, refrigerate it briefly until it is just firm enough to spread. If you want to use this as a filling as well as a frosting for a layer cake, double the recipe. Also, if used as a filling, spread about 1/4 cup of marmalade thinned with 1 tablespoon of rum on the bottom cake layer, then cover it with filling.

INGREDIENTS:

1 lb. cream cheese, at room temperature

1 C. confectioners' sugar

Scant 1/2 C. orange marmalade

1 tsp. grated orange zest

3 Tbs. sweet butter at room temperature

1. Cream together cream cheese and confectioners' sugar.
2. Add orange marmalade, grated orange zest, and butter. Beat until smooth.
3. Spread over cake.

Apricot Marmalade Filling

Bound to become a favorite, this is an old-fashioned type of cake filling that is not only delicious, it is really easy to make.

Special Instructions: This filling can also be made by substituting poached pitted prunes for the apricots, giving a different, flavorful result.

INGREDIENTS:

1 C. dried apricots

1 C. water

1 slice lemon (optional)

1/3 C. orange marmalade

1 tsp. fresh lemon juice

1/3 C. pecans, chopped fine

1. Poach the dried apricots by placing them in a small saucepan with the water. If you like, add a slice of lemon. Simmer gently until the apricots are nearly soft. (This is a variable, as, when purchased, some dried apricots are still moist and pliable while others resemble shoe leather.)

2. Drain, reserving any liquid. Finely chop the apricots.

3. Mix the fruit with the orange marmalade, lemon juice, and pecans. If the filling is stiff, add a little apricot-soaking liquid, 1 teaspoon at a time. If there is any liquid left over, brush it on the cake before spreading on the filling.

Cakes

Quick Plain Cake

If you could see the spills and stains on the typewritten page that has this recipe, you could tell how often my mother made this cake.

INGREDIENTS:

1¹/₂ C. cake flour

2 tsp. baking powder

¹/₈ tsp. salt

¹/₂ C. softened butter

1 C. sugar

1 egg

1 tsp. vanilla extract

³/₄ C. milk

1 C. jam

Plain icing (page 182)

1. Preheat the oven to 350° Fahrenheit.

2. Butter and flour the sides of two square cake pans and line the bottom with wax paper. Lightly butter the wax paper. Set aside.

3. Sift the flour with the baking powder and salt. Set aside.

4. Beat the butter with the sugar.

5. When well blended, beat in the egg.

6. Add the vanilla extract to the milk.

7. Add the flour mixture and milk mixture alternately to the butter, sugar, and egg mixture, beginning and ending with the dry ingredients.

8. Bake in two layers for 30 minutes, or until done.

9. Cool in the pan for 10 minutes, then turn out onto a cake rack. Peel away the wax paper.

10. When cool, cover one layer with jam; top it with the other layer.

11. Frost the cake with plain icing.

Plain Icing

INGREDIENTS:

1 C. confectioners' sugar

2 Tbs. hot water, milk, or cream

$1/4$ tsp. vanilla extract, fresh lemon juice, or rum

1.   Mix all the ingredients together.

My Mother's Jelly Roll

This is so quick and easy to make. It was another of Katzy's favorites for a last-minute dessert or something to serve if folks were stopping by.

Special Instructions: If the business of rolling up the jelly roll seems too much trouble, cut the warm cake along its width into three even pieces and make a little layer cake with jelly or jam between the layers. Since few kitchens (including mine) are equipped with a cake breaker (which looks like a comb made of long, thin wires), I use two forks held back to back to cut slices of either the rolled-up or layered versions.

INGREDIENTS:

5 eggs, at room temperature

1 C. sugar

Grated rind of 1 lemon

2 Tbs. fresh lemon juice

1 C. flour

1 C. jelly

Confectioners' sugar

1.   Preheat the oven to 375° Fahrenheit.
2.   Line a 10-inch by 15-inch jelly roll pan with wax paper.
3.   Separate the eggs.
4.   Beat the yolks, then slowly add the sugar, beating all the while.
5.   Add the grated lemon rind and lemon juice. Beat until the mixture is thick and lemon colored.
6.   In a clean bowl and with clean beaters, beat the egg whites until stiff peaks are formed. Set aside.
7.   Sift, then measure the flour.
8.   Fold half the flour and half the stiffly beaten egg whites into the egg yolk, sugar, and lemon mixture, alternating the two ingredients.
9.   Gradually fold in the remaining flour and beaten egg whites.
10. Pour the batter into the jelly roll pan, not more than $1/4$ inch deep.

11. Bake for 12 to 15 minutes. The cake should be golden, but not brown, when it is done.

12. Turn out cake upside down onto a damp dish towel. Peel off the wax paper.

13. Trim off any crusty edges.

14. Roll the cake while it is still warm, making as tight a roll as you can. Drape the damp towel over the rolled-up cake and let it cool for 5 or 10 minutes.

15. Beat the jelly with a fork. Carefully unroll the cake, then spread the jelly over the unrolled cake. Leave about a $^1/_2$-inch strip across the width of the cake on one end uncovered.

16. Roll the cake up again, rolling toward the uncovered end, and place it on a platter with the seam down.

17. Dust the top with confectioners' sugar just before serving.

Joyce Carleston's Jelly Roll

This is a recipe from Joyce's family cookbook, recipes that have been copied down, passed around, and shared with relatives and friends.

INGREDIENTS:

4 eggs

1 tsp. baking powder

$^1/_4$ tsp. salt

1 tsp. vanilla extract

1 C. sugar

1 C. cake flour

1 C. jelly

1. Preheat the oven to 400° Fahrenheit.

2. Line a $15^1/_2$-inch by $10^1/_2$-inch by 1-inch jelly roll pan with wax paper.

3. Break the eggs into the bowl of a mixer.

4. Add the baking powder, salt, and vanilla extract. Beat on high speed for 10 minutes.

5. Add the sugar and beat for 1 minute.

6. Add the flour and mix.

7. Pour the batter into the prepared pan and bake for 13 minutes.

8. Remove the cake from the pan and turn it out onto a cloth. Roll it up and let it sit until almost cool.

9. Unroll the cake and spread it with your favorite jelly or filling, then roll it up again.

Jam Cake

This moist, fruity, spicy cake would have excellent keeping qualities, that is, if it didn't get eaten up so fast.

Special Instructions: Blackberry jam and fig jam are both good in this cake, and can even be used in combination. A combination of apple butter and peach jam is also a tasty choice.

INGREDIENTS:
1 C. butter
$^1/_2$ C. brown sugar
$^1/_2$ C. white sugar
5 large eggs
3 C. cake flour
1 tsp. baking soda
2 tsp. cinnamon
1 tsp. nutmeg
$^1/_2$ tsp. allspice
$^1/_2$ tsp. cloves
1 tsp. vanilla extract
1 C. buttermilk
3 C. preserves
Confectioners' sugar

1. Preheat the oven to 300° Fahrenheit.
2. Butter and flour a Bundt pan and set it aside.
   Note: If you don't have a Bundt pan, use a 10-inch tube pan. If you don't have a tube pan, use a large loaf pan.
3. Cream the butter with the brown and white sugar.
4. Add the eggs, one at a time.
5. Sift the flour, then measure 3 cups.
6. Resift the flour with the baking soda, cinnamon, nutmeg, allspice, and cloves.
7. Add the vanilla extract to the buttermilk.
8. Add the flour mixture and buttermilk alternately, in several additions, to the creamed butter, sugar, and eggs, beginning and ending with the dry ingredients.
9. Stir the preserves with a fork.
10. Gently lifting and folding, quickly and carefully incorporate the jam into the batter.
11. Pour the batter into the prepared Bundt pan and bake at 300° Fahrenheit for 15 minutes. Then raise the temperature to 350° Fahrenheit and bake the cake for an additional 45 minutes. Use a cake tester or toothpick to be sure that the cake is baked all the way through.
12. Cool the cake in the pan on a wire rack for 15 minutes before removing it from the pan.
13. Dust with confectioners' sugar while the cake is still warm.

Jam Roly Poly

Roly Poly was originally a substantial dessert made with lard as the shortening, wrapped and tied in a cloth, and then steamed or boiled. Times and tastes change, and today a lighter version is more appreciated. This recipe has more the texture of a biscuit, and it is baked rather than boiled. The batter also makes a good topping for a peach cobbler—just sort of plop it on top of the fruit by tablespoons.

INGREDIENTS:

$1^1/_4$ C. flour

3 Tbs. sugar

1 Tbs. baking powder

1 tsp. baking soda

$^1/_2$ tsp. salt

3 Tbs. cold sweet butter

1 large egg

$^2/_3$ C. buttermilk

1 tsp. vanilla extract

$^1/_2$ to $^3/_4$ C. raspberry, blackberry, strawberry, or other jam

1 Tbs. sugar

2 to 3 Tbs. milk

Cinnamon

1. Preheat the oven to 350° Fahrenheit.
2. Line a baking sheet with parchment paper. Set aside.
3. Combine the flour, sugar, baking powder, baking soda, and salt in a food processor fitted with a pastry blade and pulse it to combine the ingredients thoroughly.
4. Cut the butter into several pieces, add it to the food processor, and pulse until the mixture is crumbly.
5. In a separate bowl, combine the egg, buttermilk, and vanilla extract. Beat until smooth.
6. Add the buttermilk mixture to the mixture in the food processor and pulse until everything is just moist and combined. Overbeating ruins biscuit dough.
7. Lay a piece of wax paper on your work surface and flour it lightly. Flour your hands, and gently pat out dough into a 9-inch by 6-inch rectangle that is about a $^1/_4$ inch thick.
8. Beat the jam to make it more spreadable.
9. Leaving a $^1/_2$-inch border all the way around the edge of the dough, spread on the jam.
10. Roll the Roly Poly up from the long side. Place it on the prepared baking sheet with the seam on the bottom.
11. Dissolve sugar in the milk, then brush it over the top of the Roly Poly.
12. Dust with cinnamon.
13. Bake for 30 to 35 minutes, or until golden brown and baked through.
14. Place the baking sheet on a wire rack and allow the Roly Poly to cool before slicing. Serve warm or at room temperature.

Bohemian Kolachen

Kuchen dough is a sweet yeast dough, malleable and willing to be shaped into a coffee cake, little turnovers, or embellished into these Bohemian kolachen.

Special Instructions: The apricot marmalade filling or prune marmalade fillings on pages 180–181 are also delicious in this kolachen.

INGREDIENTS:

1 C. milk

$^1/_2$ cake compressed yeast

1 tsp. sugar

2 Tbs. butter

$^3/_8$ C. sugar

$^1/_2$ tsp. salt

$^1/_8$ tsp. mace

$^1/_8$ tsp. nutmeg

$^1/_4$ tsp. cinnamon

1 egg yolk

3 C. flour

1 Tbs. marmalade, peach jam, or other preserve

3 Tbs. milk

1 Tbs. sugar

1. Scald the milk and let it cool until lukewarm.
2. Crumble the compressed yeast into a cup, adding $^1/_2$ cup of tepid milk and 1 teaspoon of sugar. Let this mixture sit so the yeast can "proof" (activate).
3. Add the butter to the remaining milk, with $^3/_8$ cup of sugar, the salt, mace, nutmeg, and cinnamon. Stir well.
4. When the sugar and spice mixture is at room temperature, add the beaten yolk of 1 egg and blend well.
5. Stir in the yeast, now bubbling and active, and 2 cups of flour.
6. Start kneading, adding more flour, up to 1 cup more.
7. Knead the dough until smooth and springy.
8. Cover with a damp towel and let rise until double in bulk and very light.
9. Punch down the dough and pat or roll it out to about $^1/_2$ inch thick.
10. Thoroughly butter a shallow baking pan.
11. Cut the dough into 3-inch rounds, place them in the buttered baking pan, and flatten the center to create a raised ring.
    Note: Dip your fingers in some flour so the dough does not stick to them.
12. Place the marmalade, peach jam, or other preserve in the center of the dough.
13. Let it rise a second time.

14. Lightly warm the 3 tablespoons of milk and brush the kolachen with it. Sprinkle with sugar.
15. Bake at 375° Fahrenheit for 15 to 20 minutes, or until golden brown.

Apricot Coffee Ring

This recipe is one my sister has been making ever since she first saw it in the *Houston Chronicle* sometime in the 1960s. Of course, like cooks everywhere, she's changed a little thing here and a bit there. Haya told me that it is a lot of work, but worth it. "It is," she says, "a good project on a wintry day when one is home doing a variety of things and can pop into the kitchen for the various stages of preparation." Then she adds with a grin, "Of course, one might just recline on the sofa, reading a novel and noshing on cheese and crackers or chocolate bonbons, rising only when the dough itself has risen." This recipe makes two rings, and Haya says they freeze well.

INGREDIENTS:

1 pkg. dry yeast

1 tsp. sugar

1 pinch powdered ginger

$2/3$ C. tepid water

$2/3$ C. milk

4 Tbs. shortening, margarine, or butter

6 Tbs. sugar

1 tsp. salt

$4 2/3$ C. flour

2 eggs

1 C. apricot jam, plum jam, marmalade, peach jam, raspberry jam, or blackberry jam

2 tsp. grated orange rind

2 tsp. orange juice

1 egg yolk

1 Tbs. cold water

1. Mash the yeast with the sugar and powdered ginger.
2. Add the yeast mixture to the tepid water. Set aside to "proof" (activate).
3. Scald the milk.
4. Add the shortening, margarine, or butter, together with 6 tablespoons of sugar, to the milk.
5. Allow this mixture to cool to lukewarm.
6. Mix the salt with the flour.
7. Add half of the flour to the milk, shortening, and sugar mixture and beat it well with a wooden spoon.

8. Beat the eggs and add them to the batter, together with the proofed yeast. Beat well.

9. Add the rest of the flour, beating well to make a soft dough.

10. Turn the dough onto a lightly floured surface, cover it with a damp cotton dish towel, and let it rest for 10 minutes.

11. Turn the dough into a large greased bowl and let it rise for 2 hours, or until doubled and light.

12. Punch down and divide the dough into 6 equal pieces.

13. Roll each piece into a thin rectangle, about 20 inches by 5 inches.

14. Mix together the jam, grated orange rind, and orange juice.

15. Spread $1/6$ of the jam and orange mixture onto each rectangle.

16. Roll each rectangle like a jelly roll, from the long side, pinching the ends closed.

17. On a greased cookie sheet, braid three strands and fasten them into a ring.

18. Repeat with the additional three strands.

19. Brush the top of the coffee rings with egg yolk mixed with cold water.
    Note: Try to avoid any drips down the side onto the cookie sheet.

20. Cover them with a damp cloth and let them rise for about an hour, or until doubled in size.

21. Bake in a 375° Fahrenheit oven for about 30 minutes, or until golden brown.

Linzer Torte

This is the kind of elegant European pastry my father and I would bring to Adolph and Carola when we went to visit. I don't remember ever bringing one home for our family to enjoy. Perhaps it was a "company" thing, something done as a token of appreciation for being invited over. This is really not that difficult to make, and even if it doesn't come out looking as pretty as a picture, well, I never much wanted to eat a picture.

INGREDIENTS:

1 C. sweet butter

1 C. sugar

3 eggs, separated

1 Tbs. brandy or framboise

Grated zest and juice of 1 lemon

1 C. finely grated almonds

2 C. flour

1 tsp. baking powder

1 C. raspberry jam

1. Preheat oven to 350°Fahrenheit.
2. Cream together the butter and sugar.
3. Add the egg yolks, brandy or framboise, and the grated zest and juice of the lemon. Beat this mixture until thick and lemon colored.
4. Add the finely grated almonds.
5. Sift the flour twice. Measure 2 cups and sift it again with the baking powder.
6. Add the flour mixture to the egg and almond mixture.
7. Beat the egg whites until stiff. Incorporate half of them into the dough, then fold in the remaining half in 3 portions.
8. Use about $2/3$ of the dough to line a springform pan. The dough should be somewhat thicker on the bottom than the sides.
9. Fill the torte with raspberry jam.
10. Roll out the remaining dough and cut it into $1/2$-inch strips. Make a crisscross lattice over the top of the torte.
11. Bake for 55 to 60 minutes, or until light golden brown.

Cookies

Aunt Frumeh's Cookie Cake

My sister, Haya, recommends these cookies, mentioning that the recipe comes from a time when there were food shortages and strict rationing in Israel in the early 1950s. She says that for such simple ingredients, these cookies are surprisingly tasty. When Haya makes the cookies today, she often uses up the last bits from several jars of preserves, spreading them across the top of the dough in horizontal stripes. That way she gets several different flavors of cookies in one batch.

INGREDIENTS:

3 C. plus 3 Tbs. flour

3 tsp. baking powder

1/2 C. sweet butter or margarine

5 Tbs. sugar

1 egg

1 tsp. vanilla extract

Grated rind from 1 lemon or 1 orange

1/4 C. milk, fruit juice, or water

1 C. jam

1. Preheat the oven to 350° Fahrenheit.
2. Sift together the flour and baking powder. Set aside.
3. Cream the butter or margarine with the sugar.
4. Beat egg, vanilla extract, and grated lemon or orange rind into the butter mixture.
5. Add the flour and baking soda alternately with milk, fruit juice, or water, beginning and ending with the dry ingredients. This makes a rather stiff dough.
6. Press half the dough into a rectangular 9- by 12-inch pan.
7. Spread the top with jam.
8. Grate the remaining batter over the top of the cake, using the coarsest side of a grater.
9. Bake for 20 to 25 minutes, or until golden.
10. Cool and cut into squares.

Filled Cookies

This is your basic type of filled cookie. But just about any sort of plain cookie rich with butter and eggs is okay (though I would avoid chocolate, gingerbread, or anything emphatic in its flavor). Jack Lenzo remembers almond cookies sort of glued together with jam. Meringue-type kisses can be paired up, too, and sugar cookies are another traditional kind of jam- or preserved-filled cookie.

INGREDIENTS:

3 C. flour

2 tsp. baking powder

$^1/_2$ tsp. salt

$^3/_4$ C. sweet butter at room temperature

1 C. sugar

2 large eggs

$^1/_4$ C. milk

1 tsp. vanilla extract

1 C. apricot jam or other thick preserves

1. Preheat the oven to 375° Fahrenheit.
2. Sift the flour. Measure 3 cups.
3. Sift the baking powder and salt into the flour.
4. Cream the butter with the sugar.
5. Beat the eggs with the milk and vanilla extract.
6. Add the egg mixture to the creamed butter and sugar mixture.
7. Gradually add the dry ingredients in 4 portions, blending thoroughly.
8. Wrap the dough in plastic wrap and refrigerate for 1 hour.
9. Working with a small portion of the dough at a time, roll it out onto a lightly floured board. Leave the dough that is not being worked in the refrigerator.
10. Cut half the cookies into 3-inch rounds and the rest with a donut cutter.
11. Place 1 teaspoon of thick preserves, such as apricot jam, in the center of one round cookie, then top the round cookie with one that has a center cutout. Seal the edges by pressing them down with the tines of a fork.
12. Place the cookies on a lightly buttered cookie sheet and bake them for 15 minutes, or until light golden in color.
13. Remove to a rack to cool.

Thumbprint Cookies

This is an easy cookie to make, and fun for children, who help in the shaping (and eating).

INGREDIENTS:

²/₃ C. butter

¹/₃ C. sugar

1 tsp. vanilla extract

2 eggs

1¹/₂ C. flour

¹/₄ tsp. salt

³/₄ C. walnuts

1 C. apricot, plum, blackberry, raspberry, or strawberry jam

1. Cream together the butter and sugar, beating until light.
2. Add the vanilla extract.
3. Separate the eggs. Reserve the whites in a clean bowl. Add both egg yolks to the butter and sugar mixture and mix well.
4. Combine the flour and salt.
5. Mix thoroughly. Wrap the dough in plastic wrap and refrigerate it for at least one hour.
6. Preheat the oven to 350° Fahrenheit.
7. Beat the egg whites very slightly and place them in a shallow bowl. Chop the walnuts fine and place them in a second shallow bowl.
8. Shape the dough into 1-inch balls. Roll them lightly in beaten egg white, then in the finely chopped walnuts. Place the balls about an inch apart on an ungreased cookie sheet.
9. Use your thumb to make an indentation in the center of each cookie. Fill it with a dollop of apricot, plum, blackberry, raspberry, or strawberry jam, or any other thick preserve. Or, use the tip of a spoon to make an X-shaped indentation, teasing the points apart to hold a dab of jelly or jam.
10. Bake for 15 to 17 minutes, or until lightly golden brown. Cool on a wire rack.

Hamantaschen

My brother, Ben, remembers the hamantaschen from New York City bakeries. Those were probably made without cream cheese in the dough. However this recipe, which my friend Selma Miriam gave me, is so simple to make and easy to work with that it is my preference. Traditionally served at Purim (a Jewish holiday that commemorates the deliverance of the Persian Jews from the plot of the evil Haman to exterminate them, as recorded in the Book of Esther), hamantaschen are flattish, triangular pastries symbolizing the tricornered hat that Haman wore. So delicious that they're eaten all year round, they frequently have a poppy seed filling, though a jamlike filling made from prunes or apricot preserves is also popular. I also like raspberry jam. Whatever kind of preserve you decide to use, just make sure it is thick rather than runny.

Special Instructions: These cookies go stale within a few days, so only bake what will be eaten in about three days. Bear in mind that you can roll out just a portion of the dough, fill, shape, and bake it. Leave the rest of the dough, tightly wrapped in plastic wrap, in the refrigerator, for up to three days.

INGREDIENTS:

1/4 C. unsalted sweet butter, at room temperature

1/2 C. full-fat cream cheese, at room temperature

1/2 tsp. vanilla extract

Grated zest of 1 orange

3/4 C. sugar

1 large egg

2 C. flour

1 tsp. baking powder

1 C. apricot or raspberry jam

1. Cream together the butter and cream cheese.
2. Add the vanilla extract and the grated orange zest.
3. Slowly add the sugar, beating all the while.
4. Beat in the egg.
5. Add the flour and baking powder. Mix well, but do not overbeat.
6. Form the dough into a thick disc. Wrap it in plastic wrap and refrigerate for a minimum of 30 minutes, until it firms up.
7. Preheat the oven to 350° Fahrenheit. Prepare two cookie sheets by lightly buttering them.
8. Lightly flour your rolling pin and work surface. Roll the chilled dough until it is rather thin, just about 1/8 inch. Cut the dough into 3-inch-diameter circles. *Note: If you don't have the right size cookie cutter, just use the tip of a paring knife and a glass with the right diameter as a template.*
9. Brush the edge of each circle of dough with plain water.
10. Pile 2 teaspoons of apricot or raspberry jam in the middle of each round. The prune and marmalade filling described earlier is also good.
11. Imagine a triangle, then fold up three pieces of dough outside it. Pinch the corners together. The filling should show in the middle.
12. If you are preparing all of the dough, keep the second baking sheet with the shaped cookies in the refrigerator while the first one bakes.
13. Bake for 20 to 25 minutes, until the hamantaschen are pale gold but not browned. Cool them on a wire rack.

Rugelach

Here's another cookie that uses a cream cheese dough that is cut into triangles, spread with a filling, then rolled up.

INGREDIENTS:

1 C. sweet butter, at room temperature

$^{1}/_{2}$ lb. cream cheese, at room temperature

$^{1}/_{4}$ C. sugar

1 tsp. vanilla extract

2 C. flour

$^{1}/_{2}$ C. apricot jam

Almond/strawberry jam or walnut/currant filling (see recipes on page 195)

Topping (see recipe on page 195)

1. Cream together the butter and cream cheese.
2. Add the sugar and vanilla extract. Mix well.
3. Sift the flour, then measure 2 cups. Add it to the batter and mix only until the flour is lightly incorporated.
4. Gather the dough into a ball, cover it with plastic wrap, and refrigerate for 2 hours or overnight.
5. Prepare a filling and the topping from the recipes below.
6. Take the dough out of the refrigerator and divide it into 4 pieces. Rewrap 3 of them and return them to the refrigerator.
7. Lightly dust your work surface and rolling pin with flour. Roll the dough into a 9-inch-diameter circle about $^{1}/_{8}$ inch thick.
8. Cut it into 12 triangular pieces, pizza style. Without separating them, spread the triangles with just a little of the apricot jam, about $^{1}/_{2}$ teaspoon per slice. Then top each triangle with the almond/strawberry jam or walnut/currant filling. Make sure the filling is spread evenly and pressed lightly into the dough.
9. Starting at the wide end, roll the triangle up and place it on a cookie sheet lined with parchment paper, pointed down and $1^{1}/_{2}$ inches away from the next cookie. Gently bend it into a crescent shape.
10. Refrigerate the shaped cookies for about half an hour to firm them up again.
11. When you are ready to bake the cookies, preheat the oven to 350° Fahrenheit. Brush the rugelach lightly with just a little of the topping.
12. Bake for 18 to 20 minutes, or until light golden brown.
13. Cool on a wire rack.

Almond/Strawberry Jam Filling

INGREDIENTS:

1 C. strawberry preserves

1 C. finely chopped almonds

1.   Combine all ingredients.

Walnut/Currant Filling

INGREDIENTS:

6 Tbs. sugar

$^1/_4$ C. firmly packed light brown sugar

$^1/_2$ tsp. cinnamon

$^3/_4$ C. dried currants

1 C. coarsely chopped walnuts

1.   Combine all ingredients.

Topping

INGREDIENTS:

1 tsp. cinnamon

2 Tbs. sugar

$^1/_4$ C. milk

1.   Combine all ingredients.

Sauces

Just as preserves thinned with a liqueur can be used as a simple sauce for cakes, they can also add a delicious burst of flavor and savor to meat. Consider barbecue or grilling. Often enough, grilled meat will be started off with a marinade or a dry rub. These require some advance planning. A glaze is a quick, last-minute way to add flavor and appeal. Choose the jam, jelly, marmalade, or preserve of choice; orange marmalade, apricot jam, and currant jelly are just a few options. They need to be thinned out to make them easier to brush on the meat. What you want to do is create a tangy blend of sour and salty with the sweet. Soy sauce is one option, lemon or lime juice another, or liquor, such as rum, vodka, or bourbon, a third. A spoonful of mustard, some black pepper, a scraping of fresh ginger, or some fresh or dried chili pepper to taste, and you're on the way to creating the specialty of the house.

A glaze goes great with all kinds of poultry, from chicken to duck or goose, and it also complements rich meat such as pork, from chops and roasts to spareribs and ham. Just remember that the sugar in the preserves will readily blacken and burn, so when cooking over the coals, brush the glaze on at the finish, 15 minutes or so before the meat is done. Oven roasting is a different matter.

Basic Barbecue Sauce

INGREDIENTS:

$^1/_2$ C. orange marmalade, peach jam, plum butter, or other preserve

$^1/_2$ C. ketchup

$^1/_4$ C. soy sauce

1. In a small bowl, stir the preserves with a fork.
2. Add the ketchup and soy sauce and mix well.

Basic Orange Marmalade Glaze

INGREDIENTS:

$^1/_4$ C. orange marmalade

2 Tbs. butter

1 Tbs. Worcestershire sauce

1. Combine all the ingredients in a microwave-safe container.
2. Zap for about 1 minute, until hot but not boiling.
3. To use: Brush half the glaze on a roasting chicken as it goes into the oven and the rest about halfway through the roasting period. If used with duck, first prick the skin over the breasts and thighs with the tip of a sharp knife. Pour a kettle of boiling water over the duck to loosen up the fat. Place the duck in a roasting pan. Then brush with glaze as the duck goes into the oven. Brush with the rest of the glaze halfway through the roasting period.

Apricot or Orange Glaze for Ham

Each year we buy half a pig from our friends Jack and Cheryl Gaskill of Blue Jingler Farm, from whom we also buy eggs laid by their pastured chickens. These hams need to be simmered in a huge pot of water for a couple hours before they go into the oven. If you are starting with an oven-ready ham, skip ahead to step 4.

INGREDIENTS:

Bone-in ham, fresh or fully cooked

Whole cloves

1 C. apricot jam or orange marmalade

$^1/_3$ C. dry mustard

1 C. brown sugar

1. Simmer the fresh bone-in ham until it's ready for the oven.
2. Remove the skin and most of fat from the ham.
3. Score the remaining fat into a diamond pattern with a sharp knife. Insert one whole clove into each diamond.
4. Thoroughly mix the apricot jam or orange marmalade with the dry mustard. Spread this mixture over the whole surface of the ham. Pat brown sugar over the jam and mustard layer.
5. Bake in a 325° Fahrenheit oven until done, about 15 to 18 minutes per pound.

Variation: Substitute Dijon mustard for dry mustard, combine with the apricot jam, $^1/_2$ C. brown sugar, and $^1/_4$ tsp. cloves, and spread over the ham.

Tangy Marmalade Marinade

INGREDIENTS:

$^1/_2$ C. orange marmalade

$^1/_2$ C. orange juice

$^1/_2$ C. ketchup

$^1/_2$ C. Worcestershire sauce

1. Stir the orange marmalade with a fork in a small bowl.
2. Add the orange juice, ketchup, and Worcestershire sauce. Stir well.
3. Use to marinate pork or poultry.

Variation 1: Use pineapple juice in place of the orange juice and soy sauce in place of the Worcestershire sauce.

Variation 2: Substitute $^1/_4$ cup fresh lemon juice for orange juice.

Tangy Marmalade Sauce with a Bite

Not all marinades are sloshable. Some are thicker and more gloppy. Thicker ones need to be patted onto the meat, which should be given a longer marinating period—from overnight to 24 hours, depending on how thoroughly you want the flavors to penetrate. The meat should be turned several times for even distribution of marinade and flavor. This not only makes an interesting marinade, it is great as a dipping sauce as well.

Special Instructions: If you grate the horseradish in a small food processor, turn your face away when you take the lid off. The pungent root will bring tears to your eyes and clear your sinuses. If you buy prepared horseradish, splurge on a fresh jar—horseradish ages and loses its bite when kept for a while, even in the refrigerator.

INGREDIENTS:

1^1/$_2$ C. orange marmalade

5 Tbs. coarse brown mustard

5 Tbs. finely grated horseradish

1. Break up the orange marmalade with a fork in a bowl.
2. Add the remaining ingredients.
3. Pat evenly all over meat and refrigerate overnight or up to 24 hours, turning periodically.

Herbed Orange Marmalade Sauce

This pleasant, easy sauce is a simple way to dress up pan-roasted chicken. It's fine with skinless, boneless breasts, even better with skin-on thighs. You can use it for grilled chicken, too. When I buy duck, I usually bone-out the breasts, leaving the skin on, and pan cook in a cast-iron frying pan. This may not be duck bigarade, but it's not bad.

INGREDIENTS:

$^{1}/_{4}$ C. orange marmalade

$^{1}/_{2}$ C. orange juice

$^{1}/_{4}$ C. coarse brown mustard

$^{1}/_{2}$ tsp. fresh rosemary leaves

1 Tbs. olive oil

4 to 6 chicken breasts or thighs or duck breasts

1. In a pint measuring cup, combine the orange marmalade, orange juice, and coarse brown mustard.

2. Stir well and add the snipped fresh rosemary leaves.

3. Pour the olive oil into a heavy frying pan over moderately high heat.

4. Brown the chicken or duck breasts for about 1$^{1}/_{2}$ minutes on each side. Set aside.

5. Pour the marmalade and juice mixture into the skillet in which the chicken or duck breasts were sautéed. Bring it to a simmer over moderate heat, stirring and scraping to incorporate the brown crispy bits at the bottom of the skillet. Cook until the sauce has thickened slightly.

6. Return the chicken or duck to the pan and simmer, covered, for about 5 minutes.

7. Remove the lid and baste the chicken or duck with the sauce. When you baste the poultry, also check to make sure the sauce doesn't burn or caramelize.

8. Cover, cook for another 3 minutes, and baste again.

9. Repeat, then check to see if the juices run clear when the chicken or duck is pierced with a sharp knife, indicating it is done.

Marmalade Glaze for Poultry or Pork

Special Instructions: This makes a delicious glaze for boneless pork tenderloin cutlets, too.

INGREDIENTS:

$1/4$ tsp. dried mustard powder or $1/2$ Tbs. Dijon mustard

$1/2$ teaspoon cold water

$1/4$ C. orange marmalade

1 tsp. fresh lemon juice

$1/4$ tsp. Worcestershire sauce

1 Tbs. olive oil

2 boneless chicken breasts or thighs

$1/4$ C. white wine

1 finely minced garlic clove

1. Combine the dried mustard powder or Dijon mustard with the water, mixing until smooth. Set aside.
2. In a small bowl, stir the orange marmalade with a fork to break it up.
3. Add the lemon juice, Worcestershire sauce, and the previously prepared mustard.
4. Pour the olive oil into a heavy frying pan over moderately high heat. Brown the boneless chicken breasts or chicken thighs for about $1^1/2$ minutes on each side. Set aside.
5. Add the white wine to the frying pan. Bring to a slow boil while scraping up any brown crispy bits.
6. Blend in the marmalade mixture
7. Return the chicken to the frying pan, together with the garlic.
8. Cover and simmer for about 5 minutes.
9. Remove the lid and baste the chicken with the sauce.
10. Cover and cook for another 3 minutes.
11. Remove the lid and baste again.
12. Repeat, and check to see if the juices run clear when the chicken is pierced with a sharp knife, indicating it is done.

Grape Jelly Sauce

This works with elderberry jelly or blackberry jam, too. It is especially nice with some of the savory jellies described in Chapter Seven, such as Grape-Elderberry Jelly with Thyme and Juniper (page 87) or Grape Jelly with Thyme and Balsamic Vinegar (page 86).

INGREDIENTS:

6 medallions venison or boned duck breast

1/2 C. chicken stock

Freshly ground pepper to taste

3 Tbs. grape jelly

1 Tbs. sour cream or whole milk yogurt

1. After sautéing the medallions of venison or boned duck breast, set them aside and keep them warm.
2. Add a little stock to the pan and turn up the heat, stirring to scrape up the scrumptious brown bits.
3. Add freshly ground pepper, to taste, and jelly, stirring all the while.
4. When the sauce begins to reduce and get syrupy, add the sour cream or whole milk yogurt to enrich the sauce.
5. Ladle a tablespoon's worth over each medallion and pass any extra around in a heated sauceboat.

Swedish Lingonberry Sauce

INGREDIENTS:

1/2 C. lingonberry jam

1 Tbs. preserved ginger in syrup, finely grated

1. Mix together all the ingredients. Serve with pan-fried Baltic herring and mashed potatoes or little Swedish meatballs and mashed potatoes.

Of course, if you like, you can use a more involved recipe.

Sauce Marchand de Vin

INGREDIENTS:

4 venison chops

2 Tbs. butter

$^1/_2$ C. sliced scallions (both green and white portion)

1 C. red wine (Beaujolais works well)

$^1/_2$ C. grape jelly

$^1/_4$ tsp. Worcestershire sauce

Salt to taste

4 to 5 Tbs. butter

Freshly chopped parsley

1. Sauté the venison chops. Set them aside and keep them warm.
2. Melt 2 tablespoons of butter in the same skillet in which the venison chops were sautéed.
3. Add the sliced scallions. Cook for a few minutes, stirring frequently, until tender.
4. Stir in the red wine. Bring it to a boil and reduce to $^1/_2$ cup.
5. Stir in the grape jelly until incorporated.
6. Add the Worcestershire sauce and salt to taste. Remove the pan from the heat.
7. Stir in 4 or 5 tablespoons of butter, 1 tablespoon at a time, until the sauce is slightly thickened.
8. Sprinkle with fresh chopped parsley.
9. Pour a tablespoon or two of the sauce over each chop, passing the remainder around in a heated sauceboat.

Cumberland Sauce I

Currant jelly is popular in English cookery as an accompaniment for venison. Just spooning it out of a jar is one thing; using red currant jelly as an ingredient in a sauce is something else again, an improvement that's an order of magnitude better.

Special Instructions: This should have the texture of a thick cream and is served warm. Use as a sauce for duck, goose, ham, or spareribs (and remember to use it to baste the spareribs while cooking them, too).

INGREDIENTS:

1 C. red currant jelly

$^1/_2$ C. orange juice

$^1/_4$ C. fresh lemon juice

2 tsp. cornstarch

$^1/_2$ C. port wine

1 Tbs. grated orange zest

2 Tbs. Cointreau or other orange-flavored liqueur

1. Combine the red currant jelly with the orange juice and $^1/_4$ cup of lemon juice in a saucepan.
2. Bring the mixture to a boil, then turn down the heat to a simmer.
3. Blend the cornstarch with $^1/_4$ cup of port wine, whisking until smooth. Add to the jelly mixture, stirring constantly.
4. Continue heating the sauce at a brisk simmer, stirring constantly.
5. When the mixture begins to thicken, add another $^1/_4$ cup of port and the grated orange zest.
6. Just before serving, stir in the Cointreau or other orange-flavored liqueur.

Cumberland Sauce II

Special Instructions: This sauce is quite thin, and is served at room temperature, or even cold. Use with cold venison.

INGREDIENTS:
1 shallot
1 Tbs. orange peel
1 Tbs. lemon peel
1 C. red currant jelly
1 tsp. Dijon mustard
1 C. port
Juice of 1 orange
Juice of 1 lemon

1. Chop the shallot. Snip the orange and lemon peel into fine strips.
2. Blanch the shallot and citrus peel by dropping them briefly into boiling water, then cold water. Pat dry.
3. Melt the red currant jelly in a saucepan. Add the blanched shallot, orange peel, and lemon peel, together with Dijon mustard. Blend well.
4. Add the port plus the orange and lemon juice.

Miscellaneous

Marmalade-Glazed Carrots

Special Instructions: Dark orange sweet potatoes can be substituted for the carrots.

INGREDIENTS:
2 C. chopped carrots
1/2 C. chicken or vegetable stock
1 to 2 Tbs. butter
3 Tbs. orange marmalade, apricot jam, or peach jam

1. Cut the carrots into 2-inch-long pieces or use a waffle cutter, a wavy metal blade that gives vegetables the same appearance as ruffle potato chips, only you'll cut them thicker than the potato chips.
2. Braise the carrots in the stock, adding the butter and agitating the pan occasionally until they are done.
3. When carrots are just about done, add the marmalade, apricot, or peach jam. You want just a hint of sweetness, not a palate-cloying candy coating.

Marmalade-Glazed Sweet Potatoes

You want the deep orange sweet potatoes for this recipe. Some folks call them yams. This recipe is sweeter than the previous one.

INGREDIENTS:

3 lbs. sweet potatoes

2 Tbs. olive oil

1 tsp. salt

1 tsp. freshly ground black pepper

3 Tbs. sweet butter

1/4 C. orange marmalade

2 tsp. brown sugar

1.   Preheat the oven to 325° Fahrenheit.
2.   Peel the sweet potatoes and cut them into large chunks.
3.   Put the potatoes in a sturdy plastic bag together with olive oil, salt, and pepper. Jumble everything around until the sweet potatoes are lightly coated with oil and seasonings.
4.   Arrange the sweet potatoes in a single layer in a jelly roll pan or shallow casserole dish. Bake for 30 minutes.
5.   Meanwhile, in a saucepan, melt the butter. When just melted, combine it with the orange marmalade and brown sugar.
6.   Remove the casserole of yams from the oven. Place the potatoes in a large mixing bowl.
7.   Drizzle the marmalade mixture over the sweet potatoes and gently toss them until the pieces are evenly coated.
8.   Return the mixture to the casserole, return it to the oven, and cook for approximately 15 minutes more, or until the yams are tender and glazed.

Cranberries and Cheese

INGREDIENTS:

Small wheel of Brie
¹/₂ C. or more DeeDee's Cranberry Chutney
1 loaf crusty bread

1.	Slice the Brie in half like a layer cake.
2.	Spread the cheese with DeeDee's cranberry chutney and reassemble it.
3.	Serve with slices of good crusty bread as an appetizer.

Texas Meatballs

Here is an unusual recipe that my daughter shared with me. She got it from a friend in The Woodlands, outside Houston. "Here is the crock pot recipe that I promised you. It is for an appetizer for a party. It sounds disgusting but trust me, it is *really good!*" Strange as the recipe sounds, it turns out that it is one that friends of mine recommend highly. Tammy Sassaman describes it as having a sweet and pungent flavor, and says she uses it with little cocktail hotdogs as well as meatballs.

INGREDIENTS:

1 8-oz. jar chili sauce
1 8-oz. jar grape jelly
24 precooked meatballs

1.	Mix together the chili sauce and grape jelly.
	Note: Mira said that it is important that the chili not have any beans. Also, the jars should be the same size, 8 ounces or larger.
2.	Put jelly and chili sauce in a crock pot together with the precooked meatballs.
3.	Simmer on low for at least 1 hour before the party, and serve right from the crock pot.

Monika Nicholson gives the recipe her own twist. She puts one package of prepared frozen meatballs in a crock pot, pours a jar of chili sauce over the meatballs, and then adds only two to three heaping tablespoons of grape jelly. One time, when she happened to be out of grape jelly, she used damson plum jam that she had made and found it just as tasty. "This meatball recipe is so simple and yummy that most people just can't believe that there are only three ingredients! I learned this recipe from my sister-in-law, who now has the task of making meatballs for any family function."

APPENDIX A: RECIPE LIST

Jam, Jelly, Marmalade, Conserves, and Fruit Butter

Apple

Currants

Elderberry

Figs

Ginger

Gooseberry

Grape

Using Preserves

Miscellaneous Baked Goods

Muffins and Scones

Sweet and Savory Sauces

Miscellaneous

APPENDIX B: RESOURCES

Canning Supplies

A well-equipped kitchen usually has an array of saucepans, a larger Dutch oven, and measuring cups and spoons. The only supplies you have to purchase are jelly jars (the 8-ounce and/or 4-ounce size) and two-piece canning lids. Once you have the jars, they'll be used and reused again and again. The sealing rings are also reuseable. It's just the flat lids that are used once and then discarded. Jars are purchased a dozen at a time and come complete with the two-piece lids. The replacement flat lids are purchased in boxes of 12.

Alltrista (www.alltrista.com) is the parent company of Ball, Kerr, Bernardin, and Golden Harvest brands, operating mainly in the United States and Canada. They sell to wholesale and retail customers, offering (among other products) home canning jars, jar closures, and related food products. Under the Ball trademark, some hardware stores and other places offer a boxed kit that included a large enameled canning pot; a wire rack that holds the jars, 6 pint jars, and their lids; a wide-mouthed plastic funnel; a lid lifter (a small plastic wand with a magnet to lift lids out of hot water); a bubble remover; and a pamphlet on canning and preserving.

Should your local hardware store not carry canning supplies, there are other options. As well, there are other bits and bobs that might be a little more difficult to find but are nice to have. These sources are listed for your convenience only and do not carry any guarantee on my part. Any source not included does not imply anything more than an oversight.

Home Canning Supplies & Specialties

P.O. Box 1158
Ramona, California 92065
Telephone: 760-788-0520
www.homecanningsupply.com
Carries a wide range of supplies from water bath canners, water bath canner starter kits, canning and jelly jars, canning tools, and more.

Canning Pantry, a division of Highland Brands, LLC

10470 S. Redwood Road #415
South Jordan, Utah 84095
Telephone sales: 800-285-9044
Telephone support: 801-280-3241
www.canningpantry.com
Offering all sorts of canning equipment and supplies, a water bath canner package with canning tools, and much more.

Lehman's

Kidron, Ohio
Telephone orders: 877-438-5346
Customer service: 888-438-5346
www.lehmans.com
Lehman's offers "products for simple, self-sufficient living," and their catalog of nonelectric supplies is popular with the Amish. They offer a Victorino-style food mill that clamps to a counter or table and a "Foley" food mill that sits over a bowl or pot. They sell not just one apple peeler, you have your choice of the Reading 78 apple peeler (said to peel more than 10 apples a minute), a "most versatile peeler," and a hand-cranked apple peeler. As well, they sell an orange peeler. Choose between Lehman's best cherry pitter and their old-fashioned cherry pitter or a punch rod cherry pitter complete with a see-through waste container for the pits. They also sell all sorts of handy gadgets, down to a tweezerlike strawberry huller, and lots of other practical equipment and supplies.

Williams-Sonoma

Telephone orders: 800-541-2233
www.williams-sonoma.com
Williams-Sonoma carries a diversity of kitchen tools, serving dishes, pots and pans, table linens, and more. They have outlets in a number of malls across the country, and they also feature both catalog and Internet sales. Look for their top-of-the-line food

mill with three interchangeable straining disks, an elegant cherry-pitter, fancier-than-usual canning jars, and more.

Sur La Table
Pike Place Farmers' Market
Seattle, Washington
Telephone orders: 800-243-0852
Telephone assistance: 866-328-5412
www.surlatable.com
Cookware, housewares, knives, appliances and more. A fabulous place to browse, whether in the store, in their catalog, or on their Internet Web site.

Nurseries

Whenever possible, I prefer to buy plants at a local nursery. Sometimes, though, a mail-order or Internet vendor offers plants not available in your neighborhood. If it's just a different kind of apple tree or blackberry bush and you know they grow in your area, that's one thing. Make sure that something completely unfamiliar is suitable for your backyard, though; for example, oranges won't grow in New Jersey, but a dwarf variety might make a lovely houseplant.

Raintree Nursery
391 Butts Road
Morton, Washington 98356
Telephone: 360-496-6400
www.raintreenursery.com
Unusual fruits, berries, grapes, fruit and nut trees, orchard, garden, and landscape supplies.

One Green World
28696 South Cramer Road
Molalla, Oregon 97038-8576
Telephone: 503-651-3005
Mail-order source for 17 kinds of blackberries, blueberry bushes, cranberries, currants, and gooseberry bushes, elderberry bushes, and strawberry plants, as well as unusual fruiting plants such as hawthorne, mountain ash, sea buckthorn, and serviceberry. They also carry ornamentals and a range of fruit trees, including figs and both quince bushes and quince trees, berries, and orchard and garden supplies.

Cummins Nursery

18 Glass Factory Bay Road
Geneva, New York 14456
Telephone: 315-789-7083
www.cumminsnursery.com

Cummins Nursery carries fruit trees of special interest—a superb diversity of uncommon varieties of main crop and cider apples, heirloom and exotic varieties of apples, especially winter-hardy apples, apricots, sweet and tart cherries, Japanese and European plums, pears (including perry pears for perry, a drink like cider, but made from pears rather than apples).

Burnt Ridge Nursery & Orchards

432 Burnt Ridge Road
Onalaska, Washington 98570
Telephone: 360-985-2875
www.burntridge.com

Specializing in plants that produce edible fruit, such as blueberry, currant, and gooseberry, elderberry bushes, and Rosa rugosa, they also offer plants of uncommon bush fruits, such as seaberry, serviceberry, aronia, and hawthorne.

Four Winds Growers

www.fourwindsgrowers.com

Specializing in citrus trees, Four Winds offers a diversity of oranges, mandarins, tangerines, lemons, limes, grapefruits, kumquats, and exotics such as calamondin and *etrog* citron.

Located in California, Four Winds Growers accepts mail orders outside that state. In Northern California, the San Joaquin and Central Valley areas, and the Los Angeles Basin, their trees are available in many nurseries and garden centers.

BIBLIOGRAPHY

AFRC Institute of Food Research. *Home Preservation of Fruit and Vegetables*. 14th ed. London: HMSO Books, 1989.

America's All-Time Favorite Canning & Preserving Recipes. Des Moines, Iowa: Better Homes and Gardens Books, 1996.

Ferber, Christine. *Mes Confitures: The Jams and Jellies of Christine Ferber*. Translated by Virginia R. Phillips. East Lansing: Michigan State University Press, 2002.

Freitus, Joe. *Wild Preserves*. Boston: Stone Wall Press, 1977.

The Good Cook, Techniques & Recipes: Preserving. Alexandria, Va: Time-Life Books, 1981.

Hogan, Elizabeth L., ed. *Sunset Home Canning*. Menlo Park, Calif.: Sunset Publishing, 1993.

Kander, Mrs. Simon. *The Settlement Cook Book*. 13th ed. Milwaukee, Wisc.: The Settlement Cook Book Company, 1951.

Kochilas, Diane. *The Glorious Foods of Greece*. New York: HarperCollins Publishing, 2001.

Lesem, Jeanne. *The Pleasures of Preserving and Pickling*. New York: Alfred A. Knopf, 1975.

Plagemann, Catherine. *Fine Preserving*. New York: Simon and Schuster, 1967.

Sternberg, Rabbi Robert. *The Sephardic Kitchen*. New York: HarperCollins Publishers, 1996.

Wejman, Jacqueline, with essays by Charles St. Peter. *Jams & Jellies*. San Francisco: 101 Productions, 1975.

Wilson, C. Anne. *The Book of Marmalade*. Philadelphia: University of Pennsylvania Press, 1999.

Woloson, Wendy A. *Refined Tastes: Sugar, Confectionery, and Consumers in Nineteenth-Century America*. Baltimore: The Johns Hopkins University Press, Baltimore, 2002.

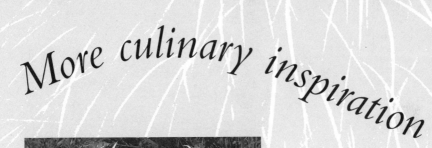

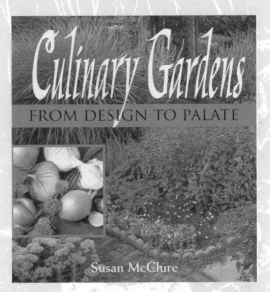